Collaboration in Media Studies

This volume offers new perspectives on knowledge production through various forms of togetherness. Via diverse cases of collaboration in Media Studies, from methodological contemplations to on-the-field social practices, the book proposes reflections and inquiries around collective research, media, and action.

The collection rethinks how scholarly endeavours feature different ways of doing and being together, identifying new and more diverse communicative spaces, challenging dichotomies, and encouraging critical perspectives. Scholars of a variety of disciplines recontextualise collaboration beyond the very nature of conventional academic approaches, to embrace vast connotations of media studies – from actions building connections across research and practice to transdisciplinary methodologies through analogue and digital realms.

This book will be an invaluable resource for scholars and post-graduate students from various fields of media studies, who carry an interest in collaborative and collective aspects of media as practice and research, as well as those in a variety of social science disciplines, participatory action research, media sociology, audience studies, intercultural communication, qualitative research methods and participatory communication.

Begüm Irmak is working as an executive manager in education and a part-time lecturer at Istanbul Bilgi University, Bahçeşehir University, and Beykoz University. She received her MSc degree from the London School of Economics in Sociology – Contemporary Social Thought in 2011 after graduating from the Sabancı University's Social and Political Sciences Programme in 2010. She received her PhD in Communication from Bilgi University. Until 2015, she worked in an advertising agency as the project leader of an international brand.

Can Koçak is a Lecturer in Media and Cultural Studies at the University of Sussex. Before his current post, he taught at King's College London, Department of Digital Humanities. He received his PhD in Communication from Istanbul Bilgi University with a thesis that focused on the representation of intellectuals in Nuri Bilge Ceylan's films after receiving his master's degree in Film and Drama at Kadir Has University with an interdisciplinary research derived from *Persona* (Ingmar Bergman, 1966).

Onur Sesigür is a Lecturer in Media and Communications at Coventry University, with a background in media studies, music and sound production. His current work revolves around streaming music and the topic of playlists, on which he recently published a book titled *Playlisting: Collection Music, Remediated*. Apart from his primary research interests in music and culture industries, he also studies digital cultures, transmedia storytelling and game studies.

Nazan Haydari is a Professor of Media Department at İstanbul Bilgi University, Turkey. Her research area consists of intercultural communication, feminist media studies, critical media pedagogy, and radio studies with a particular interest in collaborative research. Haydari is the co-editor of *Case Studies in Intercultural Dialogue*. Some of her articles appeared in *Gender and Education*, *Journalism Studies*, *Feminist Media Histories*, and *Innovations in Education and Teaching International*. She holds a PhD in Telecommunications and an MAIA in Communications and Development from Ohio University. Currently, she is working on a book manuscript on the oral history project with women radio broadcasters of the 1970s in Turkey and a project on the mapping of feminist and LGBTİ podcasts in Turkey.

Routledge Research in Cultural and Media Studies

True Crime in American Media
Edited by George S. Larke-Walsh

Branding Berlin
From Division to the Cultural Capital of Europe
Katrina Sark

Sustainable Resilience in Women's Film and Video Organizations
A Counter-Lineage in Moving Image History
Rosanna Maule

London as Screen Gateway
Edited by Elizabeth Evans and Malini Guha

Social Media and the Cultural Politics of Korean Pop Culture in East Asia
Sunny Yoon

Desire and Consent in Representations of Adolescent Sexuality with Adults
Edited by Maureen Turim and Diane Waldman

Culture-Bound Syndromes in Popular Culture
Edited by Cringuta Irina Pelea

Multilingual Fiction Series
Genres, Geographies and Performances
Nahuel Ribke

Collaboration in Media Studies
Doing and Being Together
Edited by Begüm Irmak, Can Koçak, Onur Sesigür and Nazan Haydari

For more information about this series, please visit: www.routledge.com

Collaboration in Media Studies
Doing and Being Together

Edited by
Begüm Irmak, Can Koçak,
Onur Sesigür and Nazan Haydari

LONDON AND NEW YORK

First published 2024
by Routledge
4 Park Square, Milton Park, Abingdon, Oxon OX14 4RN

and by Routledge
605 Third Avenue, New York, NY 10158

Routledge is an imprint of the Taylor & Francis Group, an informa business

© 2024 selection and editorial matter, Begüm Irmak, Can Koçak, Onur Sesigür and Nazan Haydari; individual chapters, the contributors

The right of Begüm Irmak, Can Koçak, Onur Sesigür and Nazan Haydari to be identified as the authors of the editorial material, and of the authors for their individual chapters, has been asserted in accordance with sections 77 and 78 of the Copyright, Designs and Patents Act 1988.

All rights reserved. No part of this book may be reprinted or reproduced or utilised in any form or by any electronic, mechanical, or other means, now known or hereafter invented, including photocopying and recording, or in any information storage or retrieval system, without permission in writing from the publishers.

Trademark notice: Product or corporate names may be trademarks or registered trademarks, and are used only for identification and explanation without intent to infringe.

British Library Cataloguing-in-Publication Data
A catalogue record for this book is available from the British Library

Library of Congress Cataloging-in-Publication Data
Names: Irmak, Begüm, editor. | Koçak, Can, editor. | Sesigür, Onur, editor. | Haydari, Nazan, editor.
Title: Collaboration in media studies : doing and being together / edited by Begüm Irmak, Can Koçak, Onur Sesigür, Nazan Haydari.
Description: Abingdon, Oxon ; New York, NY : Routledge, 2024. | Series: Routledge research in cultural and media studies | Includes bibliographical references and index.
Identifiers: LCCN 2023047726 (print) | LCCN 2023047727 (ebook) | ISBN 9781032486277 (hardback) | ISBN 9781032486284 (paperback) | ISBN 9781003389972 (ebook)
Subjects: LCSH: Mass media—Research—Methodology—Case studies. | Authorship—Collaboration—Case studies.
Classification: LCC P91.3 C53 2024 (print) | LCC P91.3 (ebook) | DDC 302.23072—dc23/eng/20240102
LC record available at https://lccn.loc.gov/2023047726
LC ebook record available at https://lccn.loc.gov/2023047727

ISBN: 978-1-032-48627-7 (hbk)
ISBN: 978-1-032-48628-4 (pbk)
ISBN: 978-1-003-38997-2 (ebk)

DOI: 10.4324/9781003389972

Typeset in Sabon
by codeMantra

Contents

List of contributors ix
Acknowledgements xiii

1 Introduction: Doing and being together 1
BEGÜM IRMAK, CAN KOÇAK, ONUR SESIGÜR
AND NAZAN HAYDARI

PART I
Doing research together
15

2 Women's radio history in Turkey: The politics of reflecting together in oral history research 17
NAZAN HAYDARI, ÖZDEN ÇANKAYA
AND CEM HAKVERDI

3 The artist's book: Working towards a collaborative methodology in art and design 27
MELIKE ÖZMEN

4 Duo autoethnographic approach to peer-to-peer collaboration in PhD process 44
BEGÜM IRMAK AND AYÇA ULUTAŞ

5 Podcasting as a methodological tool for research conversations with makers 59
NURGÜL YARDIM MERIÇLILER

6 Performance as a way of discovering oneself within the other 74
CAN KOÇAK

PART II
Doing media together
87

7 Human rights-based narratives of war: A journalistic tool for promoting human rights 89
ATHINA SIMATOU

8 Digitally mediating cultural trauma through virtual reality 102
ELENI PNEVMATIKOU AND ANGELIKI GAZI

9 'Alone together': Reconnecting death stranding's broken sense of sociality 116
ONUR SESIGÜR

10 Twitch Developers as a 'company-led community' 128
SARPER DURMUŞ

PART III
Acting together
141

11 From a political protest to an art exhibition: Collaboration and dialogue through artistic research 143
IŞIL EĞRIKAVUK

12 Resonance in intercultural encounters: Mapping a critical perspective on communication in pluralised societies 156
THERESA KLINGLMAYR

13 Acting together, reflecting together: Two ethnographic accounts of Jamaica's first 'pride event' in 2015 169
DAVID LOWIS AND SIMONE KIMBERLY HARRIS

14 Reflections on teaching the ethics of digital communication technologies 186
YUSUF YÜKSEKDAĞ

15 Transmedia charity initiatives in Turkey: The case of *Adım Adım* 202
DILEK GÜRSOY

Index 219

Contributors

Özden Çankaya is a Professor of media and communication. She had also worked as a radio producer and auditor in the national broadcasting of the Turkish Radio and Television Institution (TRT) between 1970 and 1981. She is the author of Türk Televizyonunun Program Yapısı (Programming Structure of Turkish Television), Bir Kitle İletişim Kurumunun Tarihi: TRT (The History of a Mass Communication Institution: TRT 1927–2000), the co-author of İstanbul Radyosu Anılar, Yaşantılar (Istanbul Radio, Memories, and Experiences), and many other articles in media studies. Cankaya has also written several film and television scripts and produced radio programs.

Sarper Durmuş previously held positions in journalism and publishing prior to embarking on his postgraduate studies. He now has a PhD in Communications from Istanbul Bilgi University where he also teaches undergraduate courses on media studies and journalism. His general interests are digital platforms and global media.

Işıl Eğrikavuk is an artist and academic, whose research specialises in performance, dialogue-based art and artistic research. She has an MFA from the School of the Art Institute of Chicago and a PhD from Istanbul Bilgi University. She has been working as a researcher and a faculty member at the Berlin University of Arts (UdK) since 2017. Eğrikavuk is the founder of the other garden, a collaborative artistic research space that focuses on issues of ecology, diversity and radical care within the UdK.

Angeliki Gazi is an Assistant Professor in Digital Research Methods in the Department of Communication, Media and Culture, Panteion University of Social and Political Sciences. Angeliki Gazi holds a PhD and MA from National and Kapodistrian University of Athens, specialising in media psychology and a bachelor's degree in Psychology, from the University of Ioannina, Greece. Her research interests concern the fields of Identity, Emotions, Relationships in Cyberspace, Interpersonal, Intergroup Communication, Identity and Emotions via Mediated Experience Applications, Social Media, Mobile Phones, Locative Media – Personal Relationships in

Technopsychological Systems and Hybrid Environments. She is a founding member and Chair of the Division: Media Psychology and Technology of the Hellenic Psychological Association.

Dilek Gürsoy is an Assistant Professor in the Visual Communication Design program at Istanbul Bilgi University in Turkey. With an academic background in design thinking and communication studies, Gürsoy earned her PhD from Istanbul Bilgi University in 2018. She is the author of *Transmediality in Independent Journalism: The Turkish Case* (Routledge, 2020), which reflects her research interest in transmedia studies. Her most recent work is 'Method Case Study: The Transmedia Journalism Design Thinking Toolkit', which was published in 2023 as a section within the *Research Handbook on Design Thinking* edited by K. Straker and C. Wrigley.

Cem Hakverdi is a faculty member at Alanya University, Faculty of Art and Design. He holds a BA in Journalism, an MA in Cinema and Television and a DFA in Film Design. He is a documentary filmmaker with a specific interest in cultural heritage, minorities, environmental activism, and animal rights.

Simone Kimberly Harris is an LGBT activist and creative industries and tourism consultant in Jamaica. She is active in arts and advocacy interventions for the LGBTQ community and has been on the frontline of innovative programmes to provide access to safe spaces for LGBTQ creatives. Her artistic works such as The Tribe and Lady Blade Ophelia Stratum have premiered on major platforms in Europe, the UK, and Canada. She holds a BSc in Psychology from the University of the West Indies, a master's in Business Administration from Everest University, and a master's in Music Business Administration from Florida Atlantic University.

Nazan Haydari is a Professor of Media Department at İstanbul Bilgi University, Turkey. Her research area consists of intercultural communication, feminist media studies, critical media pedagogy, and radio studies with a particular interest in collaborative research. Haydari is the co-editor of *Case Studies in Intercultural Dialogue* by Kendall Hunt. Some of her articles appeared in *Gender and Education*, *Journalism Studies*, *Feminist Media Histories*, and *Innovations in Education and Teaching International*. She holds a PhD in Telecommunications and an MAIA in Communications and Development from Ohio University. Currently, she is working on a book manuscript on the oral history project with women radio broadcasters of the 1970s in Turkey and a project on the mapping of feminist and LGBTİ podcasts in Turkey.

Begüm Irmak is working as an executive manager in education and a part-time lecturer at Istanbul Bilgi University, Bahçeşehir University, and Beykoz University. She received her MSc degree from the London School of Economics in Sociology – Contemporary Social Thought in 2011 after graduating from the Sabancı University's Social and Political Sciences

Programme in 2010. She received her PhD in Communication from Bilgi University. Until 2015, she worked in an advertising agency as the project leader of an international brand.

Theresa Klinglmayr is a PhD candidate and research assistant in the Division of Transcultural Communication, Department of Communication Studies, University of Salzburg. She obtained her master's degree at the University of Salzburg with a thesis dedicated to the discursive construction of culture within integration debates. In her research, she focuses on interculturality and current discourses on migration within the Austrian context. Her interests lie in the fields of diversity and communication, discourse analysis, and qualitative methods.

Can Koçak is a Lecturer in Media and Cultural Studies at the University of Sussex. Before his current post, he taught in the Department of Digital Humanities, King's College London. He received his PhD in Communication from Istanbul Bilgi University with a thesis that focused on the representation of intellectuals in Nuri Bilge Ceylan's films after receiving his master's degree in Film and Drama at Kadir Has University with an interdisciplinary research derived from *Persona* (Ingmar Bergman, 1966).

David Lowis is currently a PhD candidate at the Berlin University of the Arts, as well as being a Visual Content Creator in the German Bundestag. He has an academic background in Social Anthropology and International Development. In 2015, he conducted three months of ethnographic research with the Jamaican LGBTQ rights organisation 'J-FLAG', and has worked as an LGBTQ activist in a variety of capacities since.

Nurgül Yardım Meriçliler is a London-based architect, communications specialist, and researcher. She earned her PhD in Communication from Istanbul Bilgi University (2023), with a focus on London makerspaces. Nurgul holds a Bachelor of Architecture from Middle East Technical University (2009), where she was awarded the Archiprix mansion prize, and an MSc degree in Interdisciplinary Urban Design from Istanbul Technical University (2011). With experience in global architectural practices, Nurgul currently manages the Anylab Experimental Studio as a resident at Somerset House Studios. Additionally, she hosts and produces the Anylabtalks podcast, and curates the weekly newsletter Sense of Place.

Eleni Pnevmatikou is a PhD student in Media Psychology and Technology at the Panteion University of Social and Political Sciences, Athens. She holds an MA in Applied – Clinical Sociology and Art from the University of the Aegean (Sociology Department) and the University of Western Macedonia (School of Fine Arts) (2019). She graduated with Honors from the Aristotle University of Thessaloniki, School of Fine Arts, Film Department (2014, Integrated Master). Her doctoral thesis deals with healing collective trauma through VR technology. Her research fields as a researcher are collective memory, collective identity, and cultural trauma.

Melike Özmen is an Assistant Professor in the Visual Communication Design Program at Istanbul Bilgi University. She completed her BA in Visual Arts and Design/Graphic Design at the Başkent University in 2008 and her MA in Visual Communication Design at the Yeditepe University in 2012. She obtained a PhD in Communication from Istanbul Bilgi University, with her thesis on information design in 2018. Her research interests include information design, visual storytelling, urban communication, design ethics, psychogeography, and visual research methods/concept development. She is a designer/researcher/artist.

Onur Sesigür is a Lecturer in Media and Communications at Coventry University, with a background in media studies, music and sound production. His current work revolves around streaming music and the topic of playlists, on which he recently published a book titled *Playlisting: Collection Music, Remediated*. Apart from his primary research interests in music and culture industries, he also studies digital cultures, transmedia storytelling and game studies.

Athina Simatou is a PhD candidate at the Panteion University of Athens and a grantee of the State Scholarships Foundation of Greece, working on the topic of 'Journalistic Narratives and Human Rights in Conflict Zones'. In the context of her PhD research, Athina has been to Argentina, Qatar, and Uganda. Her academic background in law and social sciences has played a key role in her participation in various projects concerning human rights and intercultural communication. Part of her work has been published in the book *Public Space, Education, Communication* (Original Title: 'Δημόσιος Χώρος, Εκπαίδευση, Επικοινωνία').

Ayça Ulutaş is working as a part-time lecturer at Istanbul Bilgi University. She completed her BA degree in Business Administration from Istanbul University and received her Master of Science degree in Integrated Marketing Communications from San Francisco Golden Gate University. She started her professional career in a public relations agency in 2006 and continued to work as a Marcom Manager in many leading brands of the technology industry until 2014. She completed her PhD in Communication from Istanbul Bilgi University and her academic interests include digital media and communication, gender studies and transformative consumer research.

Yusuf Yüksekdağ is an Assistant Professor at the Faculty of Communication, Istanbul Bilgi University. He works and teaches in the fields of applied ethics, political philosophy and media studies. He has worked on migration ethics in particular, and recently he is concerned with the ethics of/on urban space, smart city and datafication ethics. He received his PhD in 2019 from the Department of Culture and Society, Linköping University, Sweden and later worked as a researcher at the Institute of Philosophy, University of Bern for a year before joining Istanbul Bilgi University.

Acknowledgements

This edited collection is the product of a long journey that has itself involved inspiring practices of collaboration and togetherness. We would like to thank all the contributors for their instrumental work and generous commitment to this book. Collaborating with every one of them was a privilege and we are sincerely grateful for all the effort, energy, and ideas they each brought to this collection. We are sincerely grateful to all our parents and families for their continuing encouragement and enthusiasm. The idea for this book emerged from the Interdisciplinary PhD Communication Conference 2021, and we are grateful to Istanbul Bilgi University's PhD in Communication programme for being the initiator of this collaborative process.

We thank Wendy Leeds-Hurwitz for being a brilliant mentor at every stage. We thank Salvatore Scifo for enthusiastically supporting us and for being there whenever we needed his input and guidance. Finally, many thanks to the great contribution of Suzanne Richardson, our commissioning editor, for her support and belief in this collection.

Begüm Irmak, Can Koçak, Onur Sesigür, and Nazan Haydari
September, 2023

1 Introduction

Doing and being together

Begüm Irmak, Can Koçak, Onur Sesigür and Nazan Haydari

Often adopting practical viewpoints, especially in pedagogical situations (Lee, 2006; Murawski & Spencer, 2011; Boboc, 2014; Stevenson & Bauer, 2019), organisational/administrative contexts (Nikoi & Boateng, 2013; Kolbaek, 2018), strategic and functional interdisciplinary research (O'Rourke et al., 2013; Derry et al., 2014), and corporate frameworks (Heath & Isbell, 2017; Rice, 2021), collaboration has been extensively studied across diverse fields in the contexts of cooperative endeavours. This practical perspective permits the extension of collaboration into media studies, enabling scholars to contemplate their own research areas through different case studies. Togetherness and collaboration have also been thoroughly explored within the realm of media studies, through varying perspectives on how people engage with media, interact with each other, and form communities. Whether they emphasise hands-on work and practical applications, discussing maker movements, hackathons, and participatory culture (Howley, 2011; Ostherr, 2018), delving into political struggles and ideological implications related to media participation (Carpentier, 2011), exploring togetherness through artistic and theoretical lenses, invoking societal and scientific reflections (Aranda et al., 2017), or focusing on the impact of technology on togetherness within the context of tourism (Molz, 2014), the works on this field highlight the convergence of media and collective engagement.

Scholars of different disciplines and contexts with varying practices and experiences recontextualise togetherness beyond conventional academic approaches. Therefore, the methodologies, practices, and inquiries provided here expand the horizons of media studies by taking into account diverse voices that span beyond scholarly thought. The concept of togetherness, as a necessity to achieve goals and not so rarely as a means to its own end, is approached by many disciplines and fields in a myriad of studies. Communication happens in united situations of various forms, and media, by definition, functions as a facilitator for such encounters. If we consider togetherness as a prerequisite of sociality, *Doing and Being Together* from a media studies perspective offers a new inquiry into knowledge production. Our intention is not to present a bulletproof notion of doing and being together, but rather to expand our understanding of media and society by focusing on the

DOI: 10.4324/9781003389972-1

collaborative and collective aspects of human agencies. In highlighting these agencies, actions and intentions become central in seemingly disparate yet essentially unified patterns. To frame such an endeavour, we offer as an entry point collective intentionality – a popular concept of philosophy dealing with social ontology – to inquire about how our world is jointly constituted. Through this approach, we highlight intentional efforts towards common goals and encapsulate the diverse and collaborative nature of doing and being together in media studies.

Collective intentionally, as structurally proposed by John Searle (1990), though hinted at and discussed under different topics and labels by much earlier philosophers and social scientists such as Epicurus (2000), Rousseau (2004), Durkheim (1982), Sellars (1974), and Weber (1991), utilises many sub-concepts or modes including joint attention, joint action, and 'skilful joint action', as recently proposed by Judith Martens (2020). Philosopher Ramio Tuomela goes as far as to forefront collective intentionality as 'the cement of society' (2013, p. x). One of the most significant features of collective intentionality is that, much like the cultural studies approach, it deals with everyday life. From seemingly trivial forms of acting together such as carrying a sofa to another room to more complex and wider applications of joint action towards grand social organisations, collective intentionality is interested in how we constitute our social world. Collective intentionality, as an umbrella concept for putting intentional effort towards a common goal, would be a suitable motto for the purpose of this collection, which is to understand acting together through cases in media studies, since it is through this perspective that the field of media studies is introduced to a practice-based framework, both academically and colloquially. To present the diverse efforts at understanding and highlighting doing and being together in media studies, this collection presents three interconnecting sections to provide a narrative frame to our collaborative efforts: Doing Research Together, Doing Media Together, and Acting Together.

Togetherness is commonly represented in media studies education in terms of collaborative media, media and society and participation, yet dispersed under other foci. As media and communication are collective in nature, ways of doing and being together are often taken for granted. Although the main focus of the book, doing and being together, is researched in eclectic contexts, the focus is often diversified in terms of contemplating implications and repercussions from a media studies perspective. Referring to existing connotations, social sciences and humanities provide various efforts to contextualise the mechanics and influences of the concept in dispersed areas of inquiry. Studies in social work (Anscombe, 2009; Pawar et al., 2014), consciousness studies (Clarke, 2015), occupational science (Wilcock, 1998; Lavalley, 2017), social psychology and social cognition (Satne, 2021), qualitative studies (Nind & Winha, 2014; Puyalto et al., 2016), participatory action research (Fortmann, 2009; Hayes, 2014), and education studies (Weiss et al., 2017) all contribute to current discussions circulating around the ideas of how to know and do together. Yet it is vital to note that the diverging point of this edited collection relies on insisting to highlight the mechanisms of collective research, media, and action. The cases in media studies presented in the collection offer insight into this discussion from diverse perspectives, looking at the same essential point of doing and being together.

The meaning and the essence of doing and being together in the title of this collection can be traced back to the foundation principles of the Bilgi IPCC (Interdisciplinary PhD Communication Conference) community, of which the collection's editors are active members. Bilgi IPCC emerged as an outcome of students and instructors at the PhD in Communication Programme at Istanbul Bilgi University in 2017. First and foremost, the main goal of the group was to provide early career researchers with an inclusive and constructive community to further their research in an interdisciplinary manner. The group's first attempt to achieve their goal manifested a series of 'Coffee Talks' where researchers could present their ongoing research, open-up discussions, or facilitate roundtables on their work. These talks were designed in a way that would inspire early career researchers for collaborative work opportunities as well as encourage publication potential.

As a further step, as discussed by several scholars (Mead & Byers, 1968; Leeds-Hurwitz, 1994; Freeman, 2008) the conference itself was imagined as a possible creative space that overcomes the competitive, often somewhat hierarchical and compressed conference atmospheres where early career researchers struggle to acquire constructive feedback and colleague support. The collaborative efforts of the PhD students together with the doctoral programme coordinator Nazan Haydari yielded its first visible outcome in Spring 2018 as a national conference themed 'Re-thinking Methodology'. Apart from the main goals of IPCC as an early career research community, the conference specifically aimed to define communication as an interdisciplinary arch where researchers from various fields from media to cinema, architecture to marketing, sociology to design would come together, embracing an inclusive approach to redefine what communication and social sciences mean from a methodological perspective. To do so, the call for the conference invited participants to explore beyond the dichotomies of qualitative and quantitative, theory and practice, and academic knowledge and everyday knowledge. Encouraged by the success of the first conference, the community organised the second Bilgi IPCC in Spring 2019, with the theme 'Inclusion/Intersection'. The call for the conference reminded participants that one of the meanings of communication is contact and invited them to take a step out of their comfort zones to contemplate about inclusion and intersection of theories, fields, questions, concepts, identities, and methods. This theme was presented as a follow-up to the methodology discussions presented in the previous year's conference since as the IPCC community began to form, the need to discuss how we do research became clear. Later that year, the outcomes of the first two years of Bilgi IPCC were compiled as a special issue, including select full papers of the first two years' presenters' work. The collection was published as a special issue (Volume 11, issue 1) in *Interactions: Studies in Communication & Culture* with the title 'Rethinking communication research methodologies: Interdisciplinary Ph.D. Communication Conference (IPCC)' (Gürsoy et al., 2020).

The plans of Bilgi IPCC to continue their now annual conference in spring, unfortunately, had to be cancelled due to the Covid-19 pandemic, as uncertainties increasingly grew in the Spring of 2020. However, the community quickly adapted to the online environment. This adaptation also facilitated an international shift, which the community had been discussing for some time. Consequently, to disseminate the publication, to re-discuss the published work, and to internationally get together on Zoom, Bilgi IPCC organised a special issue seminar in Fall 2020, this time in English. The seminar, hosted by the Bilgi IPCC organisation committee in collaboration with the editor of *Interactions: Studies in Communication & Culture*, Salvatore Scifo, allowed the authors to re-visit their published work and begin new discussions with the seminar participants. At the end of the seminar, the theme for Bilgi IPCC 2021, to be held online and in English, was announced as 'Collaborations'.

Bilgi IPCC 2021 was held as a virtual conference with participants from various disciplines and backgrounds. As organisers, we aimed to create a collaborative conference atmosphere and, to do so, we asked paper presenters, panel organisers, and roundtable facilitators to keep any un-interactive presentation to a minimum and use the allocated time to initiate discussions regarding the presented work, as well as the general topic of the encapsulating session. Considering the limits and affordances of online communication, this was particularly important for the Bilgi IPCC community since, to allow for an inclusive atmosphere of collaboration, we understood that we should facilitate interpersonal communication, subjective inputs, and an overall free-form discussion atmosphere. This attitude, we believe, is a necessary step towards a community of inquiry from a rather Cartesian model of research to which most scholars are more accustomed.

With IPCC 2022, titled 'Transitions', we delved into the ever-evolving landscape of communication, labouring, and social relations. The conference posed thought-provoking questions about the ethical implications of these changes and the relationship between analogue and digital ways of social conduct and research. We encouraged participants to reflect on the vulnerability and resilience in the divide between digital and analogue spaces, exploring the changing norms of sharing and transmitting meaning. The edition ultimately enabled us to challenge traditional notions of being 'in communication' and its singular nature, considering the effects of transitions on learning and research methods. It also prompted a holistic examination of transitions as a matter of transfer, adaptation, co-existence, contradiction, transformation, or synthesis.

IPCC 2023, titled 'Communication, Technology and Experience: Crossroad,' put inclusivity to the forefront. This edition emphasised the intersections and interconnectedness between seemingly unrelated threads, seeking to broaden the scope of communication, technology, and experience by exploring their individual journeys and how they interacted with each other. Rather than fixed titles and definitions, our focus here was on a comprehensive interpretation that accommodated diverse perspectives and encouraged interdisciplinary collaboration. The intention was to foster a sense of togetherness, reflecting the foundational principles of the Bilgi IPCC community. By embracing a comprehensive understanding of communication, technology, and experience, IPCC 2023 aimed to bring together different fields and disciplines to redefine the boundaries and possibilities of these domains.

We, as the editors of this collection and members of Bilgi IPCC define scholarship and research as a collaborative and collective knowledge production process, and perceive education as a space of dialogic learning where the hierarchies between teachers and students, and senior and junior scholars are questioned and redefined. We equally value accumulated knowledge through expertise and a new set of questions and approaches determined by the political and social contexts of different generations. Having said that as an initiative, Bilgi IPCC receives full support and continuous academic guidance from an international advisory committee for the periodical conferences and publications (see https://ipcc.bilgi.edu.tr/committees/). The faculty of the PhD in Communication programme at Istanbul Bilgi University, comprising scholars from diverse research areas, are also active members of the IPCC community. This edited collection is an activity of collaborative learning and collaborative knowledge production.

Collaboration in Media Studies: Doing and Being Together presents 15 chapters in three interconnected sections to offer a navigable structure for diverse and exploratory attempts at understand doing and being together in media studies. Thus, the sections – and the chapters presented under each – are presented in a narrative structure to widen our visions rather than pursuing a consolidated representation of togetherness as a whole. With an understanding of media as a communicative space facilitating relationships at multiple levels through the means of technology, physical space, and creativity, a selection of cases from diverse areas are included in the chapters. Furthermore, the collection is composed of chapters written by scholars from various cultures and countries including Austria, Greece, Jamaica, Turkey, and the UK, showcasing diverse cases in media studies. The focused variety of the contents of the collection hopes to provide a collective inquiry through diverse togetherness.

The edited collection is intended for scholars and postgraduate students from various fields of media studies, who teach or carry an interest in collaborative and collective aspects of media as practice in addition to media research, as a diverse selection of understandings and implications of doing and being together. The collection also provides insight for researchers, who are already working on alternative perspectives in doing and being together as an aspect of their work, in other disciplines such as social sciences, arts, and humanities. Furthermore, this collection offers a teaching resource presenting cases from media studies that specifically concentrate on the intentional collectivity that underlies the way we do media, act via media and research media. Additionally, transdisciplinary case studies from various contexts constitute significant teaching material and creative discussion tools for undergraduate courses, such as peacebuilding and communication, community studies, participatory action research, media sociology, audience studies, intercultural communication, qualitative research methods, and participatory communication.

Doing research together

The first section, 'Doing Research Together', takes a pluralistic approach to both methods and methodology in terms of encompassing collaborative endeavours. It can be considered a unifying term for the unified efforts of documenting and analysing, thus building relationships around and reflecting on the significance of knowledge production. On one hand, doing research together refers to multiple agents of research (academic and non-academic) coming together to delve into a topic, and on the other, it implies the contribution of research participants in various stages of the research process. Stressing the significance and interrelatedness of reflection and action, Heron and Reason (2006) underline the procedural necessities by concentrating on experiential knowing. They also summarise the process of researching together by stating that 'this is not research on people or about people, but research with people' (p. 145). Prioritising an engagement with the real world (Firchow & Gellman, 2021), ways of being and doing are characterised here as a continuous relationship that consists of experimenting with traditional or new methods, reflecting on the research process and outcomes as well as working together with research participants in this dynamic environment.

This section includes eclectic approaches, enabling the utilisation of various tools to implement and exercise alternative ways of being and doing. In other words, doing research together becomes an umbrella term for collective efforts in understanding the situatedness and interconnectedness in diverse research areas of media studies.

The section begins with the chapter by Nazan Haydari, Özden Çankaya, and Cem Hakverdi, who conduct oral history research with women broadcasters at Turkish Radio and Television Institution and address a collaborative act of memory reclamation through remembering, reimagining, and reflecting. Through interviews, women's media histories are presented with a feminist approach to oral history, which also underlines the creation of a space of collaborative knowledge production. Not only the collaboration between a researcher and a radio broadcaster in the research process is evident but also the collaboration between the researchers and the participants is signified through drawing on the gendered history of radio broadcasting processes.

Melike Özmen, in her three-fold effort to shed light on the relationship between an artist and a designer and their related disciplines, puts forward a scene of interdisciplinary collaboration through the case study of an Artist's Book. The first mapping is around re-visiting distinct yet related aspects of two disciplines, Arts and Design, through questioning the hierarchical structure by proposing a collaborative working methodology. The second part proposes Artist's Book as a medium to exhibit and promote artwork and initiates the necessary grounds for the last part where the creation of an Artist's Book is presented as a case study.

Begüm Irmak and Ayça Ulutaş aim to underline the implications of lived experiences of PhD journey and utilise duo ethnography as a collaborative methodology to vocalise a dialogic exploration in finding their paths and also their academic selves. Driving upon personal narratives, the authors mainly focus on both the interrelatedness and differentiations in their PhD journeys, presenting a sphere of polyvocality. At the same time, they maintain a motivation to disrupt the metanarratives constructed around the PhD experiences and present a more bottom-up approach by collaborating as two peer authors.

Nurgül Yardım Meriçliler aims to discover the different connotations of 'podcasting', and claims it could be seen as more than a communication tool (Browder et al., 2017), becoming a gateway into makerspaces that facilitate community interactions and production processes. According to Yardım Meriçliler, who forms her research around the interviews in the *Anylabtalks Podcast* she prepares and hosts, these spaces, which are fuelled by people referred to as 'makers', also open up a new understanding of the public sphere.

In Can Koçak's work on discovering oneself within the other driving on performance studies and semiology, there is an emerging effort to rediscover a 'me statement' within an 'it statement' and mapping out how two contradictory concepts are the same as one another while underlying their contrasting descriptions. Seeking out new ways of forming relationships with the 'other', collaboration is utilised as a framework to discover new ways of defining the concept itself. In this reflexive endeavour, collaboration is approached as a tool to scrutinise a media and arts case study, with offering alternative ways of conceptualising the relationship of otherness in relation to the definitions of the self.

Doing media together

The tendency to look at media as a form of practice, rather than texts or structures of production (Couldry, 2004), dates back to the beginning of the noughties, finding its theoretical underpinnings in sociology. Ann Swidler claims (2001) that research on practice should replace an understanding of culture as something that comprises internal 'ideas' or 'meanings'; the focus should rather be on practices themselves (routine, unconscious, and automatic activities) and discourse (not the actual words, but the system of meanings that allows their formulation). Building up on Swidler's suggestions,

Couldry attempts to set a new paradigm that treats media as an open-ended range of practices, or rather delves into media-oriented practice as a phenomenon in and of itself, asking what people are '*doing* in relation to media across a whole range of situations and contexts' (2004, p. 119), opting for the looseness and openness this suggests, as opposed to the fixed nature of texts or institutions created by these practices.

This section addresses 'media as practice', stemming from the idea of breaking down the understanding that agency is linked to a certain medium or mediality (Eichner, 2014). This section presents cases that establish a new understanding of agency that is simultaneously ubiquitous and nebulous (Couldry, 2004) with reference to the fluid discourse around the ways we 'do media' in our daily lives.

Athina Simatou's chapter explores the intersection of human rights, journalism, and narratives, suggesting the creation of a new genre called Human Rights-based Journalistic Narrative. Focused on amplifying empathy and awareness for war victims, this genre places human rights principles at the core of storytelling, spotlighting violations, and combatting discrimination. It also underscores the power of narratives in promoting empathy and solidarity, serving as a resource for researchers, practitioners, journalists, and war correspondents alike.

Eleni Pnevmatikou and Angeliki Gazi focus on the Pontokomi community in Greece, which was forced into displacement after a mining site started operating around the settlement. The research questions whether VR applications could be used as a possible treatment for cultural and collective traumas, helping victims connect to fond memories through social bonds and re-establish a sense of place through a collective identity.

Onur Sesigür's research starts off with the narrative of a video game, Kojima Productions' *Death Stranding*, where players are expected to form communication networks in a post-apocalyptic setting. With reference to a framework established around Sherry Turkle's notion of 'alone together', Sesigür discusses whether online contexts truly provide a sense of community or instead foster social isolation and loneliness.

In an era where concerns about techno-dystopian imaginaries and human agency have arisen (Anderson & Rainie, 2018; Jindal, 2020), Sarper Durmuş subverts the framework of 'community-led company' in business studies and introduces the term 'company-led community' as a way of comprehending Twitch Developers – a space that connects amateur third-party developers and complementor companies. Recognising that this community is formed around and managed by Twitch, an entity owned by Amazon, the article explores potential impacts, considering concepts such as platformisation, labour relations, and political economy.

Acting together

Finally, we use Acting Together, the title of the third section, as an inclusive narrative to encapsulate the change-oriented actions, where participants are not only recognised as active involvers of the process but also cooperative agents (Heron & Reason, 2006). Acting and action are substantial concepts often dealt with in an interdisciplinary manner, from philosophy to psychology, education to health, and sociology to media studies (Arendt, 1958; Davidson, 1963; Bakhtin, 1993; Baum et al., 2006; Stringer, 2004). These frameworks help not only in establishing a basis to incorporate theories around practice into media studies but also in providing possible answers to the complex question of how people define and understand practice. A critical turning point here is the tendency to acknowledge social practice as a fundamental phenomenon in social life and as a theory that forms connections between bodies and agency (Turner, 1994; Schatzki, 1999; Reckwitz, 2002). Collective action (Eldred, 2013), with its roots in collective intentionality, could also be mentioned along the lines of this tendency. With similar intentions in mind, Acting Together presents forms or contemplations of collective and intentional action, where researchers, participants, communities, or organisations put effort towards transformative intents, both consciously and spontaneously.

This section brings together cases that deal with different forms and discussions of collective action towards understanding and bettering the conditions that constitute doing and being together.

Işıl Eğrikavuk employs a collaborative and participatory case study approach to re-think the creative elements of protest and form new discussions through concepts of community art practices. Her work presents examples of acting together in creative forms during the 2013 Gezi Park protests in Turkey and observes intersections between protests and community arts. Her utilisation of practice-based research for intrinsically collective and action-oriented phenomena brings together and highlights the 'being many' aspect of 'artivism' (Malzacher et al., 2015, p. 14) as well as the active and participatory nature of communities in protest. In the cases of limited freedom of speech and the right to public protest, collective arts serve as significant spaces to meet emotional needs, such as expressing oneself freely, feeling heard, feeling accepted, connected, and safe, rather than featuring a shared artistic vision, a common ideological agenda or career-related goals.

Theresa Klinglmayer puts forward the concept of intercultural resonance to critically evaluate communication practices in multicultural communities by focusing on the everyday interactions and encounters of individuals. She highlights these encounters as subject-constituting social practices to discuss how culture arises in social action. Through mutual understanding and acting together across differences, Klinglmayer proposes resonance as a perspective in the face of the challenges of living together in pluralised societies.

David Lowis and Simone Kimberly Harris reflect upon their experiences in a flash mob event in 2015, considered to be the first Gay Pride event in Jamaica, where homophobia appears to be a serious issue. Their ethnographic accounts aim to reflect on the legacy of the event and reignite conversations regarding solidarity and activism in a post-colonial setting.

The chapter authored by Yusuf Yüksekdağ explores higher education's response to emerging digital technologies, presenting an undergraduate course emphasising ethics in data-driven communication tech. While the course employs case-based learning, involving students and the instructor in collaborative problem-solving, the chapter highlights the approach's rationale, design, and relevance to media and communication students.

And finally, Dilek Gürsoy studies the implementation of transmediality in civil society organisations as a method to form and strengthen participation through action. She proposes Adım (Step by Step), a collective charity-run initiative in Turkey, which aims to inspire social solidarity by encouraging individuals and institutions to take action through sports, to discuss the implications of action and togetherness afforded by the transmedia practice they employ. Gürsoy underlines the underlying influence of shared beliefs in transmedia storytelling to encourage community interaction, collaboration, and solidarity.

Concluding remarks

This book rethinks how scholarly endeavours highlight distinct ways of working and being together, recognising new and more diversified communicative spaces, questioning dichotomies, and fostering critical viewpoints while bringing together numerous subfields within and cases from media studies. The authors of this edited book embrace extensive meanings of media studies by taking a colloquial concept of doing and being together as a facilitator of encounters among researchers and numerous other agents, such as civil society organisations, artists, and practitioners. In this effort, doing media together, doing research together and acting together are all utilised as umbrella terms, yet they are not definitive conceptual tools to outline this area of togetherness or collaboration per se. For future explorations, these concepts can be scrutinised and expanded and in turn might include an extensive array of works that can contribute to the already existing efforts presented in this book. The authors are willing and open to see a continuation of this effort, by possibly opening a new road for re-thinking and re-conceptualising togetherness in line with collaborative efforts.

References

Anderson, J., & Rainie, L. (2018). Artificial Intelligence and the Future of Humans. *Pew Research Center*. Accessed from https://www.pewresearch.org/internet/2018/12/10/concerns-about-human-agency-evolution-and-survival/.

Anscombe, A. B. (2009). *Consilience in Social Work: Reflections on Thinking, Doing and Being*. Bathurst: Charles Sturt University.

Aranda, J., Wood, B. K., Vidokle, A., & Negri, A. (Eds.). (2017). *Supercommunity: Diabolical Togetherness beyond Contemporary Art*. London: Verso.

Arendt, H. (1958). *The Human Condition*. Chicago: University of Chicago Press.

Bakhtin, M. M. (1993). *Toward a Philosophy of the Act*. Austin: University of Texas Press.

Baum, F., MacDougall, C., & Smith, D. (2006). Participatory Action Research. *Journal of Epidemiology and Community Health*, 60(10), 854–857. https://doi.org/10.1136/jech.2004.028662

Boboc, M. (2014). Connecting Communication to Curriculum and Pedagogy in Online Environments. In Stevenson, C. N. & Bauer, J. C. (Eds.), *Building Online Communities in Higher Education Institutions: Creating Collaborative Experience* (pp. 132–156). Hershey: IGI Global.
Browder, R. E., Aldrich, H. E., & Bradley, S. W. (2017). *Entrepreneurship Research, Makers, and the Maker Movement*. https://doi.org/10.13140/RG.2.2.20230.37441
Carpentier, N. (Ed.). (2011). *Media and Participation: A Site of Ideological-Democratic Struggle*. Bristol: Intellect.
Clarke, C. (2015). *Knowing, Doing, and Being: New Foundations for Consciousness Studies*. Exeter: Andrews UK Limited.
Couldry, N. (2004). Theorising Media as Practice. *Social Semiotics* 14(2), 115–132.
Davidson, D. (1963). Actions, Reasons and Causes, *Journal of Philosophy*, 60, 685–700.
Derry, S. J., Schunn, C. D., & Gernsbacher, M. A. (Eds.). (2014). *Interdisciplinary Collaboration: An Emerging Cognitive Science*. New York and Hove: Psychology Press.
Durkheim, E. (1982). The Nature of Society and Causal Explanation (1898). In: Lukes, S. (ed.), *The Rules of Sociological Method. Contemporary Social Theory* (pp. 31–159). London: Palgrave.
Eichner, S. (2014). *Agency and Media Reception: Experiencing Video Games, Film, and Television*. Potsdam: Springer.
Eldred, M. (2013). Arendt on Whoness in the World. In: Capurro, R., Eldred, M., Nagel, D. (Eds.), *Digital Whoness: Identity, Privacy and Freedom in the Cyberworld* (pp. 79–104). Frankfurt: Ontos Verlag.
Epicurus. (2000). *Principal Doctrines*. The Internet Classics Archive. Retrieved May 19, 2022, from http://classics.mit.edu/Epicurus/princdoc.html.
Firchow, P., & Gellman, M. (2021). Collaborative Methodologies: Why, How, and for Whom? *PS: Political Science & Politics*, 54(3), 525–529.
Freeman, R. (2008). Learning by Meeting. *Critical Policy Studies*, 2(1), 1–24.
Fortmann, L. (Ed.). (2009). *Participatory Research in Conservation and Rural Livelihoods: Doing Science Together*. Chichester: John Wiley & Sons.
Gürsoy, D., Sesigür, O., & Haydari, N. (2020). Rethinking Communication Research Methodologies: Interdisciplinary. Ph.D. Communication Conference (IPCC). *Interactions: Studies in Communication & Culture*, 11(1), 3–13.
Hayes, G. R. (2014). Knowing by Doing: Action Research as an Approach to HCI. In: Olsun, J. S. & Kellogg, W. A. (Eds.), *Ways of Knowing in HCI* (pp. 49–68). New York, NY: Springer.
Heath, R. G., & Isbell, M. G. (2017). *Interorganizational Collaboration: Complexity, Ethics, and Communication*. Long Grove: Waveland Press.
Heron, J., & Reason, P. (2006). The Practice of Co-Operative Inquiry: Research 'with' Rather Than 'On' People. In: Reason, P. & Bradbury, H. (Eds.), *Handbook of Action Research: Concise Paperback Edition* (pp. 144–154). London: Sage.
Howley, K. (Ed.). (2011). *Understanding Community Media*. Los Angeles: SAGE.
Jindal, N. (2020). Exploring Human Agency in the Age of AI. *Harvard Technology Review*. Accessed from https://harvardtechnologyreview.com/2020/01/27/exploring-moral-agency-through-art-spotlight-of-sarah-newman/.
Kolbaek, D. (Ed.). (2018). *Online Collaboration and Communication in Contemporary Organizations*. Hershey: IGI global.
Lavalley, R. (2017). Developing the Transactional Perspective of Occupation for Communities: "How Well Are We Doing Together?" *Journal of Occupational Science*, 24(4), 458–469.

Lee, P. (2006). *Collaborative Practices for Educators: Six Keys to Effective Communication*. Thousand Oaks: Corwin Press.
Leeds-Hurwitz, W. (1994). Crossing Disciplinary Boundaries: The Macy Foundation Conferences on Cybernetics as a Case Study in Multidisciplinary Communication. *Cybernetica: Journal of the International Association for Cybernetics*, 3(4), 349–369.
Malzacher, F., Faucheret, A., Kaup-Hasler, V., Kirsch, K., Peternell, A. R., & Rainer, J. (Eds.). (2015). *Truth Is Concrete: A Handbook for Artistic Strategies in Real Politics*. Berlin: Sternberg Press.
Martens, J. (2020). *Doing Things Together: A Theory of Skillful Joint Action*. Berlin: De Gruyter.
Mead, M., & Byers, P. (1968). *The Small Conference: An Innovation in Communication*. Paris: Mouton.
Molz, J. G. (2014). *Travel Connections: Tourism, Technology and Togetherness in a Mobile World*. London: Routledge.
Murawski, W. W., & Spencer, S. (2011). *Collaborate, Communicate, and Differentiate!: How to Increase Student Learning in Today's Diverse Schools*. Thousand Oaks: Corwin Press.
Nikoi, E., & Boateng, K. (Eds.). (2013). *Collaborative Communication Processes and Decision Making in Organizations - Advances in Human Resources Management and Organizational Development*. Hershey: IGI Global, U.S.
Nind, M., & Vinha, H. (2014). Doing Research Inclusively: Bridges to Multiple Possibilities in Inclusive Research. *British Journal of Learning Disabilities*, 42(2), 102–109.
O'Rourke, M., Crowley, S., Eigenbrode, S. D., & Wulfhorst, J. D. (Eds.). (2013). *Enhancing Communication & Collaboration in Interdisciplinary Research*. Los Angeles: Sage Publications.
Ostherr, K. (Ed.). (2018). *Applied Media Studies*. New York: Routledge.
Pawar, M., Anscombe, A. W., & Anscombe, B. (2014). *Social Work Practice Methods: Thinking, Doing and Being*. Cambridge: Cambridge University Press.
Puyalto, C., Pallisera, M., Fullana, J., & Vilà, M. (2016). Doing Research Together: A Study on the Views of Advisors with Intellectual Disabilities and Non-Disabled Researchers Collaborating in Research. *Journal of Applied Research in Intellectual Disabilities*, 29(2), 146–159.
Reckwitz, A. (2002). Toward a Theory of Social Practices. *European Journal Social Theory* 5(2), 243–263.
Rice, R. M. (2021). *Communicating Authority in Interorganizational Collaboration*. New York: Routledge.
Rousseau, J. J. (2004). *The Social Contract*. New York: Penguin Books.
Satne, G. (2021). Understanding Others by Doing Things Together: An Enactive Account. *Synthese*, 198(1), 507–528.
Schatzki, T. R. (1999). *Social Practices: A Wittgensteinian Approach to Human Activity and the Social*. Cambridge: Cambridge University Press.
Searle, J. R. (1990). Collective Intentions and Actions. In: Cohen, P. R., Morgan, J. L. and Pollack, M. E. (Eds.), *Intentions in Communication* (pp. 401–415). Cambridge: MIT Press.
Sellars, W. (1974). *Essays in Philosophy and Its History*, Dordrecht: Reidel.
Stevenson, C. N., & Bauer, J. C. (Eds.). (2019). *Enriching Collaboration and Communication in Online Learning Communities*. Hershey: IGI Global.

Stringer, E. (2004). *Action Research in Education*. Essex: Pearson Education Limited.
Swidler, A. (2001). What Anchors Cultural Practices. In: Schatzki, T., Knorr Cetina, K., & von Savigny, E. (Eds.), *The Practice Turn in Contemporary Theory* (pp. 83–101) London: Routledge.
Tuomela, R. (2013). *Social Ontology: Collective Intentionality and Group Agents*. New York: Oxford University Press.
Turner, S. P. (1994). *The Social Theory of Practices. Tradition, Tacit Knowledge and Presuppositions*. Cambridge: Polity Press.
Weber, M. (1991). The Nature of Social Action (1922). In: Runciman, W. G. (Ed.). *Weber: Selections in Translation* (pp. 7–33). New York: Cambridge University Press.
Weiss, M. P., Pellegrino, A., & Brigham, F. J. (2017). Practicing Collaboration in Teacher Preparation: Effects of Learning by Doing Together. *Teacher Education and Special Education*, 40(1), 65–76.
Wilcock, A. A. (1998). Reflections on Doing, Being and Becoming. *Canadian Journal of Occupational Therapy*, 65(5), 248–256.

Part I
Doing research together

2 Women's radio history in Turkey

The politics of reflecting together in oral history research

Nazan Haydari, Özden Çankaya and Cem Hakverdi

This chapter draws from the oral history project titled *Women Radio Broadcasters in the History of Turkey*.[1] The project aimed at revealing memories of women broadcasters who worked within the institutional body of the Turkish Radio and Television Institution (TRT) between the late 1960s and early 1980s. What is left out when the limited archives and written texts constitute the only source of interpretation in writing the history of media, gender and media institutions? Which layers of interpretation are conceivable in understanding the complex relationship between the subjectivities of women producers, the dynamics of media institutions, and the political, cultural and historical context? What other lenses become available when we engage in the media histories through the memories, experiences and emotions of women media producers? More importantly, how does the space of broadcasting expand our understanding of feminist politics and women's activism? Initiated by these questions, the oral history research process itself has become a transformative journey where we, as the authors, collaboratively explored women's subjectivities in radio broadcasting through interviews with over 20 women broadcasters, biographical accounts, personal archives, newspaper clips and various official documents.

With the co-author Özden Cankaya being one of the key interviewees, the research embodied a dialogic relationship of the insider and outsider perspectives which gradually transformed into a collaborative process of remembering, reflecting and reimagining. Production of a documentary film was not initially a planned outcome of the research project. Since it was our priority for our interviewees to share their stories freely, at first, we did not prioritize video recording as a means of archiving. To our surprise, most of the women broadcasters we interviewed enthusiastically agreed to engage in conversation with us in front of the camera and openly shared their emotions and experiences of working in radio. Powerful narratives emerged out of the interviews with the confidence and competence of the profession as experienced broadcasters in storytelling. The documentary film which we produced much later was an attempt to make those powerful stories more accessible. Our research process facilitated collaboration and relationship in multiple levels. We, the authors, contributed to the process through our competencies in academic research, media history, radio broadcasting, feminist studies, and documentary making. The research consisted of lengthy oral history interviews with women radio broadcasters (some are three hours long), an extensive search for any possible archival materials such as photographs or radio program recordings, the process of documentary making and collective screenings of the draft documentary with the broadcasters for a final consent.

Within the growing research addressing the histories, methodologies and strategies of women's cultural productions, the potential of radio to open a new window in gender history is often underlined while women's radio programming, women broadcasters and listeners are defined as significant lenses for historical analysis (Lloyd, 2020; Mitchell, 2015; Murphy, 2016; Skoog & Badenoch, 2020). Memory work with women broadcasters of TRT constitutes a significant space to historically explore women's agency and struggles beyond organized spaces of claiming politics, thus contributing to gendered sound histories in a non-Western context. Stephens (2010) underlines the ambivalence memory work carries for new interpretations of the past. Memory work as a methodology carries further significance in a country like Turkey, where the dismissal of historical documentation and achieving have been normalized and the attempts for understanding the politics of everyday and popular culture have historically received delayed attention. The process of remembering offers insights into the motivations, priorities and experiences of women broadcasters where radio broadcasting constitutes a space of resistance and contestation within the political, social and historical history of Turkey. Their narratives were the means of exploring how power and agency were utilized by them in interaction with the programs, their listeners, other members of the radio communities and networks of relationships. The persistent presence of women broadcasters in the aural space of radio facilitated the genderisation of everyday in the 1970s.

A rich literature on interviewing, intersubjectivity, interpretation, agency and politics of archiving defines oral history research as a complex process. Feminist approaches emphasize the importance of collaboration, relationship, dialogue and conversation in this process (Cobb & Williams, 2020; Sandon, 2018; Wang, 2019). In this chapter, we perceive oral history research as a non-linear process of collective knowledge production embodied within the everyday, mediated through structured and spontaneous conversations and moments and facilitated through various web of relationships. The discussion methodologically draws from our experiences and observations in conducting oral history research and producing a documentary titled *Radio, My Love*. Firstly, we argue that the acts of re-telling and hearing the stories introduced new discussions about gender and radio broadcasting as a profession. Secondly, we share exemplary moments in our archival search to underline oral history research as a spontaneous process. Both points move us to the documentary making as a collaborative process revealing the complexities in writing feminist media histories as a conclusion to this study.

The act of re-telling and hearing stories

Feminist approaches to history and the process of interviewing open different points of discussions with women recalling emotional and personal experiences of relationships, work life, achievements, disappointments, struggles or mistakes. Self-reflexivity, the nature of exchanges between interviewer and interviewee, the responsibilities of the researchers and the politics of interpretation have been widely addressed. Portelli (2018), describes an oral history interview "as an exchange of gazes and a co-created narrative between subjects—the interviewer and the interviewee—who are both observer and observed and speak to each other across the line of their significant otherness." Thus, interview constitutes a means of archive and a research tool, but also a "narrative space" (Portelli 2018, p. 240) for new questions and new interpretations of the past to emerge. The interview, then, is a knowledge production process mediated through the politics of location, priorities and identities of the researchers and interviewees but also through the temporary conversations, occasions and relationships.

The initial step in our research process consisted of oral history interviews with women broadcasters who spent a significant period of their lifetime in TRT taking various tasks as announcer, producer, auditor or manager. Our first interviewee was Özden Cankaya, the co-author and the co-researcher of the oral history project. Özden Cankaya started working at TRT in 1970, two years after graduating from the Law School. In 1981, she was unlawfully dismissed from her position due to her oppositional view with 101 radio and television broadcasters known as *101'likler* (the 101s). During her time at TRT, Özden worked as a producer and auditor under the management of varying ideologies and witnessed various political and institutional turmoil including the military interventions of 1971 and 1980. By going through challenging times following her dismissal from TRT, she had rebuilt her career as academic in the field of media and communication and worked as a professor until her recent retirement. With her books on the institutional history of TRT, she made a considerable contribution to the understudied media history of Turkey. The interviews in our project were multiplied through snowball technique, starting with women broadcasters in the circle of Özden Cankaya where her presence was mediated through her experience in broadcasting and her position as a researcher and interviewer.

By using the concept of "transactive memory", Smith (2010) talks about the importance of group oral recordings as what makes memory "social" is talk, and that remembering is often a shared project. The presence of Özden Cankaya during the interviews stimulated the memory, at times turning into a dialogic remembering process with new perspectives of the past and a new understanding of the selves. Various emotions of pain, anger, joy, nostalgia, at times grief, lament and sorrow were also triggered in revealing certain memories. Talking about the past for women was a chance to reflect on their gender identities, struggles, the power of their works and their own experiences. The difficulty in keeping the conversation around the topic is often defined as a challenge but also as an opportunity for a new window in history (Portelli 1997; Smith, 2010). Women we interviewed had long years of experience as producers, and announcers. In answering our questions, they seemed to be practising the profession of radio broadcasting in the past. Their enthusiasm and willingness were evident throughout the interviews. The majority of them were comfortable expressing their voices and political positions in front of the camera which we read as a sign of their persistent and oppositional personalities who believed in the transformative power of radio broadcasting as well as voice as a physical and a metaphorical concept.

The concept of voice in feminist studies often refers to the politics of representation and is associated with the subjectivity and agency of women. Voice is also a metaphor with emotional, political and personal dimensions and carries the potential to break silences and make silenced voices visible. Firstly, the metaphorical meaning of voice as reflected in the narratives locates women as the agents of history. The representational space constructed through the narratives presented the experiences and struggles of women through their own sources. Before one of the documentary screenings of the initial draft, an interviewee thanked us "for listening and hearing at a time when no one listens to each other". This can be seen as a symbolic expression of the fact that the voice of a generation that struggled to be the voice of the people was not heard. Secondly, voice also has a physical and concrete meaning. Ehrick (2015) underlines the significance of conceiving women's radio speech "as a performance of the gendered body and as a challenge to a regime wherein women are disproportionately expected to be silent (or at least quiet)." Conceptualizing voice as a sonic expression of the gendered body re-visits the relationship between the voice and the body, and the presence of gendered bodies in the soundscape. During the interviews, many stories about the occasions where women's voices were banned or unwanted were shared. For example, after the 1980 military coup, women's voices and female announcers were not allowed on the radio. Or in the 1970s, women were not allowed to present Good Morning programmes on the ground that farmers and villagers did not trust women's voices. After the start of television in 1968, men broadcasters were mostly assigned to television while women were asked to stay in radio, an unknown fact of history. The narratives also addressed the way they located their own voices in the soundscape of radio, their relationship with the recording machine and the relationship they draw between their identities, voice and quality of work. For women, the microphone and sonic space of radio were means of connecting with the public and practising their power to carry certain issues in the public space. The reliable voice within the institutional definition of TRT was expected to be "plain" to keep viewers and listeners focused on the story, not the storyteller.

Alongside voice as an expression, the interviews opened a "narrative space" for the reconceptualization of "feminism" in the context of Turkey. Narratives gave us insights about how women broadcasters associated themselves with radio, their professions, their strategies to challenge the status quo, and their struggles to become the voices of the public they were in touch with. For women, radio broadcasting was not a sole professional activity or work for a living, but rather was about ways of being, producing, a means for expression, building community and transforming social issues they cared for and prioritized. At one level, those struggles constituted a personal dimension, at other level it reflected the struggle of a community gathering around certain causes, and emotions. Similarly, their preference for the topics, issues and programmes were in a way "personal responses to the artistic and political world trends of the period" (Hendy, 2012, p. 361).

The reactions and commentaries we had from our interviewees in the follow-up conversations on various occasions have given us insight into how the collective process of making oral histories helped women broadcasters and ultimately, us understand the power of radio. It was observed that sharing memories and reminiscing about the past made them more aware of their passion for their profession as radio producers. Seaton (2004) suggests considering the radio programming as "like icebergs", to address the emotional labour invested behind the whole process (pp. 156–157). The act of retelling uncovered the emotional investment behind icebergs by reassessing gender identities, careers and struggles. While some interviewees explicitly mentioned experiences of gender inequality, others said that there was no gender inequality on the radio. Some interviewees who initially stated that they did not experience any forms of discrimination due to their gender identities, later called us and asked for a re-interview. When we met again, they re-evaluated their experiences as women broadcaster to present a new narrative about the past. This can be considered as the impact of the collaborative thinking process on personal memory. Discriminatory practices women faced involved the difficulty in taking managerial positions and being assigned to work in other geographic locations or extended working hours (nöbet) bringing challenges in creating a balance between family and work life.

The process of collective thinking and reflection also affected us as researchers and changed our conceptualization of the relationship between gender and radio broadcasting, feminist historiography and documentary as a narration of the past. Özden re-evaluated her experiences as a woman broadcaster and realized that she had never considered her own experiences from a gender perspective. When she recalled her programming strategies, she became more aware of the intervention strategies she had developed. For example, she avoided making programs that reproduced women's traditional roles. Instead, in morning programs for women, she addressed gender issues through topics such as law, social rights and economics. This approach carries similarities with the intervention strategies of feminist politics in the 1990s. Nazan reassessed the gaps in feminist historiography in Turkey and what constitutes feminist politics. She became more conscious of the problematic dichotomies in feminist history and more critical of historiography based on the preassumed waves. Cem reconceptualized the relationship between archival material and documentary film to produce a film prioritizes the voices and narratives of women defining them as the agents of the history.

Knowledge hidden within the spontaneity

The lack of archives, as widely addressed in media history research, presents a series of challenges in Turkey for recovering media histories in general and gendered media histories in particular. The archives of TRT Institution were regularly destructed due to various political and ideological reasons including changes in the political structures or what can be interpreted as a "modern attitude that sets the past clearly apart from the present" (Ahıska, 2006, p. 31). As came up in the interviews with women broadcasters, certain programs such women's programs, folk music programs or cultural programs were often not seen as worthwhile archiving. What was archived were mostly the speeches of the national leaders" (Ahıska, 2006, p. 31). Technological impossibility of the past and the professional ethics about institutional ownership of the recordings, -as many women mentioned, it never crossed their minds keeping or copying the recordings– limited the availability and accessibility of certain archival material. Throughout our research, we hardly had any access to the sound recordings from the 1960s or 1970s. TRT either does not open its archives for research or demands high fees to make them accessible. Thus, memory work and interviews constitute significant archival material when potential interviewees are alive and willing to share their memories. Therefore methodological, theoretical and practical complexities of oral history research often encourage researchers to look for other documents and non-media-centric material to recover the spirit of the past beyond the windows presented through the institutional records. The revelation of hidden knowledge is often mediated by relationship, spontaneity and collaboration. We would like to explain this point with our experience in revealing knowledge about *Kadın Dünyası* (The World of Women) program.

Women's World, co-produced by Filiz Ercan and Günseli Akol, came up frequently in our interviews on women's issues and women's programs. It was remembered as a women's program that left its mark on the 1970s with its content, approach, style and organizational structure. The program was one of the women's shows that started in 1974 and aired for five and a half years, with 848 episodes and 48,000 listener letters over a significant period of time. When we started the oral history project, the host of the program, Filiz Ercan, had unfortunately passed away. We were able to reach Günseli Akol after a long research process and learned that she was in the early stages of Alzheimer's and could not remember much about her broadcasting experience. However, she did share with us three years of written program scripts, written conversations between sentences, sentences in between sentences and notes on pre-recorded segments to be included in the program. Although we did not have access to the recordings of Women's World, the scripts opened a new window of interpretation. We were able to easily trace the topics covered in the episodes and in the listener letters, as well as the song requests from the listeners. Girls' education, relationships between couples, children and parents, relationships between mothers-in-law and daughters-in-law, women's rights to divorce and work, health issues and environmental concerns were widely covered in *Kadın Dünyası*. The content and programming strategies were similar to feminist intervention strategies in media production of the 1990s.

In later stages, Nazan's spontaneous lunchtime conversation with her colleague Esra Ercan led to a discovery that the deceased Filiz Ercan was Esra's aunt and to travel to Ankara to access Filiz Ercan's personal archives kept by her husband. A box filled with personal archives of Filiz Ercan and having a conversation with her husband opened her memories and priorities to our interpretation. During our conversation, her husband shared invaluable information that Filiz Ercan had started a column entitled Kadın (Woman) under the pseudonym of Işık Baraklı in the late 1970s, published three times a week for over a year at Cumhuriyet, a left-leaning newspaper of the time. In the history, gender-neutral or male pseudonyms were often observed. In the case of Filiz Ercan, the pseudonym probably emerged as an option to write about issues that she could not reflect in the radio environment and to overcome the limitations of being a civil servant. *Kadın*'s newspaper clips kept in the box revealed similarities in format with *Kadın Dünyası* radio program, such as the use of letters from listeners. Although her Pseudonym, Işık Baraklı are listed in the public archives of Cumhuriyet newspaper, nobody we contacted including her close friends had knowledge about her *Kadın* column. In her column, she discussed women's issues such as sex education, kin marriage, the fear of marriage and namus (honour) as regulatory tools on women's sexuality. The column lasted for a little more than a year before she stopped writing it due to the editorial censorship of one of her columns. "Transmediality" (see Hilmes, 2017, p. 142; Terkanian & Chignell, 2020, p. 21) shed light on motivations and struggles of women in making their voices heard. Regardless of the oppression, censorship and limitations, women developed intervention strategies to raise their voices and maintain their oppositional positions. Moving across media platforms from radio to newspapers to magazines and books was a search for developing new strategies to communicate with the public (Çelik & Haydari, 2022) The notion of transmediality can be transcribed in the experiences of women broadcasters to address their struggles, passion, artistic styles, and priorities, along with their search for the spaces and forms of expression within and beyond radio.

Radio, my love

Following this notion of transmediality, the documentary film *Biz Radyo Çok Sevdik* (Radio, My Love), as an edited and compiled together representation of narratives, produces experiences and observations of its own.

At first, Cem had reservations about turning oral history interviews into a documentary due to the lack of an archive. As he watched the interviews and we collectively reflected on the significance of the women's stories, he realised that a narrative that conveyed emotion to the viewer was possible. Murch (2001) points out that by the end of the film, the viewer does not remember the camera, the actors' performances, the editing or even the story. The audience only remembers what the movie made them feel. For Murch (2001), emotion is more valuable than the sum of everything else and is the one thing that cannot be sacrificed at any cost. If the emotion is right and the story moves in a unique and interesting way with the right rhythm, the audience will ignore the more technical problems. The documentary film *Biz Radyo Çok Sevdik* successfully traces the emotional, personal and political stories of women broadcasters. It mainly relied on the women's own narratives. A male voice was used in one of the representative listener letters. Music and radio announcements of the time and the images of military coups were also incorporated into the film. The montage style consists of complementing sections from the women's voices and narratives to present the collective voices of women. The documentary further constitutes an accessible space of narration to conceive the voices of women broadcasters as both "medium and message, in the abstract and in the concrete." An embracement of both physicality of voice and the representative power of the stories in the visual space of documentary (Haydari et al., 2023) provides a unique opportunity to place women's voices as the subject and object of history.

In order to provide the interviewees with the opportunity to reflect on their subjectivity as well as our take on their narratives, we had individual or group screenings with them for their final consent of the editing before launching the documentary. Those screening sessions were also turn into another form of collective thinking and reflecting. Thinking together about the sequence and editing process of the documentary also allowed for a new interpretation of women's history.

The documentary, as a conclusion, paying greater attention to the cultural lives of those who laboured within the TRT walls, visualised and diversified the study that allowed us to sense more clearly its overall fluidity as a heterogenous structure embodying various forms of struggles rather than a 'total institution' of the state or the voice of the authority. Hendy suggests that life stories can advance our understanding of bodies such as TRT as complex "emotional communities" rather than as "total" institutions (2012, p. 361). The collective voices of women in the documentary help us see women as part of the emotional communities. This approach also challenges the notion that TRT broadcasters as a somewhat characterless 'official' implementing the regulatory decisions without questions and showing any signs of agency whatsoever. Accounting for the multitude of emotional engagements that shape collective memories allows for a broadening of the scope of what counts as women's activism, ways of being well beyond the organized movements.

Note

1 The oral history project, Women Radio Broadcasters in the History of Turkey, conducted by Nazan Haydari and Özden Cankaya between 2019–2022, was supported by Istanbul Bilgi University Scientific Research Fund.

References

Ahıska, M. (2006). Occidentalism and registers of truth: The politics of archives in Turkey. *New Perspectives on Turkey*, 34, 9–29. doi: 10.1017/S0896634600004350.

Çelik, B., & Haydari, N. (2022). Parrhesia as journalism: Learning from the truth- and justice-seeking women journalists of twentieth century Turkey. *Journalism Studies*, 23(13), 1607–1624. doi: 10.1080/1461670x.2022.2096667.

Cobb, S., & Williams, L. R. (2019). Histories of now: Listening to women in British film. *Women's History Review*, 29(5), 890–902. doi: 10.1080/09612025.2019.1703542

Ehrick, C. (2015). *Radio and the gendered soundscape: Women and broadcasting in Argentina and Uruguay, 1930–1950*. Cambridge: Cambridge University Press.

Haydari, N., Sesigür, O., Ulutaş, A., & Irmak, B. (2023). Sound as technologies of the self for feminist pedagogy. *Gender and Education*, 35(5), 421–436. doi: 10.1080/09540253.2023.2194888.

Hendy, D. (2012). Biography and the emotions as a missing 'narrative' in media history. *Media History*, 18(3–4), 361–378. doi: 10.1080/13688804.2012.722424.

Hilmes, M. (2017). Entangled media histories: A response. *Media History*, 23(1), 142–144. doi: 10.1080/13688804.2016.1270753.

Lloyd, J. (2020). *Gender and media in the broadcast age: Women's radio programming at the BBC, CBC, and ABC*. New York: Bloomsbury Academic.

Mitchell, C. (2015). Re-sounding feminist radio: A journey through women's community radio archives. *Feminist Media Histories*, 1(4), 126–127. doi: 10.1525/fmh.2015.1.4.126

Murphy, K. (2016). *Behind the wireless: A history of early women at the BBC*. London: Palgrave MacMillan.

Murch, W. (2001). *In the blink of an eye: A perspective on film editing*. California: Silman-James Press.

Portelli, A. (1997). *The Battle Of Valle Giulia: Oral history and the art of dialogue*. Madison: University of Wisconsin Press.

Portelli, A. (2018). Living voices: The oral history interview as dialogue and experience. *The Oral History Review*, 45(2), 239–248. doi: 10.1093/ohr/ohy030.

Sandon, E. (2018). Engineering difference: Women's accounts of working as technical assistants in the BBC television service between 1946 and 1955. *Feminist Media Histories*, 4, 8–32. doi: 10.1525/fmh.2018.4.4.8.

Seaton, J. (2004). Writing the history of broadcasting. In *History and the Media*. D. Cannadine (ed.). Basingstoke: Palgrave Macmillan: 141–159.

Skoog, K., & Badenoch, A. (2020). Women and radio: Sounding out new paths in women's history. *Women's History Review*, 29(2), 177–182. doi: 10.1080/09612025.2019.1600648

Smith, G. (2010). Beyond individual/ collective memory: Women's Transactive memories of food, family and conflict. *Oral History*, 35, 77–90.

Stephens, J. (2010). Our remembered selves: Oral history and feminist memory. *Oral History*, 38(1), 81–90.

Terkanian, K., & Chignell, H. (2020). Nesta pain: The Entangled Media Producer. *Media History*, 26(1), 20–33. doi: 10.1080/13688804.2019.1679619.

Wang, J. H. (2019). Did they say what they thought? Gender, sound, and oral history in a Wisconsin women's radio program. *Journal of Radio & Audio Media*, 26(1), 63–74. doi: 10.1080/19376529.2019.1564998.

3 The artist's book
Working towards a collaborative methodology in art and design

Melike Özmen

The working methodologies of visual art and visual communication design are often distinctive and require different skill sets, even though art and design disciplines are similar in many ways. For instance, in exhibiting and promoting an artwork, a level of collaboration must be established between the visual artist[1] and the visual communication designer,[2] which demands interdisciplinarity. An artist's book is considered an artwork itself, but it is also an interface that provides a visual and haptic experience for its viewer to experience the artwork. Thus, the artist's book is a significant medium for revealing interdisciplinarity among art and design disciplines. It provides common ground for the artist and the designer by letting them build dialogue and explore togetherness in exhibiting and promoting the artwork.

This chapter, firstly, addresses the interdisciplinarity of art and design by opening the historically maintained hierarchical structure among those disciplines into a discussion for a collaborative working methodology. The second part focuses on the artist's book as a medium and as a significant space in exhibiting and promoting the artwork to build dialogue and collaboration through a case study of an actual artist's book created by an artist and a designer in three steps of research, analysis, and production.

The differences and similarities between art and design disciplines

The literature identifies art and design disciplines with various terms, such as fine arts, applied arts, decorative arts, crafts, and design. Nevertheless, both disciplines have a common objective: to provide communication between individuals, whether they are artists, designers, viewers, or users, by conveying ideas, emotion, or information through visual and creative means. Thus, the line between these disciplines is not sharp, if not blurred. However, there are debates if art and design are separate disciplines that fundamentally serve different purposes or if they essentially serve similar purposes by utilising similar methodologies with different approaches. These debates do not mainly pertain to the current era.

Arts, for Kant, is subdivided into mechanical and aesthetic (Kant, 2007). Mechanical art needs a purpose to be produced. Aesthetic art is subdivided

DOI: 10.4324/9781003389972-4

into agreeable art, and fine art aims to stimulate pleasure. As Mirahan-Farag states (2013), there was no distinction between fine arts and applied arts in the history of art until the implications of Kant's theory of art arose and led to the autonomy of art argument, which suggests that producing a utilitarian object obliges the producer of that object to factors such as commercial, economic, and social. That process would result in a non-autonomous artwork (Mirahan-Farag, 2013). Non-autonomous artworks embody a utilitarian aspect. Thus, they are not considered 'pure' or 'fine', but they are considered mechanical arts or applied arts. In contemporary culture, design discipline is associated with function and utilitarianism. The designer is responsible for producing something that aligns with the users' needs who will interact with or utilise that specific design product. Also, for commercial purposes, the outcome should not be ugly but beautiful. However, a work of art incorporates the right to be ugly. It is up to the artist to decide what their viewer will look at or interact with. The outcome is not related to the viewers' needs; it is related to the artist's way of self-expression.

The separation of art as fine arts and applied arts increased because of mechanisation and mass production, which detached art from its basis and caused a change in the function of art that surpassed the perspective of the 20th century (Benjamin, 2008). As the mechanical reproduction of the work of art became possible, a form of social hierarchy was produced between the creator of the original artwork and the person who reproduced it or created artworks in reproducible forms such as posters or books. This relationship resembles the contemporary relationship between the actors in the process of exhibiting and promoting the artwork.

It is possible to examine the interdisciplinarity of this process through a particular scenario. When artists prepare for their solo exhibition in a gallery space, they create a series of artworks through time to express their creative activity, imagination, and state of mind regarding a particular concept in a visual form. In this process, the selection of form, content, material, medium, technique, etc., depends on the individualistic methodology of the artist, which relies on their past experiences, particular skills, emotions, and their state of mind concerning the context in which they are creating the artworks. Through the production of the exhibition, the artist usually collaborates with a curator who develops ways in which the viewers can interpret the artworks through not only the exhibition but also publications and promotional materials. To create context, the curator contributes to the process with verbal elements, mainly text. In this step, the curator collaborates with the designer to juxtapose visual and verbal elements regarding the artworks and the context in which they will be exhibited. In such a scenario, the designer usually creates design products such as exhibition catalogues, posters, and other promotional materials. The designer uses their skills to create a visual language that communicates the content by combining text and images as design elements. In this process, the designer's methodology relies on their creative skills, their experiences regarding the visual literacy of the possible viewers/users, and how they interpret the main concept by using different methods of abstraction and utilising the design elements. In the final step of the collaboration, the designer needs to work with a printing house and with printing operators to decide on the form and the material of the publications and the promotional material, as the printing of the design products themselves requires a greater knowledge regarding the printing technology, binding techniques, materials such as ink and paper, colour specifications, bleeds, and special techniques such as coating, embossing, and folds. This scenario demonstrates the conventional means of exhibiting the artist's artworks and collaboration between four distinct disciplines.

Moreover, this scenario emphasises four accounts: the artist, the curator, the designer, and the printing operator, having a hierarchical relationship. Usually, there are three main accounts in the design process: the content provider, the designer, and the user. Clients or decision-makers are content providers. These actors are prioritised among themselves, which resembles a top–down structure. The designer is obliged to design the content provided by the decision-makers. The designer usually is not allowed to make changes regarding the content while creating the form.

Furthermore, even if the designer is trained to create designs that align with users' needs, the designer may make decisions in the design process, which depends on their trained eye. In this structure, the user is at the bottom consuming what is provided for them first by the decision-maker and second by the designer. If this structure is applied to the scenario with four accounts, the curator and the artist would be on top in the content provider zone, and the designer and the printing operator would be in the middle. Users/viewers of the outcome would be at the bottom. The artist creates the visual content, and the curator creates the written content. They hand over the visual and written content to the designer. The designer creates another visual form by utilising a suitable medium according to the users'/viewers' needs. If the suitable medium is print, the designer will communicate with a printing operator and exchange information regarding the printing process. The actors on the first two levels of the process can exchange the content with each other until they have a common understanding. Once the product is finished, the user/viewer can interact with it.

Creating an artwork, writing a body of text, or creating a design product are all processes involving meaning-making on both ends. The artist creates an artwork, or the curator writes a text regarding the artwork to convey a meaning or a message. Once the viewer interacts with the artwork, they create a personal meaning in their minds. Likewise, once the viewer reads the text regarding the artwork, the meaning-making process repeats itself. In this process, meaning-making is only about the viewers' interaction with the visual and written content. Even if it is planned before, the outcome of the meaning-making process depends on the viewers' experience.

Moreover, the designer creates a design product with the same content. Once the user interacts with the design product, different attributes, and elements of the design product direct and guide the user through their meaning-making process. Attributes and design elements such as information architecture, typography, colour, medium, page numbers, physical or digital form of the design product, orientation and alignment of the visual and written content, general layout, etc., affect the user experience. The user will be guided through their experience by reading or viewing the content in a particular order, with typographic elements of different sizes and colours, contrast, movement, harmony, emphasis, and hierarchy amongst design elements. The meaning or message the user will construct has been decided beforehand. The viewer of the artwork and the text is free to shape their own experience and meaning-making process, but for the user, the experience is already planned by the designer. Therefore, the actors in this process should work independently in their creative processes. However, overall, they need some form of collaboration to accomplish the inherent interdisciplinarity of the design process.

The debate about whether fine arts and applied arts are separated is one angle of the greater discussion about whether creatives can overcome the issues of specialisation and lack of independence for one's output without some form of collaboration with others. In his book *The Craftsman*, Richard Sennett discusses the kind of lateral thinking necessary for creating successful structures, institutions, and devices, which allows technicians to benefit from the bearers of embodied knowledge but mere manual labourers; and he states that the distinction between the head and the hand is not intellectual but social (Sennett, 2008). As stated above, four different accounts embody knowledge specific to their disciplines and expertise, and their collaborative knowledge plays an essential role in the process of exhibiting the artwork. Thus, the hierarchical relationship between these accounts does not stem from the intellectual superiority of one another. However, it stems from the roles associated with these accounts throughout history.

Furthermore, there were attempts to deconstruct the conceptual and social separation and hierarchy between fine arts, applied arts, and their actors. One of the leading examples of this approach was the Bauhaus School, which overcame the divisions between fine arts and applied arts by integrating its curriculum and training the students equally in art and technically expert craftsmanship (Ruhrberg et al., 2000). This approach constitutes the foundations of contemporary art and design education. It indicates interdisciplinarity apart from the social and economic factors that created the social hierarchy and practical distinctions between art and design disciplines. Instead, it focuses on collaboration among individuals with particular skills and knowledge to combine these into an enriched outcome. The concept of interdisciplinarity in this approach is similar to Morrison's (2015) definition of the term, which is a set of fundamental skills that enable individuals with distinct areas of expertise to collaborate effectively. Despite Morrison's definition emphasising the distinctions among areas of expertise, interdisciplinarity requires both similarities and differences to be effective. For instance, both art and design disciplines involve concept development, planning, and visualisation. The artist carries out these processes, visualises their expression as an artwork, and makes meaning. The viewer is at liberty to interpret the artwork and construct their own understanding. The designer carries out the same processes considering users' needs. Their goal is to convey a pre-established message to the user. The user interprets the meaning intended by the designer. They are not necessarily required to develop their own interpretation when interacting with the design product with a specific function. However, the designer can adopt the user's perspective and incorporate their own experience as part of the user experience in the design process.

In the creation of the artist's book subject to this chapter, Zeynep Beler[3] and I assumed the roles of the artist and the designer, respectively. We formulated a collaborative working methodology for exhibiting and promoting the artwork in the artist's book format, which differs from the conventional exhibition medium. Our backgrounds in art and design disciplines are of importance in this process. We both have experience in visual arts, visual communication design, printmaking, and exhibition curation. We wanted to decrease the number of actors and disciplines involved in the process to focus particularly on the interdisciplinary aspects of art and design disciplines. The artist's book as a medium provided us with a flexible field of research and practice with fewer actors.

Artist's book as a medium

As an exhibition platform where the efforts and methodologies of the collaborators are preserved, the artist's book is a compelling study object to examine how practical and conceptual predicaments might work together, as in ways artist's and designer's particular areas of expertise overlap and diverge. Artist's books originated in the 20th century as an established art form. They appeared in every significant movement in art and literature and realised works within avant-garde, experimental, and independent groups whose contributions have identified 20th-century artistic activity (Drucker, 2004). Artist's book was a way to fairly disseminate one's works in a print-dominated world and showcase them in a format challenging and independent of the gallery and the conventional exhibition.

The term artist's book varies in terms of authorship and form. There are artist monographs, which are in the form of retrospective assessments of an artist's work or surveys of a living artist's career. However, W. J. Strachan distinguishes 20th-century monographs from their earlier realisations using the term *livre d'artiste* (Adamowicz, 2009). There are also art zines, which are magazines/books, focusing on an artist's work generated around a specific concept rather than retrospective assessment. Both artists' books and art zines can be self-published, but traditionally, artists' books are sponsored by galleries, patrons, museums, etc., and produced in limited numbers to maintain their exclusivity. Art zines result from a collaborative effort in which a group of artists comes together, produces individual artwork centred on a particular concept, and publishes/exhibits the artwork in print format. Although the artworks are distinct, there is a connection between them and a dialogue that takes place between the artists and their artworks, as they originate from the same overarching concept. This process resembles the term used by art historian Yves Peyré, *livre de dialogue*. He defines the term as the equality of two expressions arising in a new form[4] (Peyré, 2001). This term gives equal importance to the collaborators of the artist's book instead of imposing a hierarchy. However, there are different opinions regarding the inherent collaborative aspect of an artist's book as a medium. According to Stephen Bury, an art historian, artist's books are books or book-like objects that an artist has had significant control over in terms of their final appearance. These books are intended to be works of art in their own right rather than simply reproductions of artist's work, books about artists, or books that only contain text or illustrations by artist (Bury, 1995). Bury's definition of the artist's book gives it a form and a function as an artwork. However, it also imposes a hierarchy and positions the artist among any possible collaborators in the process. His definition also strictly limits the possible content of an artist's book. Limiting the content in such a way also limits the form that would derive from the content. Hence, it disrupts an artist's creativity and ability to engage in dialogue with other actors. The artist's book is not only a work of art but also a design product. Thus, there is a user of the book as a design product and a viewer of the book as an artwork.

As a design product or as an artwork, the artist's book establishes a dialogue between different actors of art and design disciplines, including the artist, designer, viewer, and user. Moran suggests that interdisciplinarity is inherently transformative, goes beyond mere collaboration of different disciplines, and can create novel forms of knowledge by engaging with distinct fields (Moran, 2002). Likewise, the artist's book transforms the traditional book format in such a way that it resembles an interface[5] on different levels. On the first level, art and design disciplines meet and interact with each other via the artist's book. Artist and designer combine their expertise and knowledge to produce the artist's book. On the second level, the artist's book constitutes an interface in terms of meaning-making. The viewer experiences the artwork in the book and constructs meaning in their mind. The user experiences the book as an object or a design product and constructs a different meaning in their mind as they are guided through the pages via design elements and principles. On that level, the artwork and the text are pieces of information designed to create a semantic relationship between the design product and the user. In other words, it is a product of Information Design. Artist and designer construct an interface within the semantics framework and create a visual communication language for the viewer to interact with the book as an object. On the third and final level, the artist's book as an object is a physical interface. It provides a haptic experience, a necessary but generally inhibited component of experiencing artworks. Handling or touching artwork in a gallery or a museum is usually forbidden. However, the artist's book should be held, viewed, and touched to be experienced. On that level, the book's physical state, such as the book cover's material, the printing method, the weight, type, and texture of the paper, the binding method, etc., which the artist and designer decide together, becomes significant. The book format is unique as it allows the viewer/user to perceive different creative processes of the artist and designer united. Furthermore, the viewer/user can experience the artist's book, choose the context, and interpret the content on their terms as an active collaborator in the process.

As the artist and the designer, we aim to build a dialogue with each other and other actors in the design process through an interdisciplinary approach for this research. The artist's work focuses on the production of subjectivity by technologies of representation, in particular photography, cinema, and social media, that infiltrate all areas of daily life. She often works in the book format because it allows her to merge and shuffle these varying forms of personal narrative and experience of subjectivity. She has previously made and distributed various self-published artist's books and zines. I identify as a designer and a researcher, and my work combines design research and practice. My research interests include information design, the designer's experience as a user in the design process, visual storytelling, urban communication, experience design, and how our everyday life experiences are affected by technology and design. I work on these subjects in terms of temporality. I have practical experience as a designer in various media, including print, digital, photography, and video, and I previously designed books for my design projects. As the artist and the designer, we are experienced in book format and visual storytelling with different media. Therefore, our collaboration and dialogue are built upon the basis of both our similarities and differences.

The artist and I conducted a case study to demonstrate our collaborative working methodology for an artist's book as an outcome of this research.[6] The artist provided her artwork and text for this case study, and we created an artist's book called Z. by utilising our methodology. Our aim is that our approach to creating the artist's book will integrate both art and design disciplines, as well as involve research and practical application. Another main concern is providing common ground for these disciplines rather than prolonged social hierarchy and indicating functional and conceptual similarities rather than distinctions in creativity.

The case study

The case study took place between 7 April 2021 and 8 May 2021. However, the idea of creating an artist's book together emerged while we were locked up because of the pandemic between January 2020 and February 2021. Our living conditions were severely changed because of the pandemic, which affected our creative processes and how we identify ourselves as artists or designers. The artist and I were focused on our creative processes at our homes, and we exchanged many ideas in hours-long Zoom meetings with each other and our friends. At the time, the artist started a new series of digital paintings and was also working on a text comprising the concept of borrowing and cut-up methods using a combination of online text scramblers. She destabilised and glitched texts from an array of artist biographies and swapped out the pronouns of texts to read like the biography of a female subject referred to as Z. She used biographies of male artists of Western history such as Beethoven to fabricate the text because these biographies have interesting platitudes which could go for any artist when you take them out of context. She stated that her goal was to create an artist-bot, mining her identity from the debris of the internet, changing the pronouns, and stringing them together. The artist explained her scenario of an artist's book to me in one of our online meetings. She wanted to create an artist's book with her new digital works. However, instead of identifying as the artist, she wanted to refer to Z. as the book's artist. We decided to start the design process of an artist's book in which the artist would be the content provider, I would be the designer, and the persona Z. that is created by the artist would be referred to as the artist in the book.

Design process: research

The main aim of the research, as the initial step in the design process, was to examine six different artist's book examples we had access to reveal similar collaborative processes among the actors of the examples. As mentioned in the earlier paragraphs, the tactile experience of the artist's book carries great importance in the design process. Each of the selected books differed from the others in terms of form, such as different sizes and pages, in terms of collaborating actors such as artists, designers, printing houses, curators, editors, publishers, and artists' books that are outcomes of an exhibition or not. These differences are indicated in Table 3.1 and Table 3.2 shows collaborator actors for each book other than the author/artist and publisher.

Each of these books also differed from the others in terms of who provided the content, how the content was produced, and who decided on the visual language, such as utilising visuals, texts, typography, colours, book covers, materials, and other design elements of the book. Table 3.3 shows the characteristics associated with visual language and design elements of the selected artist's books. Each of these books indicated in Tables 3.1, 3.2, and 3.3 differed from the others visually in terms of their content.[7–8]

Design process: analysis

In the analysis of the selected artist's books, the differences and similarities in their form, content, and the actors involved are highlighted. The discussed artist's books, B1–B6, showcase diverse approaches in terms of content,

Table 3.1 Artist's books selected for research and analysis

Book	Title	Author/Artist	Year	Edition	Size	Pages	Language
Book 1 (B1)	Broken English Goodbye	Eren Su Kibele Yarman	2021	300	16 × 20 cm	88/pages are not numbered	English
Book 2 (B2)	fragMENtaTION 32, Make an Exception of Me	Zeynep Beler	2017	30	28 × 22 cm	16/pages are not numbered	English, Turkish
Book 3 (B3)	Halep Salonu	Wim Delvoye	2013	Not mentioned	15 × 20.5 cm	63	English, Turkish
Book 4 (B4)	Golden Age of Chaos and Clusterfuck	Theo Elias, Tuukka Kaila, Kosminen-Kollektiivi, Konsta Ojala, Robert. Parkinson, This Might Not Work	2017	100	24 × 17.5 cm	86/pages are not numbered	English
Book 5 (B5)	İçerik Magazine, No:6	Various Artists/ Participants	2016	Not mentioned	21 × 15 cm	80/pages are not numbered	Turkish
Book 6 (B6)	AYP, PEN, KİM	Hera Büyüktaşçıyan	2015	500	22 × 13.5 cm	113	English, Turkish, Armenian

36 Melike Özmen

Table 3.2 Collaborator actors for each book

Book	Editor/Curator	Designer(s)	Publisher	Content provider (Text, Visuals)	Printing house	Other actors credited in the book	Accompanied by an exhibition
(B1)	Editor: Ali Taptık	Eren Su Kibele Yarman	ONAGÖRE	Artist, curator	İstanbul: Ofset Yapımevi	Proofreading: Duygu Demir Binding: Ofset Yapımevi	No
(B2)	Curator: Necmi Sönmez Editor: Mine Haydaroğlu	Not mentioned	Yapı Kredi Yayınları	Artist, curator	İstanbul: Promat Matbaacılık	Not mentioned	No
(B3)	Curator: Brahim Alaoui	Not mentioned	Not mentioned / Unknown	Artist, curator	Not mentioned in the book	Gallery: Arndt, Berlin, Germany	Yes – Art International Istanbul, 2013, Gallery Arndt
(B4)	Not metioned	Artists	Rooftop Press	Artists	Helsinki: Printed by artists	Binding: Participating artists	Yes – Golden Age of Chaos and Clusterfuck, 2017, Myymälä2 Gallery
(B5)	Not mentioned	Not mentioned	Not mentioned / Unknown	Artists	İzmir: Meta Basım Matbaacılık Hizmetleri	Not mentioned	No
(B6)	Editor: Hera Büyüktaşçıyan	Utku Lomlu, LOM	Hera Büyüktaşçıyan	Artist	İstanbul: Ofset Yapımevi	English translator: Alexander Carter, Aslı Seven Armenian Translator: Sevan Değirmenciyan	Yes – 56th Venice Biennale, 2015, The Pavilion of Republic of Armenia

The artist's book 37

Table 3.3 Visual characteristics of the selected artist's books

Book	Visual language is decided by	Types of text	Types of text production	Types of images	Types of image production	Special printing technique/Type of binding
(B1)	Artist	1) Visual element (typographic forms, utilised as a design element), 2) placeholder (plain explanatory text, credits, commentary, etc.)	Produced by artist	Photographs illustrations	Found/Curated by artist, produced by artist	No/Softcover
(B2)	Artist	1) Visual element (typographic forms, utilised as a design element), 2) placeholder (plain explanatory text, credits, commentary, etc.)	Produced by artist (1), curator (2), editor (2)	Artwork	Produced by artist	No/Softcover
(B3)	Designer (Not credited)	1) Placeholder (plain explanatory text, credits, commentary, etc.), 2) artwork identification tags (name, size, technique, year, etc.)	Produced by curator (1), not mentioned (2)	Photographs	Artwork photography/Photographer not mentioned	Book cover – Leather embossing/Leatherbound softcover
(B4)	Artists	1) Placeholder (plain explanatory text, credits, commentary, etc.), 2) artwork identification tags (name, size, technique, year, etc.)	Produced by artists (1) (2)	Artwork	Produced by artists	No/Softcover
(B5)	Artists	1) Visual element (typographic forms, utilised as a design element), 2) placeholder (plain explanatory text, credits, commentary, etc.)	Produced by artists (1), not mentioned (2)	Artwork	Produced by artists	No/Softcover
(B6)	Designer	1) Visual element (typographic forms, utilised as a design element), 2) placeholder (plain explanatory text, credits, commentary, etc.)	Produced by artist (1), artist/editor (2)	Photographs artwork	Produced by artist	Book cover – Silver debossing/Clothbound hardcover

design, and collaboration. B1, credited to the artist as a writer, designer, and illustrator, features a collection of illustrations, poems, and stock visuals like space images and marine imagery. The visual language in B1 employs continuous visual and verbal montage with fragmented yet legible text. B2, an insert for a magazine, doubles as an artist's book, credited to the artist as the content provider. However, the artist is not credited as the designer in the book. The texts in B2 include an introductory statement by the curator and typographic forms created by the artist from various sources.

B3 serves as a catalogue of artist Wim Delvoye's artwork, with texts consisting of the curator's commentary and artwork identification tags. B3 showcases the artwork in a conventional form. Thus, both texts and visuals used in the book have a specific purpose. The artworks showcased in B3 are sculptures and installations. Thus, the artwork had to be photographed and edited to be printed. However, the photographer, the printing house, and the designer are not credited in the book.

B4 showcases artworks of various artists, and art collectives, Theo Elias, Tuukka Kaila, Kosminen-Kollektiivi, Konsta Ojala, Robert Parkinson, and This Might Not Work. It documents the process of creating an exhibition and the book is identified as one of the artworks in the exhibition. The artists involved in the process are credited as content providers and designers.

B5, an art zine and artist's book, revolves around the theme of 'copy' and features text fragments and visual elements created collaboratively by 13 artists. The visual elements are produced by participating artists as artworks. However, B5 does not indicate the names of the artworks or the artists. All the artists are credited as participants in the book.

B6, related to the work 'Letters from Lost Paradise' at the Venice Biennale, is designed in three languages with a unique typographic layout. The designer is specially credited in the book. It is in three languages, English, Armenian, and Turkish and each language is indicated with a different colour in the book. It is designed in a traditional format with two-facing pages. However, the texts as typographic forms start in one spread and overflow to the next spread, which creates continuity and movement in the overall design.

The analysis reveals that B6's approach aligns closely with the writer's vision, where all participating actors, including the designer, are duly credited. In contrast, B3 diverges from this ideal by overly emphasising the curator's role and neglecting other actors involved in the process. Notably, B1's publisher, ONAGÖRE, and B4's publisher, Rooftop Press, exemplify an open and collaborative approach to publishing, embracing equal voice and interdisciplinarity. ONAGÖRE states they embrace principles of equal voice among actors of culture and art environment in Istanbul (*Hakkımızda/About*, n.d.). This statement suggests they recognise possible actors in the process and are open to collaboration. Rooftop Press states that they see publishing as an artistic practice and their publications as a space for contemporary art (*Rooftop Press, Helsinki*, n.d.). The first part of their statement intrinsically suggests interdisciplinarity and collaboration, as publishing and artistic practice are two separate disciplines. The second part of their statement suggests that they are not bound or inhibited by the characteristics of neither print medium nor book as a medium. B4 and B5, with multiple artists collaborating on specific themes, inspire the concept for Z.'s artist's book, focused on cutting, copying, and reinterpreting information.

In summary, the analysed artist's books offer a rich landscape of approaches to content, design, and collaboration. B6 aligns well with the desired approach, crediting all participants. The discrepancy in B3 highlights the importance of recognising the contributions of all actors. Meanwhile, the publishers' stances in B1 and B4 emphasise openness and collaboration, providing inspiration for Z.'s artist's book concept.

Design process: production

At the beginning of the production process, the artist shared her digital artwork and text with me. We had a preliminary discussion on the book examples, and we created three lists to base our production: concept list, digital object/element list, and attributes list. The lists are indicated in Table 3.4.

In this study, Information Design is a tool for facilitating the interaction between the artist's book and the viewer/user. As a designer, I aim to position this book as an object and an interface and create a visual language for the viewer/user to comprehend the book's contents. Together as a team, we decided on how to translate the tactile actions of a digital graphical user interface into the physical interface of the book, such as translating sliding windows glitch to accordion spreads or stacking of digital layers to the stacking

Table 3.4 Concept list, digital object/element list, attribute list

Concept list	Digital object/Element list	Attribute list
Digital	Layers	Grey out
Glitch/Bug	Windows	Size
Mimesis-imitation	Frames	Scale
Repetition	Grid	Resolution
Borrow	Icons	Opacity
Copy/Cut paste	Text box	Flatness
Scramble	Glyphs	Snap
Leakage	Buttons	Rotation
Movement	Cursor	Colour (RGB)
Transparency	Hourglass	Pixelation
Stacking	Spinning beach ball	Overflow
Masking	Bounding box	Alignment
Flexibility	Crop marks	Proportion
Virus	Mesh	Quantity
Algorithm	Scripts	Distortion
Temporality	Pixel	
Cluster	Noise	
Memory		

of physical spreads and deciding on the overall visual language by using the lists we created together.

In the process, the artist provided 19 pieces of digital artwork. After our preliminary discussion, I decided to narrow the number of artworks from 19 to 10 to create an efficient design based on the number of signatures for printing. We decided together which artworks would be eliminated from the book. Once the number of artworks to be used in the book was decided, I started to work on the book's dimensions. I created two alternatives which include the physical form and visual design of the artist's book. In May 2021, I sent these examples to the artist with photographs of simple mock-ups for each format.[9]

The first book example is an accordion book format. We chose this format with the artist because we thought it mimics certain aspects of the digital environment, such as scrolling, cropping, and movement. The accordion format is also distinguished from the conventional book format as the spreads are not limited to two-facing pages. Instead, every consecutive two pages create a new spread like a chain. I used visual design elements in this first example to create layering and stacking on the spreads. The size of the book is 16 × 18 cm.[10]

The second book example resembles the traditional artist's book format. Artist's books have a widely accepted format, which is partly preserved in the design of this book. Examples that are analysed in the analysis chapter are similar to each other in terms of their physical forms. However, the second example presented in this chapter subverts the format via different sizes and layers of booklets stacked on each other. This example also mimics certain aspects of the digital environment, such as layers, frames, stacking, and windows. The size of booklets from top to bottom is 13 × 8 cm, 14 × 6 cm, 14 × 10 cm, and 16 × 24 cm. I did not put any content in Booklet 1, as I wanted to elaborate on the two examples with the artist first.[11]

After I designed two different book examples, the artist and I arranged a video call to discuss and work on the design alternatives together. Through our live session, we decided to continue with the second book example, but we wanted to keep specific attributes of the first example. Once we decided on the physical format, I opened the software on my computer and shared my screen with the artist. As we continued discussing, I changed and rearranged the layout and the design elements. First, we worked on Booklet 4, which contains digital artwork. After discussing the layout and the spreads, we decided to increase the number of artworks from 10 to 15. This book section resembles the conventional artist's book format the most. It contains artworks without any visual disruption or intervention and the labels of the artworks. The labels contain the name and date of the artworks alongside scrambled scripts.

Secondly, we worked on Booklet 3, which contains the text. To preserve the nature of the artist's text, I created typographic expressions by disrupting the order of the text. The artist approved the semantic relationships between the text and the typographic expressions. The first page of Booklet 3 also resembles the conventional artist's book format. It mimics a legible and comprehensible text but progressively becomes more illegible and macular as the viewer/user proceeds with the experience. To exaggerate this attribute, we started with a page number, and after the first spread, we stopped using page numbers as a design element. Booklet 2 only consists of one spread. Once opened, the viewer/user can see the colophon. The glitched text continues in this booklet, but actual information regarding the artist's book can also be seen. Booklet 1, which was left empty on purpose, is where the first and second book format alternatives are combined. We decided to use the accordion format and layout from the first alternative in Booklet 1. This booklet serves as a conceptual summary of the artist's book. It prepares the viewer/user to decipher the book's content like a Rosetta stone, so we decided to position Booklet 1 above other booklets. This process resulted in a complete first draft of what is eventually planned to become a published artist's book.[12]

Overall, we figured out a common methodology to get the most benefit from this collaboration regarding the end product and the case study. To begin, we conducted research by analysing six different examples of artist's books to examine their visual language and design process. Next, we compared and contrasted these books to identify similarities and differences. Following this, we proceeded to create our own artist's book. During the production stage, we generated three lists – the concept list, the digital object/element list, and the attributes list – to guide our production process. I created two physical mock-ups and two layout examples for our book using these lists. The artist and I then reviewed these options and selected the second layout example. We collaborated on revisions for this layout and completed the first draft of our artist's book.

Conclusions

The collaboration and interdisciplinarity between art and design disciplines are restrained within the boundaries of social hierarchy amongst the actors of processes within these disciplines. There is a hierarchy between the curator and the artist, the artist and the designer, the viewer of the artwork and the artist, the designer, the user, and so on. This research points out the disputes and hierarchy between art and design disciplines and how this relationship has been formed throughout history. After positioning the causes of the issue, this research offers a collaborative and interdisciplinary methodology for these disciplines in terms of exhibiting and promoting the artwork via a case study.

As a result of the case study, two key topics surfaced: finding common ground and building dialogue. These subjects should be considered in any creative process involving actors from art and design disciplines. Primarily, both disciplines have more common ground than differences. Even in terms of education, the foundational subjects of these disciplines are substantially similar. Both disciplines base their foundation on colour theory, composition, abstraction, visual culture, etc. After absorbing foundational knowledge, students of these disciplines construct their creative methodologies. Through time people with similar abilities and tendencies position themselves in the hierarchical structure of these disciplines and act like they do not have common ground. The case study explained in the chapter demonstrates that it is possible to let go of the hierarchical structure and build dialogue between these disciplines by respecting and understanding each other's creative processes. Instead of ordering around or criticising each other, the actors should find a way to understand each other's needs and trust each other's individual experiences of each other to build dialogue.

This research and case study demonstrates the relationship between two actors and a specific part of the creative process. For future projection, it would be possible to continue the design process by adding more actors from different disciplines, printing the proposed artist's book, and documenting the rest of the process to demonstrate different scenarios.

Notes

1. Visual artist will be referred to as an artist in this chapter.
2. Visual communication designer will be referred to as a designer in this chapter.
3. Zeynep Beler will be referred to as the artist.
4. Translated from French: 'l'e´galite´ de deux expressions dans le surgissement d'une forme Nouvelle'.
5. An interface is a point where two or more systems, subjects, and organizations meet and interact (*Oxford Languages | the Home of Language Data*, n.d.). It is a surface forming a common boundary of two or more bodies, spaces, or phases (*Definition of INTERFACE*, 2019), or it is a situation, a way, a place where two or more systems come together and influence each other (*INTERFACE | Meaning in the Cambridge English Dictionary*, n.d.).
6. Zeynep Beler and I presented our case study at the IPCC 2021 Interdisciplinary PhD Communication Conference (Özmen & Beler, 2021). Her statements mentioned in the chapter terms of the case study are from the conference presentation.
7. Link to B1 visuals: https://tinyurl.com/b1visual
8. Link to B6 visuals: https://tinyurl.com/b6visual
9. Book example 1 and Book example 2 mock-ups: https://tinyurl.com/bookexamples1and2
10. Book example 1 visuals: https://tinyurl.com/bookexamples1and2
11. Book example 2 visuals: https://tinyurl.com/bookexamples1and2
12. Book example 1 and Book example 2 visuals: https://tinyurl.com/bookexamples1and2

References

Adamowicz, E. (2009). The Livre D'artiste in Twentieth-Century France. *French Studies*, 63(2), 189–198. doi:10.1093/fs/knp061

Benjamin, W. (2008). *The Work of Art in the Age of Mechanical Reproduction*. (J. A. Underwood, Trans.). London: Penguin Books.

Bury, S. (1995). *Artists' Books: The Book as a Work of Art, 1963–1995*. Aldershot: Scolar Press.

Definition of INTERFACE. (2019). Merriam-Webster.com. https://www.merriam-webster.com/dictionary/interface

Drucker, J. (2004). *The Century of Artists' Books.* New York City: Granary Books.

Hakkımızda / About. (n.d.). *Onagore.dukkan.im.* https://onagore-lokal.myshopify.com/pages/onagore-istanbulda-mesrutiyetde-bulusuyor

INTERFACE | meaning in the Cambridge English Dictionary. (n.d.). Dictionary.cambridge.org. https://dictionary.cambridge.org/dictionary/english/interface

Kant, I. (2007). *Critique of Judgement.* Oxford: Oxford University Press.

Mirahan-Farag, M. (2013). The Segregation of Applied Arts from Fine Arts and the Status of Fashion. In P. Hana (Ed.), *An Anthology of Philosophical Studies* (Vol. 7, pp. 145–155) essay, Athens: Athens Institute for Education and Research.

Moran, J. (2002). *Interdisciplinarity.* Oxon: Routledge.

Morrison, D. (2015). *The Underdetermination of Interdisciplinarity: Theory and Curriculum Design in Undergraduate Higher Education* (Publication No. glathesis:2015-6094) [Doctoral dissertation, University of Glasgow]. https://theses.gla.ac.uk/6094/

Oxford Languages | The Home of Language Data. (n.d.). Languages.oup.com. Retrieved August 4, 2023, from https://en.oxforddictionaries.com/definition/interface

Özmen, M., & Beler, Z. (2021, May 7–8). *Working Towards a Collaborative Methodology in Art and Design: The Artist's Book* [Conference presentation]. IPCC 2021 Interdisciplinary PhD Communication Conference. Istanbul, Turkey. https://ipcc.bilgi.edu.tr/ipcc-2021-v2/

Peyré, Y. (2001). *Peinture et poésie: le dialogue par le livre, 1874–2000.* Paris: Gallimard.

Rooftop Press, Helsinki. (n.d.). *Rooftoppress.fi.* http://rooftoppress.fi

Ruhrberg, K., Schneckenburger, M., Fricke, C., & Honnef, K. (2000). *Art of the 20th Century.* Newyork: Taschen.

Sennett, R. (2008). *The Craftsman.* New Haven, CT: Yale University Press.

4 Duo autoethnographic approach to peer-to-peer collaboration in PhD process

Begüm Irmak and Ayça Ulutaş

Prologue

This study is the collective effort on the lived experiences of PhD journeys of two authors who have achieved their doctoral degrees within Istanbul Bilgi University's Doctoral Program in Communications. This conversational study is a dialogic exploration into how the self-created collaborative peer relationship shapes the way they experience the PhD process and plays a role in finding their ways and academic selves. With the help of this journey, the authors aim to explore the meanings of collaborative efforts, reflecting on their personal yet interconnected studies on gender, new media and technology. This togetherness in achieving a common goal encouraged the authors to revisit the process of being a doctoral student and finding balance in everyday life endeavours through deconstructing the meanings of working together. Hence the repercussion of togetherness is aimed to be framed within the conceptualisation of peer-to-peer support in PhD studies, fuelled by personal narratives rather than meta meanings attributed to this peculiar journey.

Providing support and assistance for students in doctoral education has received considerable research attention over the past two decades. The asymmetric nature of the relationship between supervisor and supervisee, the individualised nature of working up within self-paced models dominating scholarly environments and limited opportunities for social engagement that necessitates self-motivation are well documented by the previous studies as the *raison d'etres* for the social isolation experienced by doctoral students and low doctoral completion rates and persistence (Barnacle & Mewburn, 2010; Stracke, 2010). With respect to the available support in educational environments, the attention mostly focuses on the traditional research relationship of supervision and formal academic assistance (Malfroy, 2005; Bista & Cox, 2014), which leads to a neglect of the value of more naturally developed organic forms of relationships and peer-to-peer collaboration as a valuable source of both emotional and academic support. While the limited number of research focusing on the collaborative process between students demonstrates the association of peer support with well-being and positive academic outcomes (Littlefield et al., 2015; Wegener et al., 2016), there is still a considerable gap in our contextualised understanding of peer-to-peer support in relation to individualised experiences of PhD that can fluctuate enormously. While our stories of PhD claim the prominence of supervision and bring to light the issue of peer-to-peer collaboration's role as a crucial dimension of the doctoral students' process of development, the predominant fact is that PhD experience is a multifaceted compound that cannot be defined primarily by a single component. Our social worlds need to be considered as an important part of the PhD research process and the meaning of peer support should not be obtained from the individual contexts and backgrounds of the collaborators. In parallel, as two individuals who completed their doctoral degrees in the field of technology, new media and gender, we suggest that the area of speciality needs to be considered as an additional layer of this integrative process not only in shaping the overall journey and our understandings of collaboration but also in the exploration of one own's positionality and identity as a researcher. In other words, the concept of peer-to-peer support cannot be defined strictly by an arbitrary set of rules or attitudes but is rather shaped by the relationship within which it occurs. Like the PhD experience itself, the conceptualisation of collaboration and formation of academic selves as women are the processes to be emphasised as fluid and complex.

Departing from this point of view, the authors of this study embarked on a duo autoethnographic journey by concurring on the idea that there is still a lot to learn about the academic self, embedded in the collaborative practice by reflecting on their ongoing dialogues throughout the mutual experience of the PhD process. So, the intention of the authors is not to reify the experience of doctoral education or reach a consensus on the role and definition of peer-to-peer support, but first to make sense of themselves by re-constructing their perceptions of a mutual experience through juxtaposing points of individual similarities and differences in educational and social backgrounds, and second, to provide the reader a dialogical space through a dynamic text within which they can draw their own conclusions, find their own meanings and synthesis.

As Giddens (1991) points out, self-identity is in a state of flux. Just as our identities are not fixed, meanings we ascribe to a phenomenon in our lives are not permanent but are bound to an alteration, depending on the given place, time and the people whom we are interacting with. Taking into consideration the transformative intentions of duo autoethnography, as early career researchers, the authors take the following dialogue as an opportunity for growth in self-knowledge by examining the ever-evolving process of meaning-making around the role of peer-to-peer collaboration in their PhD experience. While the topic of this study and the duo ethnographic partnership are derived from a mutual experience and everyday conversational structures, the process of meaning-making is rooted in a trust established between the authors who knew each other before the study began. As one of the critical tenets of duo autoethnography, without trust 'disclosure would not be forthcoming, nor would rigorous conversations' (Norris et al., 2012). In parallel, as the sites of the study, insight into the identities and backgrounds of the writers needs to be provided to be able to place transparency in writing and explicitness of the voices at the centre of this duo autoethnographic process.

Ayça has a BA in Business Administration and following her MS in Integrated Marketing Communications, she started her professional career as a public relations specialist and continued to work as a marketing communications manager of many leading brands in the technology industry for more than ten years. PhD is the starting point of alternative identity development and an opportunity for critically transforming her understanding of the discipline of communication and research. At this point, she pursues her individual project of self as a researcher immersed in the field of gender, media and communication studies. For her, PhD is definitely a socially isolated journey, but is not necessarily a lonely one. Though their educational backgrounds and life experiences differ, similar personalities and shared goals brought her together with Begüm, which led to a supportive collaboration throughout her journey.

Begüm has a BA in Social and Political Sciences and an MSc degree in Sociology. After completing her master's degree in London, she returned to Istanbul, to pursue a career in advertising. PhD journey transformed her both emotionally and professionally, creating room for questioning and reshaping life goals and career plans. Even though her initial goal remains the same, her role as an early career researcher has fostered eclectic meanings. Currently, she continues to take an administrative role in a family business and works as a part-time lecturer at two universities. For her, PhD is one of the most peculiar and challenging journeys she has ever encountered, and she is still counting on the collaborative relationship she has built with Ayça during this turbulent process.

Contemplating on methodology: our routes to conducting a duo autoethnographic study

Before delving into this collaborative work, we were aiming to locate a method of drawing on personal experiences to broaden our sociological imagination regarding social challenges in our fields. Scrutinising the personal yet very connected narratives, our main concern was to be able to create a reflective and dialogic atmosphere in which the experiences of both parties could be presented and analysed. Hence, duo autoethnography complies with our initial motivation in terms of providing polyvocality and disruption of metanarratives circulating around the PhD experiences and how it is constructed around the notions of loneliness and self-isolation. Rooted in the philosophical and theoretical foundations of autoethnography (Fitzpatrick & Farqhuar, 2018), duo autoethnography also presents how co-reflectivity through dialogical methods can influence research identity and alter their understandings of the research they are involved in. In this type of research, the researchers – in this example Ayça and Begüm – take on the role of study participants.

Duo autoethnography is described as a postmodern approach to qualitative research that is both creative and innovative (Ellis et al., 2011). As in the case of auto-ethnography, there is a deeply personalised interpretation of the researchers' experiences 'to extend understanding about societal phenomena' (Anderson, 2006; Wall, 2006, p. 1). First proposed by Sawyer and Norris (2015), the narrative of the self is prioritised, borrowing from postmodern philosophical and interpretivist underpinnings, in duo autoethnographic approaches. Instead of creating and relying on meta-narratives, there is a shift towards personal stories that could be scrutinised in what they term as 'dialogic tension' (Sawyer & Norris, 2015). This approach is also depicted as a form of self-narrative that requires a critically reflexive effort between the participants. Building upon Norris and Sawyer's (2015) work, Breault (2016) more recently came up with criteria distinguishing trustworthy duo autoethnography. Providing a list of 23 items to consider when evaluating duo autoethnography, he underlines the vitality of transparency rather than making claims about truth or objectivity. As prescribed, we as the participants of the research tried to present our experiences as transparently as possible through sharing our vulnerabilities. Hence, what we are offering are not conclusive or objective findings but rather suggestions based on scholarly exploration of our unique experiences.

In the literature, there are two common forms of conducting duo autoethnography, the first of which is the storytelling approach, where the narratives of the participants are presented and discussed in relation to each other, as we have adopted in this study (Hamood, 2016). The second approach encourages participants to review collectables that act as commemoration prompts (Hamood, 2016). As will be shown throughout this study, the focus is on the pre-selected topic – peer-to-peer collaboration in PhD studies – and the dialogues mainly revolved around this topic to eliminate an environment in which random chats dislocate the main points. Through utilising the primary method of duo autoethnography, that is the dialogue, the participants aim to deepen each other's understanding of the topic and at times challenge each other's views (Ruggunan & Kinnear, 2019).

Sawyer and Norris (2015) claimed that 'Duo autoethnographers use themselves to assist themselves and others in better understanding the phenomenon under investigation' (pp. 13, 2). In a similar vein, our focus is on the shared narrative of the PhD experience by contemplating two distinct voices: perspectives and positionalities. We position ourselves as duo autoethnographers 'who want to bring a critical lens to deepening their self-understanding regarding a particular topic' (Ruggunan & Kinnear, 2019, p. 7). In this sense, cooperative data gathering is an essential aspect of duo autoethnographic research, whether collaboration is conducted fully throughout the study or at certain stages of research by the participants. This study adopts the former approach in which two authors collaborate fully at every stage of the research process including data collection, analysis and writing. The long-established togetherness of the researchers during their PhD education enabled the curation of a number of dialogical experiences, which had become centralised on the role of peer support in shaping the experience of a PhD. On that note, the past experiences of two PhD candidates served as a threshold to the path of the research and the collective decision of the topics to be explored at the beginning of the data collection. Thus, the data collection included earlier WhatsApp messages and email texts, in addition to the conversational interviews and a number of self-reflection practices. Whereas this first step is an important consideration as it allows the researchers to compile their autobiographical data without the influence of each other, the main data collection method is centred on the use of natural conversational structures, which raises the level of consciousness around the current perceptions of authors' experiences. By taking advantage of video-conferencing, researchers met online every two weeks for a period of three months and exposed themselves to each other to create dialogical narratives. The time periods between the meetings opened a space for the researchers to generate their own self-reflections in the form of written memos that informed the tentative points of the discussion and guided the next conversations. On the other hand, data analysis was not separate from the data collection. Rather than a linear process, we generated further data through an iterative analysis and reflexive writing. After each draft, emergent themes were identified, sorted out based on their resonation with the objective of the study, and integrated into a coherent organisational structure. Rather than a linear process, we generated further data through an iterative analysis and reflexive writing. We co-identified themes in the data as: Questioning Our Paths to Academia, Identity in Transition, PhD is a Black Box: Creating a Safe Zone.

Questioning our paths to academia

Ayça: Though there is no explicit claim of universality, narrative of doctorate process in general have consistently predominated by the concepts of alienation, isolation and loneliness (Weidman et al., 2001; Ali & Kohun, 2007), which lead to an assumption that our experiences are necessarily compatible to one another. It is difficult to comparatively research individuals 'lived experiences of PhD as it is unique. So, prior to immersing ourselves in a dialogue about our collaborative relationship during the PhD process, it may be helpful to start with a discussion about how we ended up with an academic career as women coming from different educational backgrounds but similar social profiles. Although we haven't had the opportunity to talk about it until now, I often find myself wondering what doing a PhD really means for each of us.

Begüm: I went to college to study economics because that was what my parents dreamed of for me, to study economics and run the family business. Therefore, my enrolment in the social and political sciences at the university caused quite a lot of family conflict. But I was insistent on what I wanted. I went to England to do my master's degree in sociology because when I finished university, I was sure about my dream of becoming an academic in this field. When I returned to Turkey, my resume pointed to the path to a career in the advertising industry. But after a while, I realised that advertising was starting to seem very distant to me philosophically, and in fact, it can be said that within this period of my life, I have moved away from my dream of being an academician. I left the industry and went back to the family business and realised that my dream is still alive inside of me. When I think about it, I was sure from the beginning that I wanted to be a lecturer and hence my PhD journey started with the motivation of an academic career.

Ayça: While your story points to the divergences and convergences in our individual paths and motivations, I can see that PhD serves a common purpose for both of us: becoming an academic. Establishing myself as an academic was to be part of a community of women that produce for the benefit of all, rather than becoming a faculty member or following a new career path. But the fact is that an academic career was not something I had dreamed of or was prepared for from the very beginning, but rather something that I discovered on the way. I believe that the personalities and identities we envision for ourselves cannot be thought of separately from the individual conditions and the cultural contexts. I decided to focus on the field of marketing, which I thought would allow me to use my creativity, and I completed my master's degree in marketing communication in the USA with great pleasure and satisfaction. So, unlike you, I can speak of an investment in my educational background that completely prepared me for a professional career and praxis. After years of marketing experience, I decided to resign from an identity of white-collar career women with an increased awareness of the professional boundaries that apply to someone's self-definition to find a more meaningful way of being a productive woman. Becoming an academic is an important part of my efforts in this direction and PhD was a first step into it. The tendency to act towards the expectations of others, which is perceived more important than what one wants for herself, and the internal contradictions as a result, were the common points that caught my attention in our stories. I wonder if this has something to do with the way we were raised in relation to our similar social contexts?

Begüm: I think it's all about being a woman who is raised with certain unique ideals in adopting the dynamics of a patriarchal society. Your parents are concerned about you, they want to make sure you check certain boxes in terms of handling your life, such as the likelihood of finding a place in business life as a woman becomes a major concern after college. It is all about 'raising a girl who can stand on her own feet', or whatever that entails.

Ayça: Departing from this point and considering that PhD is a challenging journey, what can we say about the meanings and feelings we attribute to it?

Begüm: It was the way to prove myself, especially to myself. It's a pretty long process and I've dedicated this time to something I've chosen and admired. It was much about granting my own authority over how I want to see myself and what I can do well which is similar to what is described as self-authorship – 'taking responsibility for one's actions and life decisions, not simply relying on the advice or actions of others' (Barber et al., 2013, p. 868).

Ayça: It is about growing in your self-knowledge, challenging yourself to get over your internal limits and realise your potential. The term that came after I opted out of my professional career brought the traditional roles to the fore in my life. But I accepted the challenges of workload and role strain stemming from single mothering and embarked on a PhD journey to reinvent myself as a researcher. As a middle-aged woman who returned to her education life after a long time and being so practise oriented and focused on entirely different aspects of her identity for so long, I can be considered as an atypical academic in this context. Doing a PhD is not only about skill acquisitions but rather a process which involves a constant fluctuation between one's identities and construction of an academic self. In terms of that, doing a PhD for me is an identity work and an opportunity to transform myself.

Identity in transition:

Ayça: We first had to build on the role of being a PhD candidate while continuing to enact the current roles. We did not leave our past identities behind when progressing through the program. Becoming in academia encompasses several simultaneous transitions between different identities daily and an ongoing transformation into a member of academia, all of which I believe remain central to the understanding of our mutual experience of doing PhD. As female doctoral students I think we face greater challenges than men would face. I must admit that the constant negotiation I made between my maternal self and an individual goal toward my doctorate was abrasive and full of guilt. In terms of the additional volume of work PhD puts on me, there were many times when I felt stuck between self-expectations and expectations of the already existing set of life roles from me, such as time management, maternal guilt, and financial issues. Internalisation of gendered expectations interact to shape priorities in a woman's life and so the academic performance. Of course, this should not mean that all women are affected in the same way, rather gender differences in women's PhD experiences probably vary with the personal background, each woman's profile and with the field of study.

Begüm: That's a good point. The burden of the doctoral program becoming the largest, all daily responsibilities of being a working woman intermeddled, inevitably. This entanglement challenged me in terms of time management, but more so in terms of my mental well-being. The situation of staying still with yourself or the bond you establish with yourself becomes more important than anything or anyone else and this brought the feeling of being selfish towards the people in my life. There was an even bigger dilemma: I continued to stay in the private sector due to the obligations of the family business. It did cause a clash of roles. So, trying to find a place where both can exist in balance in my life was a long learning process. While progressing our research, we encouraged and supported each other to find the right balance of our commitments and roles. You need to adjust your surviving skills in all these transformations and transitions, and it seems tough in a situation where you stay isolated. I believe that the support we received from each other facilitated what I may call 'self-regulation' throughout the process.

Ayça: It was more like an identity metamorphosis for me. Transitioning from a long professional past to a life of scholarship was not easy, but more importantly, my own personal experience indicates a learning trajectory where my past, or rather as in the definition of Collinson (2004), my 'biographical baggage' was constantly negotiating with my present. I can see clearly now that this is the implicitly biggest challenge for me when I juxtapose our educational backgrounds. PhD involves a process of ongoing adaptation and transformation and 'is very much about developing an identity as a researcher in different contexts and disciplines' (Dison, 2004, p. 85). I engaged within a particular disciplinary culture of communication, which has completely different philosophical orientation, values, language, methodological choices and practices.

On the other hand, experiences like this have been a driving force for me to explore how to use different disciplinary lenses and put my former knowledge into a critical context. You know the topic of my thesis has developed out of my own experience and the decision of conducting doctoral research in the fields of gender and technology is influenced by my own identity as a woman and a single mother. In sum, the disciplinary culture you pass through on a PhD journey becomes an important component of the re-definition of self.

A vast amount of new knowledge challenged my thinking and the ways of being – a journey of what O'Sullivan (2003) refers to as 'transformative learning' that I am always grateful for. This challenge is necessary for one's academic formation, and from a wider perspective of identity, is an effective means of becoming critically reflexive.

On the other hand, collaborating with a peer studying new media technologies and gender like me made a difference. The common area of the subject we studied enabled a great exchange of ideas and gave us the ability to interpret the criticism of each other's work together, which allowed us to perceive the comments properly and respond to them effectively. It plays an important role in passing information to each other and learning how to communicate within a field in doctoral education.

Begüm: My learning experience involves a rather divergent shift in terms of adopting to the cultural environment. Even though the disciplinary landscape resonated with my educational past, the question of processing what it is like to be an academic is always there, especially about my involvement in gender studies in relation to new media and technology. That was not just establishing a new perspective, but also receiving a new tool to internalise and challenge the everyday practices of an always online and white collared woman. This relatively new kind of pressure was exactly where our collaboration came into play. The internal dialog seems to be an essential part of the process, but still, it cannot be achieved in a vacuum. External support is also necessary and can only be possible with the existence of others' narratives around self. Peer-to-peer collaboration was essential to be able to ground the redefinition of self and go beyond the constraining effects of power imbalances. Our collaboration opened an informal space for what Jefferson (1985) defined as 'trouble telling', allowing us to become a source of the narrative practices for each other and granting us the opportunity to build on each other's knowledge, to construct ourselves as a researcher through a self-reflexive effort.

Ayça: The collaborative experience we shared did evidently influence us in gaining a solid grasp of the academic landscape we are in throughout our PhD journey. Taking into consideration the limited opportunities for engagement in academic communities, our daily collaborative activities enable the internalisation of values, enactment of the meanings we learned together, in short, and makes possible the practice of self. Additionally, the point you made about the self-reflexive understanding made me realise that PhD is not / should not only about the adaptability or normalisation, but it is a journey that requires divergence of thoughts and thinkers, only in this way we can talk about a transformation and identity development. So, our collaboration not only supported us to make sense and manage our positions but also helped us to learn making our own choices in this complex terrain of academia through a reflection on the self-definitions we offered to each other. Peer-to-peer collaboration plays an important role in learning to establish an equilibrium between yourself and playing by the rules.

Begüm: At this very point, I am wondering what this collaboration will look like when we remove a common goal like completing a PhD from the picture. It will most likely transform. We brought ourselves to this duo autoethnographic study not as doctorate candidates but as early career researchers.

Ayça: Well, that's the question, isn't it? I believe it is a new way of engaging with academia for both of us. The journey taught me something very important: Neither PhD is something to achieve, nor are we the product of it. Instead 'a line of becoming has neither beginning nor end, departure or arrival, origin or destination' (Deleuze & Guattari, 1987, p. 293).

PhD is a Black Box: Creating a Safe Zone

Ayça: Can we talk a little bit about the fact that PhD is addressed as a black box (Stanley, 2015) and how we did experience it quite that way. It was like a trip to an unknown land, where I didn't know exactly what challenges awaited me and where the exits, milestones and outputs were not very visible.

Begüm: Yes, I agree with you on that. We knew which classes to choose from the beginning, so it was a rather smooth process. But after that, it was uncharted territory. While I was taking the classes, I started to feel anxious about future scenarios. Once the classes were over, I felt that I was right about feeling concerned since the preparation for the presentation of dissertation topics became one of the hardest tasks I have ever encountered during the journey. How did you experience this process, were there any similarities?

Ayça: It is quite similar since I did not know what to expect. I was only expecting that the process would be a hard one. Conducting PhD is tough, yet these were only hearsays about the process. They turned out to be true! If you are not a member of academia and got involved from the outside, you feel yourself within a black box. That was not specific to our programme I believe.

Begüm: I agree.

Ayça: There seems to be an assumption that everyone is educated on academia's basic rules and regulations. However, it was like I did not know what to expect at the entry level. Rather than an issue of being an outsider or insider, this was more like a feeling of discomfort in socialising into the culture and practices of the academic community, for a time. That creates a certain level of uncertainty, and it is hard on oneself. In that sense, keeping each other on the road and supporting one another are the most significant aspects of peer-to-peer collaboration within an environment of a black box, in which we did not know about what to expect. There were many points where I nearly decided to quit, but we collaboratively created survival strategies to cope with the challenges like the proficiency exam.

Begüm: I'd like to define it as if we were each other's control mechanisms in that sense. The notion of support is also defined and reshaped during the actual course of events. We did not know what support was like at the very beginning, we did not have any predefined rulesets for that notion. It has evolved during the journey, and I learnt that it is also a very flexible concept that was fuelled through our togetherness.

Ayça: It was something special about this specific collaboration. It also does not have a universal definition; support might have different connotations for everyone.

Begüm: I agree because if I were to isolate the PhD journey, the concept of support might carry different personal meanings. Once we entered the PhD process and met each other, the idea of support finally made sense. I believe it is also part of a learning process as well: to learn how to provide and gain support in a collaborative relationship (Jolley et al., 2015).

Ayça: In reality, we became the outer eye for one another since one is not able to reflect on herself or her work as an outsider, yet she still needs someone to conduct such an act (Holloway & Alexandre, 2012). Also, you became alienated by the process. There was no one to tell you if you are on the right path or not. For example, we can talk about the fact that we might have found many sources of support like family, friends from academia, friends outside of academia or spouses.

Begüm: I always had the struggle with the outside support regarding a certain fixed answer to every problem I have encountered: You can do it! It is such an overwhelming affirmation that it adds extra responsibility to your already existing ones while you are experiencing a setback in your process.

Ayça: Sometimes we wipe over with the feeling that the possible roads to support are being blocked. There was a need to see my journey as a PhD candidate through the eyes of an outsider looking in but the one who is walking through a similar experience to mine. It is very interesting that once we are settled in a friendship, the feeling of shame has disappeared from the picture.

Begüm: I believe that the most important difference between outside support and this peer-to-peer collaboration support lies in the fact that we were still presenting a persona to the outside world. It is as if these patterns are subconsciously present and the support you give and receive is both shaped by these pre-written rules. There is a tendency to conceal the real problems and reflect the ones that are more socially acceptable.

Ayça: I wrote down the fact that in our relationship there was no fear of judgement. There emerges honesty, open-heartedness, and sincerity, which also meant not concealing our real feelings or opinions from one another. It is possible to say it was a 'safe zone' for us. Once we think about our academic circles, they had their own hierarchical dynamics and authoritative composition, in which you refrain from presenting a negative impression. That is why this collaboration certainly created a safe zone by building up a peer-to-peer collaboration dynamic.

For us and for potentially others

Ayça: Reconceptualizing PhD not as a product but rather as part of a larger process of becoming helps me see it as part of my drive to produce meaning in developing my understanding of who I want to be in the academic context. In this connection, sharing, reflecting, practising and the feeling of being cared for have been the essential components of my journey. And, this duo autoethnographic study shed light on the existence of another process between our provision of the collaboration and the support derived from it – a process in which you and I continuously reconcile our expectations and experiences of the relationship, in so doing we constantly refine and re-define the meaning of peer support for us. Concordantly, our dialogic exploration enhanced my understanding of collaboration as relational and contextual entity, which is in constant fluidity. I also walk off this duo autoethnography having experienced an awareness of change in my perception of loneliness, which can be phrased in a series of questions: Is loneliness the meaning given to a lack of social engagement? Is it possible that despite participation in a broader social network of a particular disciplinary community or having connections with friends and family, a person still feels like they have no one during PhD? Can loneliness only be formulated in association with being socially isolated? I think the connection is established not only through having similar experiences but also the equality in relationship that eliminates the need of controlling discourse and opens a space for learning together. On the other hand, it is also important to clarify that these similarities we have with you in terms of our social profile, perspectives and personalities raise a methodological question regarding the differences of co-researchers, which is expected for polyvocal dialogue in study (Norris et al., 2012) and the disruptive function of the method (Breault, 2016, p. 3). So rather than an attempt to find a worthwhile difference and force it into the dialog, we just decided to let our recalls of the shared experience and perspectives co-emerge within the interpretive circles and in this way, we witnessed how our individual points of differences surfaced, and how they defined the divergences in our experience.

So, my experience of conducting duo autoethnography allows me to note that the method can still be applied as an effective approach to make explicit the personal differences that take part in divergent experiences of the same phenomenon, so maybe the beginning points of an ethnographic research should not necessarily be rooted in personal differences.

Begüm: Within the context of this autoethnographic study, our experiences led us to reflect on the pre-existing categories shaping the rhetoric on the PhD journey. Starting with the idea that PhD is a black box, the feelings of insecurity and hopelessness involve the co-exploration of an unknown territory. Within that framework, sharing achievements, connections, learnings, opportunities, and struggles became the focus point of the unique collaboration established. Keeping each other on track and external accountability are the two common themes of this experience, which is as much emotional as cognitive. The collaboration did not happen in a vacuum but rather was intertwined with our ongoing personal lives. The social and cultural positionings shape and re-define the meanings we attribute to collaborative practices, defining the dynamics of the relational learning process.

Creating this togetherness or co-working environment is also influenced by everyday life conditions like the COVID-19 pandemic. For two years, we did not have any physical encounters, yet we were able to create the same collaborative working space digitally. At this point, we realised the difference between the notions of 'team support' and 'collaboration', the former representing a more goal-oriented focus and pre-defined roles. The latter, especially in this case, does not comprise any pre-give roles or guidelines to follow. We as the participants of this experience created our own rules and dynamics, reflecting on each other's emotions and perceptions dynamically. After conducting the duo autoethnographic study, I realised how fragile and yet empowering this connection is, not only in terms of managing emotions but also in creating a sustainable co-working atmosphere. Moreover, I strongly believe the influence of methodological implications on our perceptions of the notions of collaboration and peer-to-peer support in PhD journeys is twofold: Firstly, the flexibility provided by the methodological framework enables us to create another safe zone in which we can expressively discuss our prior experiences as PhD candidates. Secondly, the way it requires a certain understanding of reflexivity creates a deeper level of analysis based on challenging the socially constructed notions of collaboration, support and loneliness. Although there are more similarities than differences in our backgrounds, motives and affordances, reflecting on our past experiences creates a challenging task in terms of initiating an honest dialogue about the PhD journeys.

Yet, conducting such work leaves us with more diverse questions to be addressed regarding our definitions of loneliness, support and collaborative affordances.

References

Ali, A., & Kohun, F. (2007). Dealing with social isolation to minimize doctoral attrition: A four stage framework. *International Journal of Doctoral Studies*, 2, 33–49.

Anderson, L. (2006). Analytic autoethnography. *Journal of Contemporary Ethnography*, 35(4), 373–395.

Barber, J. P., King, P. M., & Baxter Magolda, M. B. (2013). Long strides on the journey toward self-authorship: Substantial developmental shifts in college students' meaning making. *The Journal of Higher Education*, 84(6), 866–896.

Barnacle, R., & Mewburn, I. (2010). Learning networks and the journey of "becoming doctor." *Studies in Higher Education*, 35(4), 433–444.

Bista, K., & Cox, D. W. (2014). Cohort-based doctoral programs: What we have learned over the last 18 years. *International Journal of Doctoral Studies*, 9(1), 1–20.

Breault, R. A. (2016). Emerging issues in duoethnography. *International Journal of Qualitative Studies in Education*, 29(6), 777–794.

Collinson, J. A. (2004). Occupational identity on the edge: Social science contract researchers in higher education. *Sociology*, 38(2), 313–329.

Deleuze, G., & Guattari, F. (1987). *A thousand plateaus*, trans. Brian Massumi. Minneapolis: University of Minnesota Press.

Dison, A. (2004). "Finding her own academic self": Research capacity development and identity formation. *Perspectives in Education*, 22(1), 83–98.

Holloway, E. L., & Alexandre, L. (2012). Crossing boundaries in doctoral education: Relational learning, cohort communities, and dissertation committees. *New Directions for Teaching and Learning*, 131, 85–97.

Jefferson, G. (1985). On the organization of laughter in talk about troubles. In J. M. Atkinson (Ed.), *Structures of social action: Studies in conversation analysis* (pp. 346–369). Cambridge: Cambridge University Press.

Jolley, D., Griffiths, A. W., Friel, N., Ali, J. B., & Rix, K. (2015). The importance of peer support during the final stages of a PhD. *A Guide for Psychology Postgraduates: Surviving Postgraduate Study*, 36, 36–39.

Ellis, C., Adams, T. E., & Bochner, A. P. (2011). Autoethnography: An overview. *Historical Social Research/Historische sozialforschung*, 36(4) (138), 273–290.

Fitzpatrick, E., & Farquhar, S. (2018). Service and leadership in the academy: Duoethnography as transformation. *Journal of Organisational Ethnography*, 7(3), 345–360.

Giddens, A. 1991. *Modernity and Self-identity*. Stanford, CA: Stanford University Press.

Hamood, T. (2016). An autoethnographic account of a PhD student's journey towards establishing a research identity and understanding issues surrounding validity in educational research. *The Bridge: Journal of Educational Research-Informed Practice*, 3(1), 41–60.

Littlefield, C. M., Taddei, L. M., & Radosh, M. E. (2015). Organic collaborative teams: The role of collaboration and peer to peer support for part-time doctoral completion. *International Journal of Doctoral Studies*, 10, 129–142.

Malfroy, J. (2005). Doctoral supervision, workplace research and changing pedagogic practices. *Higher Education Research & Development*, 24(2), 165–178.

Norris, J., Sawyer, R. D., & Lund, D. (2012). *Duoethnography: Dialogic methods for social, health, and educational research (7)*. Walnut Creek, CA: Left Coast Press.

O'Sullivan, E. (2003). Bringing a perspective of transformative learning to globalised consumption. *International Journal of Consumer Studies*, 27(4), 326–330.

Ruggunan, S., & Kinnear, L. C. (2019). Applying duoethnography to position researcher identity in management research. *SA Journal of Human Resource Management*, 17(1), 1–11.

Sawyer, R., & Norris, J. (2015). Duoethnography: A retrospective 10 years after. *International Review of Qualitative Research*, 8(1), 1–4.

Stanley, P. (2015). Writing the PhD journey (s): An autoethnography of zine-writing, angst, embodiment, and backpacker travels. *Journal of Contemporary Ethnography*, 44(2), 143–168.

Stracke, E. (2010). Undertaking the journey together: Peer learning for a successful and enjoyable PhD experience. *Journal of University Teaching & Learning Practice*, 7(1), 111–121.

Wall, S. (2006). An autoethnography on learning about autoethnography. *International Journal of Qualitative Methods*, 5(2), 146–160.

Weidman, J. C., Twale, D. J., & Stein, E. L. (2001). *Socialisation of graduate and professional students in higher education: A perilous passage?* ASHE-ERIC Higher Education Report, 28. San Francisco, CA: Jossey-Bass.

Wegener, C., Meier, N., & Ingerslev, K. (2016). Borrowing brain power–sharing insecurities. Lessons learned from a doctoral peer writing group. *Studies in Higher Education*, 41(6), 1092–1105.

5 Podcasting as a methodological tool for research conversations with makers

Nurgül Yardım Meriçliler

The rapid advancement of information and communication technologies has opened up diverse and promising avenues for conducting research in various fields. In this context, this chapter aims to introduce and highlight the incorporation of podcasting as not just a research subject but also as a valuable research method in the realm of social sciences. Podcasting, traditionally known as a form of entertainment or information dissemination, has now emerged as a platform with immense potential for academic research. Drawing from my own experience as a researcher and interview host in the podcast medium, I have come to realise that podcasting serves as a tool for research and complements traditional academic research methodologies. Therefore, this chapter proposes an approach for making podcast interviews a cultural practice in research and content production while analysing the methodology behind conducting such interviews.

By conducting semi-structured interviews with participants and sharing them as podcast episodes, I have witnessed first-hand how podcasting enables the integration of academic knowledge with everyday experiences in a more accessible and engaging manner. I employed podcasts as innovative tools to investigate the impacts of community, space, and production on the characteristics of makerspaces in my PhD research.[1] In a wider context such as makerspaces, this structure allowed me to explore the spatial necessities of makerspaces by identifying different forms, functions, and structures through the idea of a collaborative environment. With the growing interest in makerspaces, this approach enables an exploration of spatial requirements by identifying various forms, functions, and structures within a collaborative environment. This attempt presents new ways of understanding this relatively new social phenomenon that would hopefully incite further research. Thus, my goal for this chapter is to outline and describe the process and podcasting as a research method.

Specifically, there is a need to examine whether makerspaces offer a more diverse and inclusive form of participation in the public sphere. Given that makerspaces are often seen as sites of innovation and experimentation, it is possible that they may attract a more diverse range of participants than traditional public forums. Furthermore, the collaborative and participatory nature of makerspaces may offer unique opportunities for individuals from diverse backgrounds to engage in public discourse and contribute to collective decision-making. By examining the relationship between makerspaces and the public sphere in more detail, we can gain a deeper understanding of the potential of these spaces to foster inclusive and democratic forms of participation and identify areas for further research and intervention. Therefore, I aim to address these inquiries through case studies conducted in selected makerspaces located in London, utilising the data collected from these sources. From this perspective, I will delve into an analysis of why podcast interviews can serve as an effective means of data collection. Along the way, I will ask: if podcasts are an alternative method for research, what is my motivation for conducting the podcast interviews, and what kind do they offer about locating them alongside and through other tools?

Due to the need to cover a significant amount of terrain, I have structured this chapter around four parts. This chapter begins by defining the context of the research, diving into making, makers, and makerspaces. Then I will explore interviewing as a data collection method before laying out podcast interviews. This phase, which I will call 'podcasting as a tool', is characterised by transforming semi-structured interviews into a podcast series. My discussion of the podcast interviews concentrates on perspectives, podcasting in research and for academia, and podcasting as *produsage*. In the last part, I will discuss the relationship between interviewing as a methodology and podcasting as a method of researching and the location of the researcher. I will also point out how podcasts provide unique opportunities for engaging interactive and self-reflexive communities within a makerspace context. I will also reflect on what is unique about podcast interviews concerning the participants. I will conclude with how podcasting may contribute to and support research, as well as its ethical issues.

Context: making, makers, and makerspaces

David Gauntlett's perspective, cited by Jenkins, eloquently emphasises the transformative power of making:

> through making things, you feel more of a participant in the world, and you feel more a part of it, more embedded - because you are contributing, not just consuming, so you're more actively engaged with the world, and so, more connected.
>
> (2011, p. 5)

This perspective encapsulates the fundamental idea that lies at the heart of makerspaces. It underscores the belief that making goes beyond mere creation; it fosters a deep sense of involvement and connection.

When we think of a makerspace, the first images that come to mind could be a set of colourful tools waiting for someone to use them or many 3D printers lined up to print. These images can lead to the easy assumption that one only needs to install such characteristic elements to form a makerspace. However, the content of a makerspace is far more complicated and needs to involve other parameters. Makerspaces also get several interpretations by themselves, changing with their tools and increasing the variety of makers. According to the more activity-oriented definition proposed by Bagley (2014), makerspaces are community workshops that serve as an environment for knowledge exchange and entrepreneurial experimentation. Sleigh et al. believe that a makerspace is an open-access space with facilities for different practices where anyone can come and make something (2015). Whereas Cavalcanti (2013) defines a makerspace as a manufacturing and innovation space from the workshop perspective, allowing people to proceed with various interests, including art, electronics, woodcraft, sewing crafts, mechanics, computer software, and through making. The community is a crucial part of the makerspaces; Niaros et al. (2017) define a makerspace as a community-led, open space where individuals share resources and meet regularly to collaboratively engage in creative commons-oriented projects utilising open-source software and hardware technologies. So, we keep asking the following questions: What is a makerspace today? Is it an exclusive place for craftspeople or a place to test out fabrication equipment? Is it a public community centre that provides tools and machines to help people create things together? It is no surprise these questions and other facets of makerspaces and makers have been extensively investigated. In the recent literature, there is a range of studies[2] of makerspaces under the arts and crafts movement, gender equity and feminist hackerspaces, ethical framework and sustainability, social innovation, collaboration, creativity, and alternate entrepreneurship. However, the characteristics of makerspaces for forming a community and transforming both the physical space and the public sphere have not yet been investigated in a holistic view. The potential of community engagement, architectural space, and production is still one of the least considered narratives.

To examine the makerspaces, it is also necessary to describe who a maker is. In his seminal book *Makers*, Chris Anderson provides an inclusive definition, claiming, 'we are all makers, we are born makers' (2012, p. 13). However, Dougherty associates making with social and cultural developments and represents makers as toolmakers, artisans, inventors, innovators, do-it-yourself-ers, hackers, hobbyists, tinkerers, and YouTube influencers (2016). So, makerspaces have these people – makers – as their community. Therefore, makers are what makes each makerspace unique despite the similarities in purpose, location, business model, or community engagement process. This makes sense that makerspaces are not necessarily born out of a specific set of materials or spaces but rather a mindset of community partnership, collaboration, and creation. When makers come to the makerspace, they search for new ways to create, innovate, and produce. As Ingold (2016) says, in makerspaces, we could see makers as complete beginners from diverse backgrounds or as artists, engineers, architects, and hobbyists.

According to Menichinelli, 'the term maker is very generic and universal; however, the many meanings of the term can be related together, directly or indirectly, to form a definition of who are the makers' (2020, p. 22). In line with these definitions above, my main research question is, how do we investigate the impacts of community, space, and production on the characteristics of makerspaces? From this perspective, there are sub-questions such as: how does the position of the community concern the makerspaces, what kind of relations the makerspaces have with the public sphere, and to what extent do makerspaces support production? All these questions stem from one root – the understanding of the interaction between makers and makerspaces.

I believe *makerspace* is an interdisciplinary phenomenon; it has proved challenging to limit the scope of research within the boundaries of only one discipline. Therefore, a constructivist approach is best suited to capture the richness and diversity of the topic. The constructivist paradigm regards knowledge as a 'human construction' that recognises 'multiple realities' and sees the research as a process through which the 'researcher and the participant co-construct understandings' (Hatch, 2002, p. 13). Theories relevant to the scope of this chapter come from cultural studies, communications, social sciences, and arts and humanities. I applied constructivism to my multi-case study research, in which I will explore the experiences of makers to produce a rich and deep understanding. I observed the case study methodology that Yin (1984) suggested and conducted an exploratory, holistic multi-case study. Therefore, the development of my analysis of makerspaces will be based on this extensive multi-case analysis, where I look for relations between people and their environments. Accordingly, multiple cases from various contexts are necessary to improve the external validity (Yin, 1984), so I will focus on the findings with other contexts and maintain the replication logic. One of the empirical methods for approaching makerspaces will be by visiting selected makerspaces located in London. For almost three years, I observed these makerspaces[3] by visiting them on their public open days, scheduling events, or arranging meetings with their makers or community leaders. This journey is also an essential part of the semi-structured interviews, which I will mention in detail. My main goal is to correspond to the variables of makerspaces and comprehend how they are designed, managed, and sustained for making.

Interviewing as a data collection method

The interview serves as a social technique for the public construction of the self (Kvale & Binrkman, 2009, p. 12). Relatedly, the data were gathered from makers and makerspace directors through semi-structured interviews, where the focus was originally on understanding the relationship between makers and makerspaces. Semi-structured conversations focus on makers' experiences and insights into the makerspaces they are located in. I decided to do these as podcast interviews, which I will detail in the next section.

According to Berg, interviewing is valuable not only because it builds a holistic snapshot, analyses words, and reports detailed views of informants but also because 'it enables interviewees to speak in their own voice and express their own thoughts and feelings' (2007, p. 96). Many interviews range through a continuum, from structured, to semi-structured, to unstructured or focused interviews (Bryman, 2001; May, 2001). According to Lindlof and Taylor, due to the versatile nature of interviews as a method allows for the collection of data across circumstances and settings (2011). Therefore, these settings, in our case, 'makerspaces', have an important role. Indeed, the interviews have to seek new insights beyond the settings. As Bingham and Moore describe (1959), an interview is a conversation with a purpose.

As a researcher, I try to draw on trust, thoughtful questioning and reflective listening when conducting a qualitative interview. Qualitative interview research is unique because the researcher is the instrument for data collection, and there exists an effort to insert an objective instrument between the researcher and the research participants (Edwards & Holland, 2013), in my case, the guests of the podcast. Edwards and Holland also discuss the format that the qualitative interview can take, focusing on the setting for the type of interaction that takes place; face-to-face interviews, walking and talking interviews, and online or e-interviews (2013). The medium of participation differs; there are new circumstances when technology could be used as more than a simple transactional medium but also as a way of interacting between researcher and participant. There could also be creative ways in these choices regarding the research topic, participants or tools. Moreover, interviews can also involve participants engaging in creative activities like drawing, collaging, creating diagrams, taking pictures or looking at them, walking, and so on. Mason argues that all qualitative and semi-structured interviewing have the following features in common, which I will link to podcast interviews as well:

1 The interactional exchange of dialogue (between two or more participants, in face-to-face or other contexts).
2 A thematic, topic-centred, biographical, or narrative approach where the researcher has topics, themes, or issues they wish to cover, but with a fluid and flexible structure.
3 A perspective regarding knowledge as situated and contextual requires the researcher to ensure that relevant contexts are brought into focus so that the situated knowledge can be produced. Meanings and understandings are created in an interaction, which is effectively a co-production involving the construction or reconstruction of knowledge (2017, p. 62).

In these contexts, the researcher observes the interview dynamics as well as the surroundings and the physical and non-verbal elements. Therefore, this idea is the beginning of my research method shifting from an interview to a podcast interview. I try to further diversify my research methodology by combining academic and everyday knowledge.

Podcasting as a tool for research methodology

The term podcasting was coined in 2004 by the British journalist Ben Hammersley in an article for The Guardian, and it combines the words *broadcast* and *pod*. In the context of podcasting, the term pod is derived from the word 'iPod,' which was a popular portable media player developed by Apple Inc. during that time. Therefore, we can say that the term pod refers to the idea of delivering audio content which can be downloaded and listened to at the listener's convenience. Llinares et al. argue that 'podcasting' can be more than a communication tool; it can be a method of qualitative data collection and analysis, critical inquiry, and knowledge mobilisation (2018). Podcasts are digital audio files available for downloading to a computer or mobile device via the internet, most often released in series through media players that allow subscribers to receive new episodes automatically (Haygood, 2007; Potter, 2006). I argue podcasting is more than this definition; it is an interdisciplinary collection to be explored with a media and cultural studies lens. Moreover, Mollett et al. (2017) indicate how podcasting can extend opportunities and 'diversify content' and how the podcasting equipment enables visits to 'unexpected places' (p. 165). I have been producing and hosting a podcast since 2019, where I carry out interviews with creative people under Anylabtalks.[4] I used Anylabtalks podcast as a base for my dissertation, whereby I launched a new season for makers based on selected semi-structured interviews. What makes podcasts different is their unique ability to capture in-depth and personal conversations with individuals in a more informal and conversational format. Unlike a regular interview that is publicly accessible, a podcast can provide a more intimate and in-depth look into a particular topic or theme.

Podcasts are having a moment, becoming popular every day by introducing new audiences as a modern form of broadcasting and welcoming a new generation of producers and hosts. Mollett et al. argue that knowledge workers should take advantage of this podcasting renaissance (2017). So, with this popularity and respect, how does podcasting become a research methodology tool? To answer this question, I will discuss my own experience as a producer and podcast host. This resonates with my approach to creative practice and my interests in production, enabling me to unite academic and everyday knowledge together. Anylabtalks features interviews with creatives, such as designers, architects, and makers. I have talked to more than 50 people and launched 22 episodes on podcast platforms under Anylabtalks. Relating this podcast to my research process, I launched season three of the Anylabtalks podcast, using my semi-structured interviews with makers. In my research journey, the main challenge of the interviews was reaching out to the participants. In the beginning, I invited makers as participants in my PhD research to do an interview, but most of them kindly declined. Then I asked makers and makerspace coordinators for podcast interviews, to which they were much more eager to join. I have been having in-depth discussions with creative people; each podcast episode requires preparation in background research and planning the interview and post-production, editing, and writing copies for the show notes. Alongside the data collected for the research, these episodes are also a learning experience for me. Also, being on the podcast allows the guests to speak about their research and apply their know-how to this era. At the same time, listeners of the podcast learn about academic and practical interests.

Mark Carrigan also makes elaborations (2012), which he shares in the LSE Impact Blog,[5] regarding his academic interview techniques for podcasting and why he makes podcasts in the academy. He shares that if he were to send an email to a renowned researcher, requesting a meeting to discuss their recent book, he would undoubtedly face failure. However, based on his podcasting experience, he has sent numerous such emails to academics, and surprisingly, none of them have declined (Carrigan, 2012). Similar to Mark's experience, I share the belief that scheduling interviews can be a time-consuming process. However, I have found that all the participants involved have demonstrated their eagerness to meet.

Podcasting for research and in academia

In the book *Communicating Your Research with Social Media: A Practical Guide to Using Blogs, Podcasts, Data Visualisations, and Video*, the authors dedicate an entire chapter to the topic of audio and podcasting (Mollett et al., 2017). They define podcasting as a platform that emerged in the early 2000s and emphasise its revival as an opportunity for researchers, academics, and students from any field to reach broader audiences (Mollett et al., 2017). The authors also argue that podcasting allows individuals to effectively share their work at different stages of the research lifecycle. They highlight how this resurgence in podcasting enables researchers to communicate their findings to a wider audience, making their research more accessible and impactful (Mollett et al., 2017). In this regard, both researchers and listeners could understand elaborate topics and see topics from new perspectives. Crofts et al. also stated that podcasting 'represents a shift from mass broadcasting to on-demand personalised media' (2005). By providing a context for podcasting in social and cultural practices, I observed that using podcasts as a medium for interviews allowed me to find innovative ways to do research in 'making'. From this point of view, I turned semi-structured interviews into podcast episodes by doing them as podcast interviews. From my perspective, I transformed semi-structured interviews into podcast episodes by conducting them as podcast interviews, aligning with the concept of 'doing media together'. This approach not only facilitated collaborative media production but also opened up possibilities for potential research collaborations. Moreover, podcasts in academia can help the distribution of research findings, showcase academic expertise, and reach new audiences (Harter, 2019; Kwok, 2019; Mollett et al., 2017). On the other hand, semi-structured interviews as podcast episodes also raise methodological challenges.

Indeed, creating a podcast episode can be highly time-consuming, with technical expertise and distribution skills needed. We can see podcasting in various ways, ranging from providing students with access to full lectures and pre-lecture material to an alternative strategy of giving feedback to students and supporting distance education. In this sense, Kwok (2019) believes that there is a chance to engage with the research community through podcasts. DeMarco (2022) claims that podcasts can support expanding a person's network of colleagues. MacKenzie also highlights that podcasts can be an opportunity to reach out to other scholars, eventually helping those in academia (2019). DeMarco gives the example of Hugh Osborn, the podcast host of Exocast[6] and an astronomer at the Laboratory of Astrophysics in Marseille, France (2022). Osborn presumed that inviting senior researchers to be a guest on his podcast would be a less rough way to meet them than approaching them in a more formal setting, such as a conference. Moreover, in the learning context, Aliotta et al. (2008) indicate that podcasts could be used to successfully address students' misconceptions of a subject viewed as complex. Departing from Aliotta et al.'s perspective, podcasting could be used as a learning resource. Indeed, I will also attempt to examine the potential of the podcast as a research tool by reflecting upon my research process. Podcasts can empower researchers to engage in academic and public debates in new ways, providing a more accessible form of knowledge. On the other hand, semi-structured interviews as podcast episodes will also raise methodological challenges. Preparing a podcast episode can be highly time-consuming, with technical expertise and distribution. On the other hand, podcasts are available for free on established platforms like Apple, Google, and Spotify. They can be produced relatively rapidly to communicate research at any point in the knowledge production cycle. As podcasts are accessible to a broader audience, they can engage with academic and non-academic consumers, even though they have scholarly content. In this way, podcasts contribute to engaging society and the general public with the academy by sharing knowledge and expertise.

Considering all these approaches to podcasting, how did the process of a podcast interview in the research take place? Firstly, in terms of selecting the participants to be interviewed, I separated the interviewees into three groups: makers, makerspace directors, and designers of the space. Their backgrounds, like degrees and professional jobs, were also a part of the research. Then, I designed three sets of questions thoroughly and adequately addressed three groups. These questions formed the research questions of my PhD research. Importantly, I tailored each set of questions to the circumstances of the space and participant and modified them during the interview to provide a conversational flow. The important thing is that I guided the conversation with an introduction and conclusion dedicated to the guest, as I would launch them as a podcast episode. Meanwhile, while most interviews were just between one other person and me, I also conducted a group interview with three individuals at their request, which took the form of a collective conversation.

Based on these elaborations, there were three main reasons behind the idea of transforming some of the semi-structured interviews into podcast episodes. First, the accessibility of research participants, as many were incentivised to participate in the research due to the possibility of being part of a podcast. Second, podcasting resonates with production and reflects upon my research's potential. Lastly, podcasts might enable researchers to participate in academic and public discussions in novel ways, creating knowledge that is more accessible and interesting to address the general public. Alongside the data generated in the research, these podcast episodes were also a learning experience for me.

The production of a podcast episode entails a substantial time commitment due to the technical skills and distribution efforts involved, which necessitate careful examination. It is particularly pertinent to consider how this process aligns with the transformation of semi-structured interviews into podcast interviews as a means of creating a podcast episode. In the podcast production flow of Anylabtalks, several phases can be identified. The initial phase involves conducting the interview and recording it, as the fundamental requirement of podcasting is to gather data in audio format. Moving on to the second phase, the recorded content undergoes a comprehensive review and analysis. The producer meticulously listens to the complete recordings, performing necessary edits to the track and crafting an introduction and conclusion that are relevant to the discussion and episode. The episode title is also decided in this part of the production. Transitioning to the third phase, the episode recording is transformed into a fully-fledged episode through the implementation of sound editing techniques employing specialised audio tools. Subsequently, the podcast episode is shared with the audience along with any accompanying visuals or supplementary materials obtained during the interview process. Finally, the completed podcast episode is launched online and made available on various streaming services. When considering the transformation of semi-structured interviews into podcast interviews, the process I mentioned as phases elucidates the meticulous steps involved in creating a podcast episode. By understanding the various phases and the attention given to audio quality, content curation, and participant engagement, researchers can effectively leverage podcasting as a research methodology, highlighting the significance of this practice within the realm of academic inquiry.

Podcasts as a produsage

Bruns (2008) introduced the concept of *produsage* to describe the transformative impact of the internet on collaborative content production, consumption, and interaction. This concept emphasises the open feedback system facilitated by the internet, which has enabled users to actively engage in the creation and dissemination of content. Produsage is considered to have democratised production by providing accessible tools and promoting participatory culture (Deuze, 2007; Jenkins, 2006). In relation to the culture of produsage, podcasts embody a shift from mere consumption to active content creation for public consumption. Thus, podcasting represents an embodiment of the produsage ethos, wherein individuals become active contributors to the media landscape rather than passive recipients of content.

In 2012, Markman conducted research examining the motivations that drive independent podcasters to create podcasts. The study categorised these motivations into various categories, including technology/media motives, interpersonal motives, personal motives, content motives, process motives, and financial motives. This investigation aligns with the research conducted by Nardi et al. in 2004, which explored the underlying motives behind individuals writing blogs. Moreover, by integrating research on the remediation of blogs, which examines the transformative and adaptive processes that occur when blogs are disseminated across various media platforms, a connection can be established (Rocamora, 2011). This study highlights the empowering potential of blogs, as they afford bloggers control over their self-representation and enable the circulation of alternative notions of femininity (Rocamora, 2011). Therefore, this notion of remediation can also be applied to podcasts, wherein they serve as both a medium for freer expression and a viable research methodology.

Regarding Markman's (2012) research on evolving media consumption and production practices, a central theme exists around *the long tail* (Anderson, 2009). This concept addresses the lowering of the cost of production and distributing content through the web to find niche markets. In this sense, Markman shares that many podcast producers have the same passion for 'doing radio' (2012, p. 555). So, she believes the podcaster's motivations could be related to the power of sharing. In comparison, Besser et al. (2010) examine podcast user motivations and assert that podcasting is collaborative, interest-specific, and application-oriented.

Thematic reflection and discussion on podcast interviews

Departing from Carrigan's insights and own experiences, there is some potential to critically approach the complex relationship between the process of interviewing as a research method and there are some ethical questions (2012). As podcast interviews require establishing access to potential participants for your research, after one or two episodes, it is easier to invite other guests to the podcast. Thus, if we are to understand what the potentials of podcasting are, we have to look at the engagement of podcasting alongside its interaction. In this sense, Lynn Harter stated (2019) that her purpose in creating a podcast was to engage with her audience. Besides, if we look at Anchor,[7] consumers can interact with episodes by clicking the clap or applause icon, engaging in text-based discussions, leaving voice messages for the host about an episode, and integrating the audio into their own podcast episodes. These affordances not only enable podcasting to transition from a broadcast format to an interactive format but also demonstrate the interactive nature of podcasts.

On the other hand, there is an ethical consideration of making podcasts a research tool. Ethical issues could arise in any interview research, but in the case of podcast interviews, there are some particular critical considerations. Some are related to the possibility that the interview participant may unwittingly reveal more than was intended because online profiles or environments contain information not noted in the consent agreement (Salmons, 2012). These profiles could include social media accounts, websites, or other online platforms where individuals share personal information. Such information may not have been explicitly addressed in the consent agreement or anticipated by the participant or researcher. Consequently, during a podcast interview, there is a possibility that the participant might reveal details, potentially raising ethical concerns that they do not carefully consider while sharing publicly.

According to Kvale (1996), participants have to be informed of the purpose of the research, main design features, and possible risks which could arise from their participation. Therefore, consent forms hold significance in the context of podcasts as a data collection methodology. In fact, the public accessibility of podcast episodes and the issue of genuineness in participant contributions are additional aspects that need careful consideration. During the interview phase, Kvale (1996) outlines the steps for conducting ethical interviews. According to him, making interviewees aware of issues regarding informed consent, confidentiality, and consequences is crucial (Kvale, 1996). The consent form also has to specify how the data collected is going to be used and if it will be featured in any publication in the future.

In my podcast, I envision interviews not only as research tools but also as social content that involves dialogue between hosts, guests, and the public. So, the conversation turns into an experience. According to Harter, the audience can talk back, add commentary, make noises and gestures, or contemplate ideas long after an episode ends (2019). Relatedly, according to Boyer (1996), podcasts open the possibility for debate, doing media, and co-creation of content. These views on podcasting and the significance of the medium as a research methodology come down to the conclusion that podcast interviews are about doing new media together more than they are about doing an interview.

Conclusion

This chapter tries to present a considerable challenge for me to observe the progression of research through the exploration of various methods for data collection. Moreover, it presents an opportunity to bridge the gap between academic knowledge and daily life, merging the two in a meaningful way. I hope that this article has offered a potential methodological framework in podcasting as a methodological tool for undertaking the necessary empirical work to comprehend the ongoing reconfiguration of practices within our surroundings. By engaging in this methodological research, we may gain a clearer understanding of how media is shaped and governed, enabling us to grasp its transformative nature in contemporary society. There is definitely a place for podcasts in academia and in the research milieu in particular. Though there are challenges, as addressed in this chapter, there are also steps one can take to overcome certain obstacles. I anticipate that the exploration of these research methodologies will contribute novel perspectives to the existing body of knowledge and stimulate scholarly discourse surrounding makerspaces and podcast interviews. By delving into these areas, we can open up new avenues for inquiry, challenge established notions, and inspire fruitful debates within the academic community.

Notes

1 My PhD research is titled 'An interdisciplinary perspective towards makerspaces: 5 cases from London'.
2 For the Arts and Crafts Movement, see Morozov (2014); for gender equity and feminist hackerspaces, see Fox (2015), Buechley (2013), and Chachra (2015); for ethical framework and sustainability, see Kohtala (2015), Smith, and Light (2017); for social innovation, see Unterfrauner and Voigt (2017), Hochgerner (2012), Gauntlett (2013), and Smith (2017); for collaboration and creativity, see Baichtal (2012), Britton (2012), Wenger (1998), and Menichinelli (2020); and for alternate entrepreneurship, see Fawcett and Waller (2014), Browder et al. (2017).
3 I hold an undergraduate degree in architecture and a master's degree in urban design, and now I am practising both architecture and design communication. As a designer, I had a residency bursary at Somerset House Exchange Studios, and I cultivated relationships with Makerversity. Makerversity is the most prominent resident of the Somerset House Studios. They have been supported by Somerset House since 2013, initially with free space and currently at a favourable rate which allows them to operate an affordable workspace in central London. Makerversity is also one of the case studies I concentrate on in my research. See the website https://makerversity.org
4 Anylabtalks is a podcast including interviews with creative people from art, architecture, design, and making. In every episode, conversation on ideas, interests, projects, and stories is based on the guest's creative journey. Listen on https://open.spotify.com/show/2gbC9d9NRfP6ucKlnKVldt.
5 The London School of Economics and Political Science's (LSE) Impact Blog is a hub for researchers, administrative staff, librarians, students, think tanks, government, and anyone else interested in maximising the impact of academic work in the social sciences and other disciplines.
6 Exocast is a podcast discovering and discussing beyond the solar system to explore exotic exoplanets around distant stars. It is hosted by exoplanet astronomers Hugh Osborn, Andrew Rushby, and Hannah Wakeford. See http://www.exocast.org.
7 Anchor is a free, beginner-friendly platform for podcast creation, containing tools that allow users to record and edit audio, arrange it into podcast episodes, publish podcasts to listening platforms, and monetise content by collecting listener contributions or adding advertisements into episodes. See https://anchor.fm.

References

Aliotta, M., Bates, S., Brunton, K., & Stevens, A. (2008). Podcasts and lectures. In G.Salmon & P.Edirisingha (Eds.), *Podcasting for learning in universities* (pp. 34–42). Berkshire: Open University Press.

Anderson, C. (2009). *The longer long tail: How endless choice is creating unlimited demand* (updated and expanded edn). New York: Random House Business.

Anderson, C. (2012). *Makers: The new industrial revolution* (1st edn). New York: Crown Business.

Bagley, C. A. (2014). *Makerspaces: Top trailblazing projects*. Chicago: American Library Association.

Baichtal, J. (2012). Hack this: 24 incredible hackerspace projects from the DIY movement. Indianapolis, IN: Que.

Berg, B. (2007). An introduction to content analysis. In: Berg, B. L., Ed., *Qualitative Research Methods for the Social Sciences* (pp. 238–267), Boston, MA: Allyn and Bacon.

Besser, J., Larson, M., & Hofmann, K. (2010). Podcast search: user goals and retrieval technologies. *Online Information Review*, 34(3), 395–419. doi: 10.1108/14684521011054053

Bingham, W. V. D., Moore, B. V. (1959). *How to interview* (4th edn). New York: Harper and Brothers.

Boyer, E. L. (1996). The scholarship of engagement. *Bulletin of the American Academy of Arts and Sciences*, 49(7), 18. doi: 10.2307/3824459

Britton, L. (2012). A fabulous laboratory: The makerspace at Fayetteville Free Library. *Public*, 1–5.

Browder, R. E., Aldrich, H. E., & Bradley, S. W. (2017). *Entrepreneurship research, makers, and the maker movement*. doi: 10.13140/RG.2.2.20230.37441

Bruns, A. (2008). *Blogs, Wikipedia, second life, and beyond: From production to produsage*. New York: Peter Lang.

Bryman, A. (2001). *Social research methods*. Oxford: Oxford University Press.

Buechley, L. (2013). *Thinking about making* [Keynote Presentation]. Third Annual FabLearn Conference at Stanford University, Stanford, California. http://edstream.stanford.edu/Video/Play/883b61dd951d4d3f90abeec65eead2911d

Carrigan M. (2012). Podcasts are a natural fit for communication of academic ideas. https://blogs.lse.ac.uk/impactofsocialsciences/2012/05/10/podcasts-natural-form-academic-ideas/

Cavalcanti, G. (2013, May 22). Is it a Hackerspace, Makerspace, TechShop, or FabLab? *Make: DIY Projects and Ideas for Makers*.Makezine. https://makezine.com/article/education/the-difference-between-hackerspaces-makerspaces-techshops-and-fablabs/

Chachra, D. (2015, January 23). Why I'm not a maker. The Atlantic. http://www.theatlantic.com/technology/archive/2015/01/why-i-am-not-a-maker/384767/

Crofts, S., Dilley, J., Fox, M., Retsema, A., Williams, B. (2005). Podcasting: A new technology in search of viable business models. *First Monday*, 10(9). doi: 10.5210/fm.v10i9.1273

DeMarco, C. (2022). Hear here! The case for podcasting in research. University of Toronto Mississauga. *Journal of Research Administration*, 53(1), 30–61. https://www.srainternational.org/blogs/srai-jra1/2022/01/27/hear-here-the-case-for-podcasting-in-research

Deuze, M. (2007). Convergence culture in the creative industries. *International Journal of Cultural Studies, 10*, 243–263.

Dougherty, D. (2016). *Free to make: How the maker movement is changing our schools, our jobs, and our minds.* Berkeley, CA: North Atlantic Books.

Edwards, R., & Holland, J. (2013). *What is qualitative interviewing?* London: Bloomsbury Academic. doi: 10.5040/9781472545244

Fawcett, S.E. & Waller, M.A. (2014). Supply chain game changers—mega, nano, and virtual trends—and forces that impede supply chain design (i.e., building a winning team). *Journal of Business Logistics, 35*, 157–164. doi: 10.1111/jbl.12058

Gauntlett, D. (2011). *Making is connecting, the social meaning of creativity, from DIY and knitting to YouTube and Web 2.0.* Cambridge: Polity Press.

Gauntlett, D. (2011, August 3). Studying creativity in the age of Web 2.0: An interview with David Gauntlett. Henry Jenkins. https://henryjenkins.org/blog/2011/08/studying_creativity_in_the_age.html

Fox, S. (2015). Feminist hackerspaces as sites for feminist design. In Proceedings of the 2015 ACS SIGCHI Conference on Creativity and Cognition (pp. 341–42), C&C '15. New York: Association for Computing Machinery. doi: 10.1145/2757226.2764771

Harter, L. M. (2019). Storytelling in acoustic spaces: Podcasting as embodied and engaged scholarship. *Health Communication, 34*(1), 125–129. doi: 10.1080/10410236.2018.1517549

Hatch, M. (2002). *The maker movement manifesto: Rules for innovation in the new world of crafters, hackers, and tinkerers.* New York: McGraw-Hill.

Haygood, D. M. (2007). A status report on podcast advertising. *Journal of Advertising Research, 47*(4), 518–523. doi: 10.2501/S0021849907070535

Hochgerner, J. (2012). New Combinations of Social Practices in the Knowledge Society. In *Challenge Social Innovation* (pp. 87–104). New York: Springer.

Ingold, T. (Ed.). (2016). *Redrawing anthropology: Materials, movements, lines.* New York: Routledge.

Jenkins, H. (2006). *Convergence culture: Where old and new media collide.* New York: New York University Press.

Kohtala, C. (2015). Addressing sustainability in research on distributed production: An integrated literature review. *Journal of Cleaner Production, 106*, 654–668. doi: 10.1016/j.jclepro.2014.09.039

Kvale, S. (1996). *Interviews: An introduction to qualitative research interviewing.* Thousand Oaks, CA: Sage Publications.

Kvale, S. & Brinkmann, S. (2009). *InterViews: Learning the Craft of Qualitative Research Interviewing.* Thousand Oaks, CA: Sage Publications.

Kwok, R. (2019). How to make your podcast stand out in a crowded market. *Nature, 565*(7739), 387–389. doi: 10.1038/d41586-019-00128-7

Lindlof, T. R. & Taylor, B. C. (2011). *Qualitative communication research methods.* Thousand Oaks, CA: Sage Publications.

Llinares, D., Fox, N., & Berry, R. (Eds.). (2018). *Podcasting: New Aural cultures and digital media.* New York: Springer. doi: 10.1007/978-3-319-90056-8

Markman, K. M. (2012). Doing radio, making friends, and having fun: Exploring the motivations of independent audio podcasters. *New Media & Society, 14*(4), 547–565. doi: 10.1177/1461444811420848

Mason, J. (2017). *Qualitative researching* (3rd edn). Thousand Oaks, CA: Sage Publications.

May, T. (2001). *Social research: Issues, methods and process* (3rd edn). Maidenhead: Open University Press.
MacKenzie, L. E. (2019). Science podcasts: Analysis of global production and output from 2004 to 2018. *The Royal Society Open Science*, 6(1), 1–18.
Menichinelli, M. (2020). Exploring the impact of maker initiatives on cities and regions with a research through design approach. *Strategic Design Research Journal*, 13(1), 92–109. doi: 10.4013/sdrj.2020.131.07
Mollett, A., Brumley, C., Gilson, C., & Williams, S. (2017). *Communicating your research with social media: A practical guide to using blogs, podcasts, data visualisations and video*. Thousand Oaks, CA: Sage Publications.
Morozov, E. (2014, January 13). Making it: Pick up a spot welder and join the revolution. *New Yorker*. https://www.newyorker.com/magazine/2014/01/13/making-it-2
Nardi, B. A., Schiano, D. J., Gumbrecht, M., & Swartz, L. (2004). Why we blog. *Communications of the ACM*, 47(12), 41–46. doi: 10.1145/1035134.1035163
Niaros, V., Kostakis, V., & Drechsler, W. (2017). Making (in) the smart city: The emergence of makerspaces. *Telematics and Informatics*, 34(7), 1143–1152. doi: 10.1016/j.tele.2017.05.004
Potter, D. (2006). iPod, You Pod, We All Pod. *American Journalism Review*, 28(1), 64–65.
Rocamora, A. (2011). Personal fashion blogs: Screens and mirrors in digital self-portraits. *Fashion Theory*, 15(4), 407–424. doi: 10.2752/175174111X13115179149794
Salmons, J. (Ed.) (2012). Cases *in* online interview research. Thousand Oaks: Sage Publications. doi: 10.4135/9781506335155
Sleigh, A., Stewart, H. & Stokes, K. (2015). Open Dataset of UK Makerspaces, Report, London, Nesta. https://www.nesta.org.uk/report/open-dataset-of-uk-makerspaces-a-users-guide/
Smith, A. (2017). Social Innovation, Democracy and Makerspaces. *SSRN Electronic Journal*. doi: 10.2139/ssrn.2986245
Smith, A. & Light, A. (2017). Cultivating sustainable developments with makerspaces. *Liinc em revista*, 13(1), 162–174.
Unterfrauner, E. & Voigt, C. (2017). Makers' ambitions to do socially valuable things. *The Design Journal*, 20 (1), 3317–3325.
Wenger, E. (1998). *Communities of Practice: Learning, Meaning, and Identity*. Cambridge: Cambridge University Press.
Yin, R. K. (1984). *Case study research: Design and methods*. Thousand Oaks, CA: Sage Publications.

6 Performance as a way of discovering oneself within the other

Can Koçak

Introduction

The most basic definition of 'the other' is everything that falls outside of 'me'. The scope of the concept is based on an understanding of the self, while the terms being used to describe the other are also defined by the self. If the self is among a dominant group, these categories are imposed on the other, as stereotypes are reinforced and the remaining groups are stigmatised based on their supposed spatial marginality, which comforts the self's feeling of superiority in return (Staszak, 2008). No matter how broad the definition is – a single individual, a family, a community, a nation, human beings, earthlings – the idea of self still seems to be exclusionary, confined to a basic understanding of everyone and everything that remains outside of that group.

Exclusionary, in this sense, is used in line with the Baumanian discourse of liquidity. Bauman claims (2003) that because increasing individualisation makes relationships ever more fragile, we are forced to see the other as opponents; in order not to be eliminated by them, we need to rule out certain feelings related to collaboration such as trust, empathy, and compassion. *Homo homini lupus* [A man is a wolf to another man], the saying goes, and we are advised to fear those who demonstrate the qualities of a different species. Among all the discourse around a uniform idea of 'human nature' (Roughley, 2021), every reference to biological groups – *homo sapiens*, *homo erectus*, *homo heidelbergensis*, etc – refers to a step beyond the preceding genus. While undoubtedly necessary for human evolution, this tendency to dismiss whatever or whoever is considered prior or inferior can still be observed in the way humans approach one another, as well as different species. Then again, perhaps the acknowledgement of and approach towards the other does not necessarily have to possess a dismissive nature.

> (...) the perspective of totality in knowledge includes the acknowledgement of the heterogeneity of all reality; of the irreducible, contradictory character of the latter; of the legitimacy, i.e., the desirability of the diverse character of the components of all reality—and therefore, of

DOI: 10.4324/9781003389972-7

the social. The [better, alternative] idea of social totality, then, not only does not deny, but depends on the historical diversity and heterogeneity of society, of every society. In other words, it not only does not deny, but it requires the idea of an 'other'—diverse, different.

(Quijano, 2007, p. 177)

Can collaboration be used as a framework to map out new ways of forming relationships with 'the other' and new methods to define the concept itself? Albeit a broad question that supposes for collaboration a meaning that does not span the fields of media and arts, as well as the domain of interpersonal relationships, this inquiry constitutes the main discussion of the current chapter, which refers to the terminology of both semiology and performance studies. Collaboration is approached here as a tool to shed light on a number of media texts, while the discourse on semiology is utilised to provide the theoretical framework for how meaning is formed and definitions become fixed. More specifically, this chapter focuses on how a performance enables one to rediscover a 'me statement' within an 'it statement' and makes these two supposedly different concepts the same as one another while maintaining their opposite nature.

A given role, at an initial glance, would indicate someone or something other than the performer's self. So, in order for a performer to find a 'me statement' within a role, she would need to demonstrate an ability to come up with a definition that is beyond the limits of a conventional understanding of 'me'; one that is integrated with an 'it statement'. So, both 'me' (the performer's self) and 'the other' (the role) depend on finding their presence within one another to co-exist in a performance.

In the sub-headings that follow, this chapter will first delve into the social and political underpinnings of 'the other', with a focus on the dichotomy between a community ('us') and the outsiders of that group ('them'). Building upon this, the focus will turn to how humans form meaning and establish a sense of self, through which concepts of semiology will be explored. This will help explain how constantly demarcating a 'signifier' and a 'signified' easily establishes a dichotomy between 'me' and 'the other'. While convenient in terms of how meaning is formed and conveyed, an approach as such also enables to legitimise social and political exclusion.

After acknowledging this convenience in achieving meaning as a problem, the solution here will be sought in complicating the clear distinction between the concepts of 'me' and 'the other'. One way this is possible, this chapter claims, is by utilising the rhetoric of performance studies, through which one can find a resemblance, or even congruence, between a 'me statement' and an 'it statement'.

Finding an 'it statement' within a 'me statement' in a performance would also amount to a form of establishing a new sense of identity and belonging. With reference to the conceptual framework of Deleuze and Guattari (as cited in Kaplan, 1987), deterritorialisation would indicate a distance between the signifier and the signified. The rhetoric of performance studies, then, can be used in order to approach the relationship 'me' has with 'the other' as a form of territorialisation, and this paradigm will be proposed to help initiate a new perspective on the rhetoric surrounding 'the other'.

An uncanny yet reassuring encounter: recognising the other

In the film *The Others* (Amenábar, 2001), the titular beings are portrayed as ghostly presences, threatening a young woman and her two kids. The family home, which conventionally implies safety and security, appears to be haunted, providing a setting for horror tropes to flourish. While encouraging one to reflect on how the idea of other is constructed, the film provides an example of Derridean 'hauntology', which suggests (1994) how the self is constantly rediscovered to experience the ghost as the other, re-imagining 'ontology as fluid relational constructs made possible by an attitude of hospitality toward the complex, superfluous and "ghostly" qualities of the other emergent in action' (Pineau, 2012, p. 460). As both living and non-living beings are referred to as ghosts, the narrative of *The Others* highlights the fact that acknowledging the presence of an 'other' is uncanny in and of itself.

In *Tepenin Ardı* (Beyond the Hill, Alper, 2012), the self is embodied by a small group of village folk and constructed against the 'nomads', invisible foes who are held responsible for all malice in this fictional world. While physical interference by the nomads is not seen, their idea still haunts the community through myths created about their ghostly nature. The mere possibility of an 'other' is unsettling and reassuring at the same time. It is unsettling since it creates an enemy seemingly bent on destroying the self and everything it represents. Then again, it is also reassuring, since it helps the self conveniently orient itself as opposition, eliminating any doubt around identity and belonging.

The difficulty to embrace the other is hinted at in the Biblical text, as followers are reminded to 'love thy neighbour'. Bauman starts from this commandment in 'On the Difficulty of Loving Thy Neighbour' (2003) to question whether it is possible to be a 'good neighbour', given the frailty of contemporary human bonds. He claims the dichotomy between what is considered natural and unnatural is no more present than the exact moment 'the other' comes into the city, which is a domain claimed by the self as 'citizen' and is immediately considered both an outsider and a possible perpetrator in this space, the rules of which is certainly unnatural for any newcomer. Based on Bauman's ideas (2003), one is reminded of uncertainty and insecurity as two sentiments that cause people to turn their heads towards the closest target, the other, and initiate a war of domains to eliminate these individuals, who are seen as opponents of some sort. Thus, a metaphorical fence comes between those whose – voluntary and compulsory – domains (ghettos) are already divided by physical fences, as 'us' and 'them' are divided into two sides in a constant struggle with one another.

There are many different ways to address those newcomers, who supposedly threaten the ways of living within the established community. Based on the reception of immigrants, Jacques Rancière refers (2007) to the importance of labelling, particularly the difference between the objective number and subjective perception of immigrants. He compares the 1960s and 1990s and claims that while the number of immigrants has not changed much, subjectively, the latter seems to incorporate more immigrants. The difference, according to Rancière, is in labelling: while the immigrants were proletariats back then, they have lost this political agency, adopting an 'objective' name solely based on their identity. Indeed, it appears that when this group of people loses its grip on any other name than 'other', it becomes the subject of hate and rejection.

Lacanian psychoanalysis introduces (1977) the term 'Big Other' to denote everything that constitutes the public sphere or the milieu humans inhabit, including institutions, culture, and the language used. While being a similar cause of concern with the authority it demonstrates, Lacan claims the Big Other is not a coherent entity and is rather shaped and constantly re-negotiated by the self's perception, which would also be affected by the definition of 'self'.

> Lacanians believe that the Big Other does not in fact exist: the symbolic order we live in is not coherent but is notable for its gaps. It is in fact insubstantial. But Lacan's most important observation was that, although the Big Other does not exist, it nonetheless functions as though it did, since people's belief in it is essential to the way they understand their lives. In order to find at least temporary stability in terms of our identity, we create a fantasy scenario about the consistency of the social sphere we inhabit.
>
> (Salecl, 2011, p. 59)

Calling back *Tepenin Ardı* and its depiction of nomads, the Big Other, and its authority over individual choice and collective action, is arbitrary since it is based on an understanding of the concept rather than an actual compelling force. Ideas and decisions around 'me' and 'us' are formed over an unassimilated sense of time and place, embodied in the notion of Big Other. Similar to the relationship between 'me' and 'the society', the relationship between 'my society' and 'the other[s]' is disrupted from the beginning, fostering hostility instead of hospitality. The question that still needs an answer, then, is whether the other can still be included within the self, rather than immediately being disposed of or dismissed.

As Bauman (2003), who reminds us that encountering the self is as unnatural to the other as it is for the self to encounter the other, Habermas points out the fact that if we are to speak of the inclusion of the other, we should acknowledge the possibility of others who might want to remain as others.

> The community thus constructively outlined is not a collective that would force its homogenised members to affirm its distinctiveness. Here inclusion does not imply locking members into a community that closes itself off from others. The 'inclusion of the other' means rather that the boundaries of the community are open for all, also and most especially for those who are strangers to one another and want to remain strangers.
>
> (Habermas, 1998, p. xxxvi)

While the closed boundaries around 'me' or 'us' enable a seemingly strong sense of self, it blurs the idea of the other and prevents the possibility of inclusion. Whether it is an individual, a group, or the society at large, and whether it is constructed against a single person or a community as self, the implied difference, or foreign and alien state of the other has the potential to bring into light an idea of that self, which begs the following question: what do we talk about when we talk about a 'me' or an 'us'?

Establishing a sense of self: meaning and semiology

Psychologist and psychotherapist Engin Geçtan, with reference to Martin Buber, explains (2014) that when a child is born, she has no concept of 'me' because she is experiencing a vivid motive to get in contact with the universe without awareness of any other form of existence. If the self is inhabited by 'being' and 'doing' as two primary elements, self-discovery and a sense of existing could be solely based on a sense of being, without needing to promote the element of doing (Cohen, 2018). Therefore, establishing a sense of self is quite critical for the individual in terms of how meaning is formed and conveyed through language and recognition.

Umberto Eco, in his book titled *Semiotics and the Philosophy of Language* (1986), defines a small child in front of a mirror. After seeing her reflection for the first time, the child mistakes it for reality. Following some contemplation, she realises that it is just an image, eventually understanding it is an image of her own (Eco, 1986). In line with this description, there are also studies (Courage, Edison, & Howe, 2004) that show recognising one's image in the mirror is one of the earliest forms of self-recognition, emerging before the use of personal pronouns and photo identification. However, one does not have to wait too long for the formation of these personal pronouns.

Geçtan goes on with the statement that a sense of possession is formed nearly simultaneously with a sense of self, finding its roots in the claim of ownership directed to the baby by the parent. As soon as a 'me' starts to exist, a 'my thing' comes along, projecting images of 'me' that others believe are real (Geçtan, 2014). A 'me', in this sense, is defined and determined through the relationship it has with 'it'. So, our sense of the other is clouded by our sense of possession as well as the sense of possession within the other that distorts their projection towards us.

Adopting Saussure's terminology of semiology (1985), which sees language as a system of arbitrary signs that enable any sort of relation between sounds and concepts, Jacques Lacan returns to Eco's description, comparing a child who is looking at herself through the mirror to a 'signifier' and the mirror image to a 'signified' (Köprülü, 2014). However, it should be stated that Lacan draws apart from the 'two sides of a leaf approach' (Köprülü, 2014, p. 955) of Saussure, enabling a playing field for the discourse on the unconscious. The mirror, in this sense, appears as a threshold, marking a clear distinction between the signifier and the signified.

> But the point is that vertical mirrors themselves do not reverse or invert. A mirror reflects the right side exactly where the right side is, and the same with the left side. (...) In front of a mirror we should not speak of inversion but, rather, of absolute *congruence:* the same congruence we observe when we press blotting paper onto a page written with fresh ink.
> (Eco, 1986, pp. 205–206)

The relationship of 'me' with language and a sense of possession is also present in the writings of Ludwig Wittgenstein, especially in his explanation of how the limits of one's language correspond to the limits of one's world (1974). Soykan interprets (2002) this 'world' and 'me' as two concepts other than the 'world' as the sum of all known phenomena and the 'me', which is one of these phenomena. This would mean that when 'me' talks about 'my world', the limits of that world are drawn with a language that only 'me' understands. A similar approach is adopted as the borders around 'the other' are drawn.

> [The] Difference is used to formulate and defend a specific identity of the self—usually the state, a region, or a group of people—against outsiders. In other words, anything that is abnormal or violent is removed to outside the borders of the self. The self, therefore, shores up and reestablishes its boundaries by categorizing those who are different as threats.
> (Dixit, 2012, p. 294)

Establishing anything outside of the realms of what is considered 'self' requires a proclamation of 'This is me' or 'This is us'. Then again, these kinds of symbolic identities are taken on by observing the reactions of the Big Other and positioning oneself accordingly. The subject is first placed in a language, and after adopting a symbolic identity with the help of appropriate signifiers, it starts guessing what kind of an object it is in the eyes of the Big Other and speculating over the larger social sphere it inhabits (Salecl, 2011). Therefore, just like how the other is defined in opposition to the self, the self is rediscovered in relation to the other. It is this constant loop of renegotiation among supposedly fixed terms that this chapter seeks to acknowledge. As a realm of creativity and exploration, the rhetoric of performance studies provides a useful toolkit to develop this line of thinking.

'Me statements' within 'it statements': performance studies and liminality

Shakespeare's *Hamlet* (2015) arguably features the most renowned ghost in popular culture. Revisiting his son shortly after his death, the titular character's father reveals the hidden truth; he was murdered by his brother, Hamlet's uncle. Reminding one of Derridean hauntology, this appearance provides Hamlet with a purpose, suggesting the rediscovery of a sense of self. Then again, this does not immediately translate into a fixed 'me', as the character's 'being' is distorted by his inability to 'do'. Hamlet knows what he has to do, yet is unable to do it. As soon as 'doing' is promoted as a possibility, his 'being' is impoverished by inertia (Cohen, 2018), and he is stuck in a space between 'to be' and 'not to be'. In fact, '*Hamlet* is in several ways an essay in sustained liminality (...) only via a condition of complete liminality can Hamlet finally see the way forward' (Liebler, 1995, pp. 182–184). While aspiring 'to be' and 'not to be' simultaneously, he achieves neither, as this state of in-betweenness turns into a burden, rather than a strength.

Originally conceived as a term in anthropology to define a threshold, in which participants of a ritual are standing before the rite of passage that would restructure their identity (Turner, 1974), liminality is also used in performance studies to define the state of the performer, embodied in Richard Schechner's description, 'performance isn't "in" anything, but "between"' (2002, p. 24). The performer, similarly, is neither herself nor entirely someone else throughout the performance, since performance is a transformative experience that encapsulates every movement from the original self to another being (Zarilli, 1990). Then again, it is not always easy to determine when the performance starts and when it ends, nor what the space in between covers. If the performance before the performance is referred to as A, and the performer after the performance is referred to as B, the liminal space meant by performance studies does not suggest a straight line in a linear plane. Instead, even if one is to assume that A and B are located in the same plane, the 'in-between' is not always limited to the space between A and B; there is also the possibility of the performer moving outside the plane itself and returning to B after moving among different planes. This would enable the performer to momentarily carry elements of both A and B, enriching the definitions of both 'me' and 'the other'.

Lilo Nein, a performance studies scholar, imagines (2009) a dialogue between a text and a performance, taking place after the text sees itself being performed.[1]

> Text: (…) You were fabulous. I really recognized myself in you.
> Performance: What do you mean you recognized yourself? I didn't even know you, I don't recognize you, and you can't possibly recognize me. (…)
> Text: Yes, well, I am a performance.
> (Nein, 2009, p. 209)

Text explains the fabulous nature of Performance with the fact that he has experienced self-recognition while looking at Performance. However, if we leave it at that, this would imply a hierarchy between text and performance, which would contradict the reciprocal relationship this chapter suggests 'me' and 'the other' are in. As the dialogue goes on, Text learns that he is not interrelated with Performance from the start and their relationship is one worth reconsideration: 'Performance: Admittedly, in the act of performance I am you; you appear in me. However, we are not united from the start. (…) you were not already me before me' (Nein, 2009, p. 210). This breaks down that hierarchy, turning the oppositeness into a way of existing side by side, while a constant state of rediscovery of oneself continues. Even though there is a text, the ontological nature of the performance can only be observed in the moment of enactment, not before or after it. Then again, one more question arises here about whether the performer can be placed in the same equation.

Çetin Sarıkartal points out (2010) a distinct feature of Brechtian Theatre; the fact that it radically separates 'me statements' and 'it statements', which refer to statements regarding a notion of self and the other, respectively. He goes on to explain that the Brechtian approach is not deemed interesting today, because the audience of contemporary theatre does not pay any attention to a talk of the other, rather opting for narratives that focus on a deeper understanding of 'me'. The real skilful actor, Sarıkartal suggests, finds a 'me statement' within the role they portray. This would result in an idea of going beyond a regular sense of self, being able to come up with a definition that is beyond the limits of a conventional understanding of 'me', bringing 'me statements' and 'it statements' together. While displacing and disorienting the sense of self, performance does not cause dissonance within the performer around the definitions of 'me' and 'it'. Instead, when elements of both are found within one another, the performer comprises both a 'me' and an 'it', offering a possible method into how the self can formulate its relationship with the other.

Rediscovering a lost identity: the other as territorialisation

The notion of finding oneself as the other can sometimes be caused by a loss of identity. An example of this can be seen in *Yalan* (Lie, 2002), the novel by Tahsin Yücel. The book centres on Yusuf Aksu, the main protagonist who starts to be seen as the founder of a linguistic theorem his childhood friend, Yunus, puts forward before his untimely death. Yusuf Aksu is surrounded by people who assume he is a brilliant linguist and therefore is living a 'lie', as the title suggests.

> Right from the start of the novel, the author notifies us of the conflict between *being* and *appearing*, with the use of a *paromasis*, defined as the adjoint state of words that are vocally similar but separated by meaning per their reciprocity in rhetoric. (…) Through their vocal similarities, the names of Yusuf Aksu and Yunus Aksu are put first in a state of adjointness, then a state of concentricness, and then a process of full identicalness. (…) The stylistic separation that was formed based on the paromasis disappears after a while, (…) the *you* becomes a *me*. In other words, Yunus turns into the 'other me' of Yusuf's identity. Me becomes the other, or rather me starts living as the other.
> (Aktulum, 2015, pp. 111–113)[2]

Yusuf Aksu, along with the theorem, takes the last name of his childhood friend. He chooses to live the rest of his life with this loss of identity, which has been a result of the *paromasis* between the names Yusuf and Yunus. On the other hand, the narrative presents an observable difference between 'being' and 'appearing', revealing Yunus Aksu's 'being' as opposed to Yusuf Aksu's 'appearing'. The people around him inadvertently call Yusuf by Yunus' name, yet this does not refer to a merging of two identities. Within the narrative of *Yalan*, there is only a single identity; that of Yunus Aksu. In this context, 'doing' is also similar to 'being', as both of these terms connote authenticity, as opposed to the fake nature of 'appearing'.

Loss of identity can also be observed when the scope of 'me' or 'self' is bigger. In fact, in many cases where the self is defined not by an individual but by a group, the boundaries around that identity ('us') are established in opposition to 'them', in line with a reinstituted dichotomy between 'inside' and 'outside'. The possibility of losing the identity appears as an even bigger threat and what emerges is a reflex to conserve.

> [Traditional] perspective allows for a consideration of the influence of the internal forces on state identity, but it assumes that the external is a fixed reality that presents itself to the pregiven state and its agents. In contrast, by assuming that the identity of the state is performatively constituted, we can argue that there are no foundations of state identity that exist prior to the problematic of identity/difference that situates

the state within the framework of inside/outside and self/other. Identity is constituted in relation to difference, and difference is constituted in relation to identity, which means that the 'state,' the 'international system,' and the 'dangers' to each are coeval in their construction.
(Campbell, 2005, as cited in Dixit, 2012, p. 303)

A recent trend in works that revolve around the issue of transnationality, which by itself spans the traditional borders of nations and pushes identities to become more fluid, has been the use of the term 'deterritorialisation' (Pekerman, 2012). Pekerman distinguishes between two directions that these researchers dealing with this concept have chosen so far. One focuses on how a state of deterritorialisation carries the potential to be turned into a space of resistance, the other relates it with deprivation and sticks to negative connotations of the term with reference to Deleuze and Guattari. 'Gilles Deleuze and Felix Guattari use the term "deterritorialization" to locate this moment of alienation and exile in language and literature. In one sense it describes the effects of radical distanciation between signifier and signified. Meaning and utterances become estranged' (Kaplan, 1987, p. 188). Finding a 'me statement' within someone else and finding an 'it statement' within oneself, in this sense, would amount to a form of territorialisation, of finding one's place due to that reduced distance between signifier and signified.

Seemingly in contrast with the paragraphs above, Eco claims (1986) that mirrors, in fact, do not produce signs, explaining this in a way that would bring into mind the dialogue between text and performance; the fact that the mirror image and the person standing in front of the mirror are not in a relationship of antecedent-consequent. In addition, since 'the mirror image cannot be used to lie' (Eco, 1986, p. 216), there cannot be a contrast between *being* and *appearing*, because there is no *appearing* in this context. There are also no mediators in between, the only medium is the mirror itself (Eco, 1986) and meaning has to be rediscovered each time. Therefore, much like *Yalan*'s narrative, which highlights the difference between being and appearing, Eco's reading of mirrors, which claims there is no appearing to be spoken of, also brings together being and doing. Territorialised by their simultaneous act, the mirror image *does* what the person *is*.

Conclusion

This chapter asks whether the rhetoric of performance studies can help re-evaluate the most basic understanding of the 'other', and integrate a 'me' within the 'it', or the 'other', and an 'it' or 'other' within 'me'. A follow-up question worth asking here is: what would happen if *homo homini lupus* meets collaboration?

In the final act of *The Others*, the woman and her kids are revealed to be dead. Since the story is told from their point of view, the audiences assume these characters are the victims, but in fact, it is them who are haunting the house and its inhabitants. By subverting expectations, the film makes a point about labelling; it seems that identifying something as 'the other' is enough to demonise it or turn it into a villain. The ending of *The Others* is an indication of how easy it is for 'me' or 'us' to turn into the 'other' when circumstances allow. The narrative also serves as an inquiry into how 'me' can also become an 'other', if the story is told from the other's perspective.

Names and the stereotypes they create are undoubtedly important while establishing the self both socially and physically (Zwebner et al., 2017), yet this is precisely why they are restrictive; they do not tell the whole story. Semiology reminds us that the signifier and the signified do not have an absolute bond; even though the signifier points out to the signified, it does not contain an element that refers to the very essence of the signified within itself (Barthes, 1968). Capturing the essence of 'the other' as a signified, then, requires for the concepts of 'self' and 'the other' to be evaluated under a different light, potentially that of performance studies, and within a framework of collaboration.

What the rhetoric of performance studies brings to the table here is a displaced declaration of being, a notion of bringing oneself into existence with reference to the other. For 'it' to exist, 'me' cannot be absent, and 'me', likewise, can only be present in the presence of 'it'. This is because the constant rediscovery between the two concepts enables room for them to be the same as and the opposite of each other at the same time. Performers are *being* and *doing* in-between – neither themselves nor their role, they ensure collaboration among the self and the other by discovering 'me statements' within 'it statements'. This is a state of territorialisation that finds its roots in displacement, of all places.

Notes

1 Nein refers to the text as 'he' and performance as 'she' without providing an explanation for this choice. This chapter will use the same pronouns while referring to the two concepts.
2 My own translation.

References

Aktulum, K. (2015). Tahsin Yücel'in *Yalan* Adlı Romanında Yazınsal Bir İzlek Olarak Aşırmacının Portresi. [The Portrait of the Plagiarist as a Literary Theme in Tahsin Yücel's Novel titled *Yalan*]. In N. T. Öztokat (Ed.), *Söylem, Söylen, Yazın: Tahsin Yücel'e Armağan* [Discourse, Myth, Literature: A Gift for Tahsin Yücel], pp. 104–136. İstanbul: Can.
Amenábar, A. (2001). *The Others* [Film]. Cruise/Wagner Productions.
Alper, E. (2012). *Tepenin Ardı* [Beyond the Hill; Film]. Bulut Film.
Barthes, R. (1968). *Elements of Semiology*. New York: Hill and Wang.

Bauman, Z. (2003). *Akışkan Aşk: İnsan İlişkilerinin Dayanıksızlığı* [Liquid Love: On the Frailty of Human Bonds]. Istanbul: Alfa.
Cohen, J. (2018) *Not Working: Why We Have to Stop*. London: Granta.
Courage, M. L., Edison, S., & Howe, M. (2004). Variability in the Early Development of Visual Self-Recognition. *Infant Behavior and Development*, 27(4), 509–532.
Derrida, J. (1994). *Specters of Marx: The State of the Debt, The Work of Mourning, and the New International*. P. Kamuf, Trans. New York: Routledge.
Dixit, P. (2012). Relating to Difference: Aliens and Alienness in Doctor Who and International Relations. *International Studies Perspectives*, 13, 289–306.
Eco, U. (1986). *Semiotics and the Philosophy of Language*. Bloomington: Indiana University Press.
Geçtan, E. (2014). *Zamane* [These Days] (4th ed.). İstanbul: Metis.
Habermas, J. (1998). *The Inclusion of the Other: Studies in Political Theory*. C. Cronin and P. de Greif, Trans. Cambridge, MA: MIT Press.
Kaplan, C. (1987). Deterritorializations: The Rewriting of Home and Exile in Western Feminist Discourse. *Cultural Critique*, 6(Spring), 187–198.
Köprülü, Ö. (2014). Bilinçdışı ve Dil. [Unconscious and Language]. *Journal of Turkish Studies*, 9(3), 951–958.
Lacan, J. (1977). *Ecrits: A Selection*. A. Sheridan, Trans. New York: W.W. Norton.
Liebler, N. C. (1995). *Shakespeare's Festive Tragedy: The Ritual Foundations of Genre*. London: Routledge.
Nein, L. (2009). *TRANSLATE YOURSELF! A Performance Reader for Staging*. Vienna: self-published.
Pekerman, S. (2012). *Film Dilinde Mahrem: Ulusötesi Sinemada Kadın ve Mekân Temsili*. [Intimacy in Filmic Language: The Representation of Woman and Space in Transnational Cinema]. Istanbul: Metis.
Pineau, E. (2012). Haunted by Ghosts: Collaborating with Absent Others. *International Review of Qualitative Research*, 5(4), 459–465.
Quijano, A. (2007). Coloniality and Modernity/Rationality. *Cultural Studies*, 21(2–3), 168–178.
Rancière, J. (2007). *Siyasalın Kıyısında* [On the Shores of Politics]. Istanbul: Metis.
Roughley, N. (2021). Human Nature. In N. Zalta (Ed.), *The Stanford Encyclopedia of Philosophy*. https://plato.stanford.edu/entries/human-nature/.
Salecl, R. (2011). *The Tyranny of Choice*. London: Profile Books.
Sarıkartal, Ç. (2010). Klasik Metinleri Bugün Buradan Anlatmak [Recounting Classical Texts Here and Now]. *Tiyatro Araştırmaları Dergisi*, 29(1), 67–79.
Saussure, F. d. (1985). *Genel Dilbilim Dersleri*. [Course in General Linguistics]. Ankara: Birey ve Toplum.
Schechner, R. (2002). *Performance Studies: An Introduction*. London: Routledge.
Shakespeare, W. (2015). *Hamlet*. London: Penguin Classics.
Soykan, Ö. N. (2002). Wittgenstein Felsefesi: Temel Kavram ve Sorunlar. [Philosophy of Wittgenstein: Basic Concepts and Problems]. *Cogito*, 33(Fall), 40–79.
Staszak, J. F. (2008). Other/Otherness. In N. Thrift and R. Kitchin (Eds.), *International Encyclopedia of Human Geography*, pp. 43–47. Amsterdam: Elsevier.
Turner, V. (1974). Liminal to Liminoid in Play, Flow, and Ritual: An Essay in Comparative Symbology. *Rice University Studies*, 60(3), 53–92.

Wittgenstein, L. (1974). *Tractatus Logico-Philosophicus*. Atlantic Highlands: Humanities Press.
Yücel, T. (2002). *Yalan*. [Lie]. Istanbul: Can.
Zarilli, P. (1990). What Does It Mean to "Become the Character": Power, Presence and Transcendence in Asian in-Body Disciplines of Practice. In R. Schechner and W. Appel (Eds.), *By Means of Performance: Intercultural Studies of Theatre and Ritual*. New York: Cambridge University Press.
Zwebner, Y., Sellier, A., Rosenfeld, N., Goldenberg, J., & Mayo, R. (2017). We Look Like Our Names: The Manifestation of Name Stereotypes in Facial Appearance. *Journal of Personality and Social Psychology*, 112(4), 527–554.

Part II
Doing media together

7 Human rights-based narratives of war

A journalistic tool for promoting human rights[1]

Athina Simatou

Violent conflicts have always been the cause of every human rights violation. In 2022 alone, 42 highly violent conflicts were recorded worldwide, of which 21 were classified as limited wars and 21 as wars (HIIK, 2023). Egregious human rights violations have been reported during the armed conflicts, including attacks on civilians and civilian objects, tortures, extrajudicial killings, burning of whole villages, beheadings, massacres, injuries, enforced disappearances, abductions of women and girls, sexual violence, including rape and gang rape, early marriages, arbitrary arrests, and detentions (Amnesty International, 2023). For example, as a result of the Russian invasion of Ukraine, millions of civilians were forced to flee, creating the largest refugee flow in Europe since World War II (Amnesty International, 2023), while over ten million refugees and internally displaced people were caused by wars and climate crises in Mozambique, the Democratic Republic of Congo and Somalia (Amnesty International, 2023, p. 54). While war victims have not been treated by the international community in a manner commensurate with their suffering, the level of international protection appears to be inadequate and inappropriate. A recent report by Amnesty International (2023) points to deeply racist and discriminatory practices by the European Union community against people from countries outside the region such as xenophobic hate crimes in Germany (p. 173), the criminalisation of solidarity in Italy (p. 212), the arbitrary detention of asylum seekers in Japan (p. 214), and the arbitrary detention and discriminatory and humiliating mistreatment of Haitian asylum seekers by US authorities (p. 389), along with the difficulties refugees face in 'accessing essential needs' in Jordan due to inadequate funding of international assistance (p. 215), the refusal of the United Arab Emirates to recognise the rights of refugees (p. 382), and the efforts of the United Kingdom government to circumvent international obligations under the UN Refugee Convention (p. 385). These alarming realities highlight the need for 'human rights discourses' at the forefront of public policies, raise public awareness, and promote empathy for the most vulnerable war victims.

Considering the role of the media as the primary source of human rights information (Heinze & Freedman, 2010) and its ability to immediately mobilise the public (Apodaca, 2007) and transform human suffering (Fairclough, 1995),

90 *Athina Simatou*

this chapter explores how journalistic practices can use the principles of human rights to expose human rights violations both inside and outside war zones. Simultaneously, it draws on the idea that narrative is the most powerful tool for promoting human rights culture and enhancing positive feelings (Barreto, 2006, 2011; Rorty, 1998) to combat racism, discrimination, and exclusionary practices towards war victims. Therefore, this chapter proposes the concept of 'Human Rights-based Journalistic Narrative', a narrative genre of journalism that takes the approach of human rights organisations and advocates and uses narrative techniques to raise awareness and spread empathy and solidarity across different cultures and societies. In this way, empathy and solidarity become the central emotions that unite not only people, but especially media professionals, journalists, human rights defenders, and civil society organisations working together towards the goal of 'creating' a stronger human rights culture.

The relationship between human rights and journalism

Journalism and human rights present crucial key points of intersection, as the freedom of expression, and in particular the freedom of the press, is enshrined in the Universal Declaration of Human Rights (1948, Article 19) as cornerstones of human rights and democracy. There is also a remarkable degree of overlap between journalism and human rights subjects, since a large part of the journalistic coverage concerns topics directly or indirectly related to human rights (International Council of Human Rights Policy, 2002, p. 27). Human rights address such a wide range of issues and extend to so many aspects of human activity that there are human rights norms for almost any possible occasion (Heinze, 2012). That being so, 'almost all news has the potential for a human rights news frame', according to Powers (2016, p. 322), and the concept of human rights news 'is always potentially under negotiation' (p. 323).

Journalists, as the 'producers of information for the general public', are the ones who choose which stories to cover and on which of their aspects to shed light (Internews Global Human Rights Program, 2012, p. 61). As such, the media is emerging as the dominant diffuser of human rights information and news (Apodaca, 2007; Heinze & Freedman, 2010) and as the communicator of human suffering (Zhang & Luther, 2020), playing an important role in the way issues such as the human pain or vulnerability of the victims of violence are perceived by the public (Zhang & Luther, 2020).

Besides, journalists often witness incidents of human rights violations (Batario, 2009; Shaw, 2012) and establish through their work unofficial evidence of those abuses (Ovsiovitch, 1993; Shaw, 2012). Evidence like this has been used in the past by human rights organisations and advocates, in order to draw attention to the violations taking place worldwide and for the prevention of further violations. One such attempt was made by Amnesty International in the 1960s, when the organisation tried to raise awareness through the media about the torture of political prisoners by the Greek military junta, and the country withdrew from the Council of Europe (Powers, 2016).

Apart from being a 'necessary bulwark' for the protection of human rights (Shaw, 2012, p. 28), the media also functions as a pole of diffusion of ideological and political representations, shaping this way the public beliefs around human rights (Drywood et al., 2019). The dynamics of the media to influence public policies and debates, and provoke political change (Ovsiovitch, 1993) goes hand in hand with the belief that news coverage can raise public awareness (Beman & Calderbank, 2008; Heinze & Freedman, 2010), educate people about human rights (Beman & Calderbank, 2008; Ovsiovitch, 1993), bring social change (Downman & Ubayasiri, 2017), and cultivate a prolific ground for the upsurge of activities of support towards people who are suffering (Zhang & Luther, 2020). According to a study by the International Council on Human Rights Policy (2002), 'the selection and presentation of human rights stories in media coverage influence our perception of the world around us in many ways' (p. 113).

The difficulty of accessing the conflict zones, as well as the immensity of human suffering, make the role of journalists as transmitters and shapers of reality even more essential and important. Furthermore, if the report of the first modern war correspondent, W. H. Russell, about the Crimean War, resulted in the fall of the British government and the resignation of the UK's Prime Minister (Tumber, 2009), then the power that war correspondents hold as carriers of social and political change is indisputable. In a more recent example, the widespread media coverage of the so-called 'genocide' in Darfur affected public opinion to such an extent that the international community was forced to put pressure on the Sudanese government to stop the persecution (Rose, 2013). Besides, as the Institute for War and Peace Reporting mentions (Batario, 2009, p. 13), in the cases of Rwanda and former Yugoslavia, war crimes prosecutors used press reports as evidence to lead their suspects to the International Criminal Court.

Is there an ethical obligation for journalists to report on human rights?

The moral responsibility of the media can be attached to a theory of journalism ethics and the activist journalism theory where journalists should be 'more than stenographers of fact' (Ward, 2009, p. 299) to seek social reform by 'challenging the status quo, opposing wars' and 'promoting social causes' (Ward, 2009, p. 299) and mobilising the public against unjust policies (Ward, 2009). According to the Internews Global Human Rights Program (2012), 'journalists have a moral obligation to promote human rights all the time and in every story because media are "watchdogs"' (p. 61) and 'human rights are a moral compass for good journalism' (p. 62). This moral principle of journalists, generated by virtue of their profession, extends to their obligation to inform and educate the public, raise awareness, witness, monitor, investigate, and report on human rights abuses of all forms (Batario, 2009; Shaw, 2012).

It is an ethical duty attributed to journalists, especially in the democratic setup, where they are considered as the ones responsible for checking and exposing any governmental misconduct, providing a 'platform' for an active public dialogue (Apodaca, 2007; Balabanova, 2015; Soma & Chakraborty, 2017) and mobilising citizens to participate in the public sphere.

The human rights-based approach to journalism can be characterised as the approach that gives voice to the voiceless through people-oriented stories. Based on international human rights standards, norms, and a holistic approach to human rights, it contains specific principles and guidelines, such as the duty to promote the universality of basic human rights (Batario, 2009; Beman & Calderbank, 2008; Hamelink, 2001; Heinze & Freedman, 2010; Rose, 2013; Shaw, 2012) and establish 'linkages to human rights standards' (Beman & Calderbank, 2008, p. 24). A human rights-based approach suggests that people are placed at the centre of the stories (Batario, 2009), the reporting is highly descriptive or humanised (Heinze & Freedman, 2010, p. 495), all affected parties, especially the most disadvantaged and vulnerable, participate in the stories (Batario, 2009; Beman & Calderbank, 2008), the audience develops a greater knowledge and understanding of its rights and of the way its problems are translated into human rights issues (Hamelink, 2001; Rose, 2013; Shaw, 2012), the duty bearers are held accountable for the deprivation of the rights (Batario, 2009; Beman & Calderbank, 2008; Rose, 2013), inequalities, unjust and discriminatory practices are identified (Batario, 2009; Beman & Calderbank, 2008), the big picture of the violations is given, in order to understand the extent of the problem (Batario, 2009, p. 43), visual, audio, or audiovisual material is included in journalistic pieces whose main narrative means is the text, because 'seeing is believing' (Batario, 2009; pp. 75–76), the rights involved are clearly stated (Batario, 2009, p. 42) and/or the concept of human rights is placed at the forefront of the stories (Beman & Calderbank, 2008, p. 26), and the abuses are covered in a way that solutions to the problems stated are included (Rose, 2013).

Inspired by the moral responsibility of journalists, human rights journalism reveals human rights abuses, focuses and critically reflects on the victims and the perpetrators to prevent further abuses and promotes and protects human rights (Shaw, 2012). It is a 'journalism with a human face, a journalism that cares for the people' (Shaw, 2012, pp. 37–38). To do so, it applies the human rights-based approach to journalism seeking to add the advancement of human rights to journalists' everyday obligations (Rose, 2013, p. 85). Thus, if journalists and journalistic organisations are inspired by a theory of moral correctness (journalism ethics), then the effort to underline human rights as issues of the public agenda and cultivate emotions of empathy towards the victims of violence can fall under the umbrella of the human rights journalism and human rights-based approach. After all, human rights journalism is on the opposite pole from the war, based on the idea that 'the ideal cosmopolitan society is where peace and human rights co-exist' (Shaw, 2012, p. 21).

Human rights as a topic of news

The close relationship between journalism and human rights does not seem to be taken into consideration as a point of concern by journalistic practices with a limited systematic analysis (Heinze & Freedman, 2010; Pollock, 2014) making it quite difficult to map out the relationship between journalistic practice and human rights. Ovsiovitch (1993) in one of the first studies on the topic argued that human rights were covered by the media to a very small extent, while chronic human rights violations were unreported, a finding that was confirmed by later studies too (see Hamelink, 2001; International Council of Human Rights Policy, 2002). In 2002, the International Council of Human Rights Policy study provided important feedback about the serious ignorance and confusion on the part of journalists concerning the concept of human rights, even though it noted an increase in the value of human rights as news items and the number of stories about human rights due to the many humanitarian crises taking place.

Inadequate media coverage of human rights issues was also noted by Klein (2011), where he argued that despite the global human rights crisis, the language of rights is seldom found even in the most sophisticated print media, a finding that underlined the gap between real human rights situations and the media interest in them. Heinze and Freedman (2010) were also highly critical when they claimed that the media does not give real importance and value to human rights, and often fails to properly capture the reality of violations around the world. Heinze (2012) has also underlined that even in their most egregious abuses human rights are not given the highest value and do not constitute the primary focus of the reporting. Research has shown that the media and journalists often prefer to report on warfare, clashes, and acts of terrorism rather than on human rights, humanitarian issues, or the death toll per se (Powers, 2016). The European Institute of Peace recorded that in 2016, only 3% of Syrian war stories published by global media were relevant to humanitarian issues (European Institute of Peace, 2016).

Heinze (2012) emphasises the disproportionate media coverage of conflicts. He claims that human rights events taking place in Afghanistan, in Israel against Palestinians, and in Iraq against Americans have received far more attention than the abuses committed in the armed conflicts of the Democratic Republic of Congo, Syria, and Libya (Heinze, 2012; Heinze & Freedman, 2010). More recently, Mead (2019) complained about the bias and lack of objectivity in the portrayal of human rights cases (p. 12).

The lack of adequate and high-quality reporting on human rights can be attributed to the fact that the media is 'ill-equipped to deal with human rights issues' (Hamelink, 2001, p. 5), which needs 'background, context and in-depth analysis' and long-term processes (Hamelink, 2001, p. 5). It has been observed that journalists confuse human rights law with the law of war, struggle to recognise and distinguish between different human rights issues and find it difficult to interpret the diverse protection mechanisms and the human rights treaties (International Council of Human Rights Policy, 2002). The complexity of human rights notions and issues is one of the difficulties faced by journalists when covering human rights events. Other challenges include the fear of sources of information to talk to journalists, the need for continuous training, the belief that human rights do not sell, the fear of repercussions from the advertisers or the owners of the media organisations, and the affiliation of media outlets with specific political parties and interests (Batario, 2009; Ovsiovitch, 1993; Rose, 2013).

Reporting on human rights during the war is even more challenging since the risk is always present (Creech, 2018) and journalists are never safe. The lives of journalists are constantly threatened, and they are often subject to abuses, such as attacks, killings, enforced disappearances, imprisonments, harassments, threats, and abductions (Amnesty International, 2021; Batario, 2009; Human Rights Watch, 2021; Koul, 2018). Besides, reporters often face difficulties in accessing the war zones and finding primary sources of information. The recent research of Zhang and Luther (2020) on the Syrian war attributed the lack of primary and meticulous narratives of 'human suffering' to the fact that there are not enough journalists reporting from the field (p. 416), while at the same time, the Assad regime imposes very strict restrictions on journalists' access to information.

Why narratives matter? Human rights and narratives

Narrative as a tool to create a culture of human rights based and inspired by Richard Rorty's work titled 'Human Rights, Rationality, and Sentimentality' (1998), was re-interpreted and recontextualised by J. M. Barreto (2006, 2011). Moving away from the foundationalism and the metaphysical theories of human rights, Rorty seeks to radically reshape human rights theory and practice (Barreto, 2011; Rorty, 1998), since he identifies, in human history, practices of dehumanising individuals and social groups, practices which distinguish between 'humans', on the one hand, and 'sub-humans', 'pseudo or quasi-humans', and 'non-humans', on the other. He records discrimination between men and women, whites and blacks, adults and children, and Christians and Muslims (Barreto, 2011, pp. 110–111; Rorty, 1998). The removal of these practices of discrimination will come with the development of our sensibility towards other people, in whose place we are called to put ourselves and find what unites and not differentiates us (Barreto, 2011). Ethics of human rights is, thus, based on the 'ethics of emotions' which focuses on the cultivation of moral feelings ('sentimental education'), such as sympathy and solidarity, and aims to make everyone see the victims of violations as fellow sufferers with the ultimate practical goal of reducing their pain (Barreto, 2006, 2011). Dealing with human rights is, therefore, directly linked with understanding human suffering and using narratives to address the problems that exist around the world (Barreto, 2011).

Narrative, thus, is not just an attractive way of communicating something. Instead, it is a tool with 'an emancipatory function' (Plummer, 1995, as cited by Elliott, 2005, p. 50) that can transform 'individual lives and the wider culture' (Plummer, 1995, as cited by Elliott, 2005, p. 50). Its power originates from its ability to be easily accessible to people, to reach large audiences and to provide deep and detailed information on events and issues that people, social actors, and governments might have no previous knowledge about, especially concerning the feelings and the experiences of the victims of abuses and the horrors they have endured.

This potential of narrative has been addressed recently by Cattaneo and Grieco (2021), who created and shared positive narratives about migrants' impact on the hosting countries, to examine the pervasive and decisive role that narratives play in the way attitudes, decisions, and behaviours are shaped (p. 795). The project concluded that narratives are potent to replace the negative opinion of the audience towards migrants with a positive one. Accordingly, the narrative's impact was proved during the 1993 Global Tribunal on Violations of Women's Human Rights, when the personal narratives of women about their everyday horrors managed to shed light on the ongoing violations against women and girls and highlighted the need to put an end to them (Meyers, 2016, p. 73).

The narrative has, therefore, the potential to raise awareness, shape attitudes and behaviours, influence decisions, call to action, increase the audience's empathy and sympathy towards the actors of the story, and ultimately bring all the changes that the narrator is aiming at – especially as far as it concerns advancing human rights empowerment and human rights law (Ali, 2014; Cattaneo & Grieco, 2021; Johnson, 2013). Thus, telling stories of people who are suffering human rights violations, such as slavery, enforced displacement, forced marriage, sexual harassment, rape, killing has emerged as one of the most potent ways to support human rights claims, advance and protect human rights, as well as solve problems (Johnson, 2013; Ochs et al's, 1989). Therefore, human rights become more of a subject of public discourse, narrative, and advocacy (Johnson, 2013, p. 243). The several authors and creators (journalists, activists, organisations, lawyers) of human rights stories claim to have different goals when portraying victims of abuses and vulnerable groups, such as victims of slavery, refugees, women, minor girls as protagonists. The goal, however, is always the same: to stop the abuses and promote and guarantee better human rights for everyone.

Narrators of slavery, aim, according to Johnson (2013), to help audiences recognise the existence of slavery, stop the judgement against the victims, educate other victims of enslavement, advocate specific interventions that will help in the prevention of further abuses, and encourage specific actions against slavery. The prohibition and abolishment of slavery is not the only target of the narratives. Their target shall also be the emancipation, rehabilitation, and inclusion of the victims in society, as well as the design and implementation of strategies (Johnson, 2013). For example, writing creative stories about women and gender issues intends to empower women and change their status quo in specific societies by developing gender education and consciousness concerning inequalities, bias, and injustice (Ali, 2014). Besides, storytelling is considered very effective when it comes to tackling sensitive issues, such as gender-related ones (Ali, 2014).

Nevertheless, existing narratives seem to be missing important qualitative characteristics, as highlighted by the research work of Brough et al. (2013), who focus on the need for refugee narratives that elaborate more on suffering and hope. Similarly, Batario (2009) emphasises that the journalistic narratives of human rights simply remain on 'the struggle between good and evil' (p. 11), without delving into the whole complexity of the human rights story. Much like Batario, professor of law, Mutua (2001) also suggests that the dominant narrative concerning human rights is based on 'a three-dimensional compound metaphor' (pp. 201–202), the 'savages – victims – saviors (SVS) construction' (p. 201), which includes on the one side the 'savages' and on the other side the 'victims' and their 'saviours'.

Narrative in journalism and human rights

The use of narrative format in news as a tool for promoting, defending human rights and increasing awareness towards the victims of abuses is a proposal that has been under-studied by scholars. Even though the way news is framed has a strong impact on people's attitudes (Maier et al., 2017, p. 1014) and the influence of journalistic narratives on reader's engagement and behaviour has been widely recognised (Shen et al., 2014), only a few studies have elaborated on this topic. Nevertheless, most studies focus on the influence of the story form on the behaviour of the people and their feelings towards stigmatised groups or minorities, while the human rights issues as narrative topics do not constitute a research subject of the existing bibliography.

Shen et al. (2014) have concluded that a very effective way to generate feelings of empathy and support is with narrative news, which focuses on the negative consequences of political issues. Almost the same claim was made by Oliver et al. (2012), who suggested in their study that narrative news stories provoke more compassion, positive intentions, engagement, and 'information-seeking behaviour' (p. 205) towards stigmatised groups than the non-narrative forms. Journalists themselves have also widely admitted the narrative power of their stories, as they have noted very dynamic reactions following the publication of their narrative pieces and have used the narrative methodology, to 'educate' people and change public opinion concerning certain groups of people.

As Sonia Nazario (2007), the Pulitzer Prize winner journalist, argues, journalistic stories have the potential to mobilise the audience to reflect on the issues mentioned, but also to take actions (p. 182). Besides, she believes that journalists should aim to make these stories as moving as possible (p. 182).

Her personal goal and desire, when she wrote the story of a little boy's 'illegal' journey from Honduras to the USA in 'Enrique's Journey', was to educate people about the harsh reality of an immigrant's journey and the deep poverty that leads people to risk their lives while 'escaping' their countries (p. 181).

Adopting a similar perspective, Richard Ben Cramer, another Pulitzer Prize winner journalist, expresses in his interview with R. Boynton (2005) the desire that his books and articles have the same impact as that of a novel, considering that they share the same opportunity to create a 'life-changing experience for the reader' (p. 35). Wilkerson (2007) highlights the life-changing power of the narrative when she describes readers' unique and unprecedented reactions to her story about ten-year-old Nicholas's tough, risky, and 'manful life': *'I had succeeded in transcending the stereotypes and assumptions some readers have about people who seem different from them'* (p. 176).

The journalistic narrative as a meaningful way to address human rights issues in war

An interdisciplinary approach to human rights violations in wars becomes crucial in examining the intersection between journalism and human rights and the interaction between narratives and human rights. Such approach interrelationships between the subfields of narrative, journalism, and human rights by linking them to a common goal of protecting human rights and fighting racism, exclusion, and human rights violations against victims of war. It underscores the critical role that media and journalists play in upholding human rights and identifies storytelling as a powerful tool to promote positive sentiments and actions toward suffering humanity.

Thus, it proposes a new genre of discourse, the 'Human Rights-based Journalistic Narrative', which, based on the above connections, applies the criteria of the human rights-based approach to journalism and the characteristics of narrative discourse. For the methodological purposes of this chapter, it is defined as a journalistic narrative that meets most of the following criteria:

- a high level of participation of the affected parties, placing them at the centre of the stories.
- use of human rights language and making references to human rights standards. Rights affected are clearly identified and/or the concept of human rights is placed at the forefront of stories.
- deeply descriptive and/or humanised reporting.
- assigning responsibility to perpetrators of human rights abuses and/or holding duty bearers accountable for withholding human rights and/or failing to adequately protect them.
- highlighting inequalities, unjust and discriminatory practices, and/or identifying vulnerable or disadvantaged groups.

- providing an overall picture of the violations to understand the scope of the problem.
- the violations are presented in a way that includes solutions to the problems identified.
- visual, audio, or audiovisual material is included in journalistic pieces whose primary means of presentation is text.

Therefore, the concept of 'Human Rights-based Journalistic Narrative' is proposed as a discourse genre that places the victims of wars and human rights violations taking place in conflicts at the centre of narratives in order to develop empathy and solidarity as a common emotion against fear, insecurity, and indifference, and to progressively promote human rights in contemporary societies. By recognising empathy and solidarity as core values and ultimate goals, the human rights-based approach functions as a common ground for practitioners, institutions, and organisations of various sub-fields to collaborate, network, and cooperate to strengthen human rights societies. As such, it serves as a guideline for journalists and war correspondents to promote human rights-based practices and work on human rights issues in war, a reference point for human rights scholars studying journalistic ethics and practices, and a methodological tool for human rights practitioners working with journalists to promote human rights principles.

Note

1 This chapter is based on the author's doctoral research for her PhD dissertation entitled 'Journalistic Narratives and Human Rights in War' supervised by Professor Nikos Bakounakis at the Panteion University of Social and Political Studies. The research is co-funded by Greece and the European Union (European Social Fund- ESF) through the Operational Programme 'Human Resources Development, Education and Lifelong Learning' in the context of the project 'Strengthening Human Resources Research Potential via Doctorate Research – 2nd Cycle' (MIS-5000432), implemented by the State Scholarships Foundation (IKY).

References

Ali, M. (2014). Stories/Storytelling for Women's Empowerment/Empowering Stories. *Women's Studies International Forum*, 45, 98–104. doi: 10.1016/j.wsif.2013.10.005

Amnesty International. (2021). *Amnesty International Report 2020/2021 The State of the World's Human Right*. https://www.amnesty.org/en/documents/pol10/3202/2021/en/

Amnesty International. (2023). *Amnesty International Report 2022/2023 The State of the WORLD'S Human Right*. https://www.amnesty.org/en/documents/pol10/5670/2023/en/

Apodaca, C. (2007). The Whole World Could Be Watching: Human Rights and the Media. *Journal of Human Rights*, 6(2), 147–164. doi: 10.1080/14754830701334632

Balabanova, E. (2015). *The Media and Human Rights: The Cosmopolitan Promise* (1st ed.). London and New York: Routledge. doi: 10.4324/9780203105436

Barreto, J. M. (2006). Ethics of Emotions as Ethics of Human Rights: A Jurisprudence of Sympathy in Adorno, Horkheimer and Rorty. *Law and Critique*, 17, 73–106. doi: 10.1007/s10978-006-0003-y

Barreto, J. M. (2011). Rorty and Human Rights: Contingency, Emotions and How to Defend Human Rights Telling Stories. *Utrecht Law Review*, 7(2), 93–112. doi: 10.18352/ulr.164

Batario, R. (2009). *Reporting Human Rights in the Philippines. A Field Guide for Journalists and Media Workers*. Philippine Human Rights Reporting Project. https://reliefweb.int/report/philippines/reporting-human-rights-philippines-field-guide-journalists-and-media-workers

Beman, G., & Calderbank, L. (2008). *The Human Rights-based Approach to Journalism: Training Manual, Viet Nam*. UNESCO Bangkok. https://unesdoc.unesco.org/ark:/48223/pf0000179185/PDF/179185eng.pdf.multi

Boynton, R. S. (2005). *The New New Journalism Conversations with America's Best Nonfiction Writers on Their Craft*. New York City: Vintage Books.

Brough, M., Schweitzer, R., Shakespeare-Finch, J., Vromans, L., & King, J. (2013). Unpacking the Micro-Macro Nexus: Narratives of Suffering and Hope among Refugees from Burma Recently Settled in Australia. *Journal of Refugee Studies*, 26(2), 207–225. doi: 10.1093/jrs/fes025

Cattaneo, C., & Grieco, D. (2021). Turning Opposition into Support to Immigration: The Role of Narratives. *Journal of Economic Behavior and Organization*, 190, 785–801. doi: 10.1016/j.jebo.2021.08.015

Creech, B. (2018). Bearing the Cost to Witness: The Political Economy of Risk in Contemporary Conflict and War Reporting. *Media, Culture & Society*, 40(4), 567–583. doi: 10.1177/0163443717715078

Downman, S., & Ubayasiri, K. (2017). *Journalism for Social Change in Asia* (1st ed.). London: Palgrave Macmillan. doi: 10.1057/978-1-349-95179-6

Drywood, E., Farrell, M., & Hughes, E. (2019). Introduction. In M. Farrell, E. Drywood, & E. Hughes (Eds.), *Human Rights in the Media. Fear and Fetish* (1st ed., pp. 1–5). London and New York: Routledge.

Elliott, J. (2005). *Using Narrative in Social Research Qualitative and Quantitative Approaches* (1st ed.). London, Thousand Oaks, CA, New Delhi: Sage Publications. https://uk.sagepub.com/en-gb/eur/using-narrative-in-social-research/book226488#contents

European Institute of Peace (2016, May 17). *War/Peace Reporting: Syria in Global Media*. Retrieved April 14, 2022, from https://www.eip.org/war-peace-reporting-syria-in-the-global-media/

Fairclough, N. (1995). *Media Discourse* (1st ed.). Edward Arnold.

Hamelink, C. J. (2001). Introduction Human Rights and the Media. *Critical Arts*, 15(1–2), 3–11. doi: 10.1080/02560240185310031

Heinze, E. (2012). The Reality and Hyper-Reality of Human Rights: Public Consciousness and the Mass Media. In R. Dickinson, C. Murray, & O. Pedersen (Eds.), *Examining Critical Perspectives on Human Rights* (1st ed., pp. 193–216). Cambridge: Cambridge University Press.

Heinze, E., & Freedman, R. (2010). Public Awareness of Human Rights: Distortions in the Mass Media. *The International Journal of Human Rights*, 14(4), 491–523. doi: 10.1080/13642980802645804

HIIK. (2023). *Conflict Barometer 2022*. https://hiik.de/wp-content/uploads/2023/05/CoBa_2022_00_01.pdf

Human Rights Watch. (2021). *World Report 2021*. https://www.hrw.org/sites/default/files/media_2021/01/2021_hrw_world_report.pdf

International Council on Human Rights Policy. (2002). *Journalism, Media and the Challenge of Human Rights Reporting*, Versoix, Switzerland.

Internews Global Human Rights Program. (2012). *Speak Up, Speak Out: A Toolkit for Reporting on Human Rights Issues*. https://tinyurl.com/2t9d92mv

Johnson, K. (2013). The New Slave Narrative: Advocacy and Human Rights in Stories of Contemporary Slavery. *Journal of Human Rights*, 12(2), 242–258. doi: 10.1080/14754835.2013.784664

Klein, J. (2011). The Rhetoric and Ideology of Human Rights in the Media. In D. Papademas (Ed.), *Human Rights and Media*: Vol. 6. Studies in Communications (1st ed., pp. 41–56). Warrington: Emerald Group Publishing Limited. doi: 10.1108/S0275-7982(2011)0000006005

Koul, S. (2018). Human Rights of Journalists Working in Kashmir: An In-depth Analysis. *Journal of Content, Community and Communication*, 7, 86–91. doi: 10.31620/JCCC.06.18/11

Maier, S. R., Slovic, P., & Mayorga, M. (2017). Reader Reaction to News of Mass Suffering: Assessing the Influence of Story Form and Emotional Response. *Journalism*, 18(8), 1011–1029. doi: 10.1177/1464884916663597

Mead, D. (2019). They Offer You a Feature on Stockings and Suspenders Next to a Call for Stiffer Penalties for Sex Offenders. In M. Farrell, E. Drywood, & E. Hughes (Eds.), *Human Rights in the Media. Fear and Fetish* (1st ed., pp. 9–43). London: Routledge.

Meyers, D. T. (2016). *Victims' Stories and the Advancement of Human Rights* (1st ed.). Oxford: Oxford University Press. doi: 10.1093/acprof:oso/9780199930388.001.0001

Mutua, M. (2001). Savages, Victims, and Saviors: The Metaphor of Human Rights. *Harvard International Law Journal*, 42(1), 201–245. https://ssrn.com/abstract=1525547

Nazario, S. (2007). Dealing with Danger: Protecting Your Subject and Your Story. In M. Kramer & W. Call (Eds.), *Telling True Stories* (1st ed., pp. 178–182). New York: Plume.

Ochs, E., Smith, R., & Taylor, C. (1989). Detective Stories At Dinnertime: Problem-Solving Through Co-Narration. *Cultural Dynamics*, 2(2), 238–257. doi: 10.1177/092137408900200206

Oliver, M. B., Dillard, J. P., Bae, K., & Tamul, D. J. (2012). The Effect of Narrative News Format on Empathy for Stigmatized Groups. *Journalism & Mass Communication Quarterly*, 89(2), 205–224. doi: 10.1177/1077699012439020

Ovsiovitch, J. S. (1993). News Coverage of Human Rights. *Political Research Quarterly*, 46(3), 671–689. doi: 10.2307/448953

Pollock, J. (2014). Illuminating Human Rights: How Demographics Drive Media Coverage. *Atlantic Journal of Communication*, 22(3–4), 141–159. doi: 10.1080/15456870.2014.916292

Powers, M. (2016). A New Era of Human Rights News? Contrasting Two Paradigms of Human Rights News-Making. *Journal of Human Rights*, 15(3), 314–329. doi: 10.1080/14754835.2015.1106309

Rorty, R. (1998). *Truth and Progress: Philosophical Papers*. Cambride: Cambridge University Press. doi: 10.1017/CBO9780511625404

Rose, T. (2013). A Human Rights-Based Approach to Journalism: Ghana. *Journal of International Communication*, 19(1), 85–106. doi: 10.1080/13216597.2012.737347

Shaw, I. S. (2012). *Human Rights Journalism* (1st ed.). London: Palgrave Macmillan.

Shen, F., Ahern, L., & Baker, M. (2014). Stories That Count: Influence of News Narratives on Issue Attitudes. *Journalism & Mass Communication Quarterly*, 91(1), 98–117. doi: 10.1177/1077699013514414

Soma, A. A., & Chakraborty, S. (2017). A Critical Analysis of Newspaper Reporting on Women's Issues. In G. P. Pandey, C. Joshi, & D. Paromita (Eds.), *Problems and Perspectives of the Relationship between Media and Human Rights* (1st ed., pp. 1–10). Cambridge Scholars Publishing.

Tumber, H. (2009). Covering War and Peace. In K. Wahl-Jorgensen & T. Hanitzsch (Eds.), *Handbook for Journalism Studies* (1st ed., pp. 386–397). New York and London: Routledge.

Universal Declaration of Human Rights, December 10, 1948, https://www.un.org/en/about-us/universal-declaration-of-human-rights

Ward, S. (2009). Journalism Ethics. In K. Wahl-Jorgensen & T. Hanitzsch (Eds.), *Handbook for Journalism Studies* (1st ed., pp. 295–309). New York: Routledge.

Wilkerson, I. (2007). Playing Fair with Subjects. In M. Kramer & W. Call (Eds.), *Telling True Stories* (1st ed., pp. 172–176). New York: Plume.

Zhang, X., & Luther, C. (2020). Transnational News Media Coverage of Distant Suffering in the Syrian Civil War: An Analysis of CNN, Al-Jazeera English and Sputnik Online News. *Media, War & Conflict*, 13(4), 399–424. doi: 10.1177/1750635219846029

8 Digitally mediating cultural trauma through virtual reality

Eleni Pnevmatikou and Angeliki Gazi

Introduction

Human activity (e.g., war or public interest reasons) and physical disasters (e.g., hurricanes, earthquakes, tsunamis) can lead to landscape destruction with essential consequences for the people residing there. Such events result in a horrendous change for the inhabitants' continuity of life (Fried, 1967), who are then forced to abandon their place of living. The losses of the home and the cultural bonds between the community members might cause negative feelings like loss of control, fear for the unpredicted future, sadness, stress and nostalgia for the lost homeland (Tata-Arsel, 2014). The community's cohesion is disrupted, affecting its members' individual and collective identity. At a distant time, this sentimental crisis might evolve into an individual or collective trauma.

The healing of the trauma in such circumstances is a challenge. It can be approached at a personal or a collective level as a shared experience with other community members (Koh, 2021). Healing programs might involve interventions to preserve memory, restore collective identity and the sense of belonging, support togetherness within the community and give voice to the emotions of loss and mourning to be expressed, seeking to empower the trauma carriers (Alexander, 2012). Such collective interventions could emerge from inside the community or they could be developed with external support. In the last years, intervention programs 'with rather than on people' (Heron & Reason, 2006, p. 179) have shown encouraging and promising results. Scholars claim that in interventions *with* and *within* a community, the involvement of the participants in the process is more important than the outcome itself (Laplante, 2007, pp. 433–434). These intervention strategies often involve rituals, memorials, art, media and digital technology.

In this chapter,[1] the use of virtual reality (VR) technology in healing cultural trauma, in Pontokomi's community case, is proposed. First, we investigated (i) if the community's members experience trauma due to their forced relocation for public interest reasons, which will lead to the irreversible destruction of their land, and (ii) what are the aspects of their culture, everyday

DOI: 10.4324/9781003389972-10

life and their land that they want to be preserved in memory, as a reference for the future. Secondly, we will examine (iii) if a VR platform could facilitate the experience of negative feelings caused due to the disruption of the community, and the irreversible destruction of its land. More specifically, this chapter focuses on the process of collectively designing an intervention, together with the members of the community of Pontokomi in Western Greece, using VR technology. The first inhabitants of Pontokomi were placed in the settlement a century ago, arriving from the Caucasus and other areas (of Pontos) around the Black Sea. Today, Pontokomians are obliged by the Power Public Company to leave their houses, as a second displacement. The settlement will be demolished, as the lignite in the subsoil underneath needs to be mined to generate electricity, leading in a few years to its total disappearance. So, the aim of the intervention proposed in this chapter is to empower the individuals who experience negative feelings due to their displacement. It is noteworthy that the VR platform mediates the person's experience of the place, in a sense creating a hybrid space that lies at the intersection of the physical environment and digital information. It is therefore conceivable that, by combining aspects of physical and virtual spaces, hybrid spaces can take advantage of the place-defining characteristics of both their constituent elements at the same time.

This chapter begins with defining the terms of collective and cultural trauma. The second section focuses on the trauma caused due to displacement. After presenting some indicative objectives and techniques used in trauma therapies, the third section of this chapter proposes the development of a 360° virtual environment as a collective intervention for the Pontokomi's community case, with images captured at a time when the settlement was still as its inhabitants want to remember it, so that at a future time, this virtual environment will act as a reference point for the community.

Collective and cultural trauma

The Greek word trauma means wound and is used to qualify an interruption in continuity (Koh, 2021). The first to insert and study the term collective trauma was sociologist Kai T. Erikson (1995), who defined it as 'a blow to the basic tissues of social life that damages the bonds attaching people together and impairs the prevailing sense of communality' (cited in Hanif & Ullah, 2018, p. 4). Collective trauma refers to the individuals and the society they belong to (Erikson, 1995), and occurs when those individuals share similar subjective traumatic experiences. Alexander (2012, p. 4) defined collective trauma as a 'symbolic rendering that reconstructs and imagines' the initial event and the consequent individual suffering.

A subset of collective trauma is the cultural trauma, that is socially constructed, as the cultural sociologists who have mainly approached, defined and studied it agree (Smelser, 2004; Alexander, 2004, 2012; David, 2008; Eyerman, 2013, 2015). Cultural trauma occurs in a situation or an extraordinary and potentially dangerous life-changing event interpreted by a community as violent or horrible, as a shock, interrupting what was previously experienced by the community as normality. Cultural trauma is not always realised when crises happen. Therefore, regardless of how severe a crisis is, it is not for granted that it will become cultural trauma (Demertzis & Eyerman, 2020). The term 'Holocaust', for example, has become 'the social creation of a cultural fact', which, in turn, affects 'social and moral life' (Alexander, 2002, p. 197).

Although cultural trauma is usually studied from a distant point in time, it is also possible to be studied during its occurrence (e.g., Ostertag & Ortiz, 2013; Demertzis & Eyerman, 2020). The latter is essential for developing early interventions to prevent the individuals from their negative feelings while experiencing that crisis, which could be socially processed as trauma. For example, the recent cases of hurricane Katrina, 9/11 and the COVID-19 pandemic were studied *in vivo*, as from the very beginning, they all triggered a trauma process (Demertzis & Eyerman, 2020). Recently, referring to the traumatic consequences of the COVID-19 pandemic, Demertzis and Eyerman (2020, p. 428) introduced the new term of *compressed cultural trauma*, claiming though that the pandemic 'has not evolved into cultural trauma' (yet). In other words, although the trauma drama occurs from the very beginning, the way and the extent to which it will affect the social body cannot be predicted. It will only become distinct *if* and *when* there are other social changes and it is processed accordingly (Demertzis & Eyerman, 2020).

As cultural and collective trauma share many commonalities, the distinction between the two terms is not always obvious. However, understanding those two types of psychological trauma is crucial before designing and developing any healing or mediating intervention.

Displacement and cultural trauma

During the passage of time, repetitive, habitual practices and the stability of the continuous living of a group of people in a location, cultural bonds are established between them and a community is formed. Their common space then becomes a *place* (Tuan, 1977, p. 6), a 'habit field' (Tuan, 1979, p. 418), a 'field(s) of care' (Wild, 1963, p. 47). Although individuals rarely notice this sense of continuity and togetherness, once the cultural bonds and the continuity of social life are impaired, a psychological disturbance might occur, that the individuals could interpret as more or less important for their future and for their lives. Some community members might experience negative feelings like sadness, grief, nostalgia, insecurity and fear (Tata-Arsel, 2014), a sentimental crisis or trauma (Alexander, 2004). Nevertheless, other community members might not have negative feelings and they could even feel empowered by the emerging situation (Stamm et al., 2004), perceiving it as a chance to escape or as a chance for a change.

Place, identity and memory

Through time and practice, a space that has been endowed with value is made familiar and meaningful and becomes a *place* (Tuan, 1977, p. 6), a reference point for the community and its members. Thus, it is not the mobility *per se* that creates the negative feelings and trauma, but the sense of losing the place. For instance, natural disasters are particular cases that could force a community's mobility. Therefore, they have been studied as particular cases that could lead to creating sentimental crises and trauma. An example of a natural disaster is the massive earthquake in Nepal in 2015, that led many Nepalis to move to the United Kingdom. Kalyan Bhandari's (2017) research with the Nepali diasporic community in the United Kingdom revealed the strong sense of the Nepali identity that the diasporic community tries to maintain through everyday routine and rituals. Other unexpected physical disasters that have been studied in terms of cultural trauma due to displacement are hurricane Katrina (e.g., Ostertag & Ortiz, 2013) and the nuclear catastrophe that ruined Chernobyl (Yankovska & Hannam, 2014; Hannam & Yankovska, 2017).

The 'shock to the routine' (Onwuachi-Willig, 2016, p. 337) results in a threat to or even destruction of the individual and the collective identity of the community that is experiencing the trauma. As time passes, through the 'emotional or affective attachments to [the] environment' (Tuan 1979, pp. 451–452), individuals develop a sense of belonging (Tilley, 1994) in their place of living and their community, with the other people who reside in there and with whom an individual interacts, establishing their cultural bonds with them. This sense of belonging and togetherness is crucial for an individual's socialisation, as it shapes and affects personal and collective identities, bonding them through time with the specific space and turning it into a *place* (Moores, 2012).

Those interactions between the community members, plus their experiences located in this specific place, are all recorded in memory (both the individuals' and the collective memory of the community). The philosopher and sociologist Maurice Halbwachs was the first to coin the term collective memory in 1925. According to Halbwachs' approach, memory can be recorded and memories can be recalled only through and within the social and collective context. Memory is not something stable and concrete. Memory is about the representation of past events; it is the recreation that is happening in the present time of the last recall of a specific event or feeling (Halbwachs, 1992). Memories are connected with and to a location, affect – and are simultaneously affected by – the individual and collective identities. Years before, the philosopher George Santayana (1905) had recognised the importance of remembrance and, consequently, its lack, the so-called (historical) amnesia. 'Those who cannot remember the past are condemned to repeat it', Santayana noted at the beginning of the 20th century (Santayana, 1905, cited in Berberich, 2019, p. 2). Cultural commentators focus not only on learning about the past and its remembrance but mainly on the way, 'the *how* of this commemoration and its political connotations' (Berberich, 2019, p. 4). In parallel, scholars 'have asserted that contemporary "policies of memory," or adapted "channels of memory," perform the functions of traditional ritual and liturgical memory work' (Kidron, 2013, p. 341).

Ways of dealing with trauma together with the community

One way of treating a psychological disturbance could be through medical care or psychotherapy. As an example, in their study about the (Syrian) refugees in Lesvos Island, Greece, Giannoulaki and Polychroni (2020, p. 82) claim that a psychoanalytic approach can play a vital role in this trauma's contemporary (early) treatment. For instance, a central objective of refugee care is 'facilitating the mourning process with particular attention to the identity resistance' (Giannoulaki & Polychroni, 2020, p. 81). However, in cases when the place of birth, the reference point and the roots are somehow being destroyed, or if communal infrastructures are no longer accessible, medical care and psychotherapy might not be enough, as it might be difficult for the community to regroup and rebuild itself on its own, without other kinds of external help, such as interventions designed for and together with the members of the (threatened) community.

The objective of the interventions

External help in dealing with a (potentially) traumatic condition could include collective actions, with and within the community (Laplante, 2007), to preserve the memories located in this specific place, to connect the past and the present to the future and to reinforce the process of keeping the community's collective identity. This approach is founded on the idea that it is not only the event by itself, neither the 'individual experiences of pain and suffering' nor the consequent threat to the individual identity that constructs collective trauma (Alexander, 2012, pp. 2–4). Instead, Alexander focuses on the threatened collective identity as the core of the cultural work that will characterise suffering as trauma.

Social processes of repairing a cultural trauma are frequently linked to the carriers' collective memory and, consequently, to its understanding. Collective psychological health could be restored when respective memory is restored. This health restoration could happen by facilitating the individuals and the collectivities to express their negative emotions through, for example, 'public acts of commemoration, cultural representation and public political struggle' that create 'a materiality with a political, collective, public meaning [and] a physical reminder of a conflictive political past', and by supporting their perception about their collective identity, such as memorials, museums and monuments (Alexander, 2012, pp. 12–13).

Moreover, the mental empowerment of the individuals who experience such crisis or trauma could be achieved by attempting to return to the previous normality through the *bricolage* (Levi-Strauss, 1962, p. 26) of the disturbed identities and social bonds. Notably, a study on designing an intervention for such crisis or trauma repair should examine and take into consideration: (a) the importance of memory in strengthening the resilience of individuals, (b) the way this specific community interprets the specific conditions they experience, (c) the unique sentimental experiences of the members of the community, as well as (d) the ability (or disability) of returning to the place. However, facilitators and scholars should be sceptical, as interventions for dealing with trauma carry the risk of devaluing it by 'ritualizing a continuous re-enactment' of it (Berberich, 2019, p. 4).

Techniques used in the interventions

When working together with a community to heal trauma, scholars frequently use techniques considered adequate to heal collective and cultural traumas. Various forms of narration (e.g., rituals, movies, plays) are used to give voice to the victims, helping them organise their narratives about *what* happened and *how* they experienced it. Narrating the initial (horrendous) event, as well as organising the narrative around it, could potentially both construct the trauma and facilitate its repair (Alexander, 2012). Narrations and other acts of remembrance can facilitate personal and collective memory work and mourning (Kidron, 2013). Yet, narrative control in processes of cultural trauma repair has not often been examined by cultural trauma theorists.

Social processes of constructing cultural trauma and repair can also be digitally mediated (Ostertag & Ortiz, 2013). The most direct, impartial, indisputable and effective way for a present condition or a moment to travel in time is through visual media (Banks, 2008), through the audiovisuals: the images (still and moving) and the sound. On top of this, visual and electronic media allow the user to expand the limitations and the boundaries of physical settings and locations (Meyrowitz, 1985). This is probably the reason why most memory projects use pictures and videos as the technical means to capture collective memories.

This study's innovative proposal is about developing a memory project not only through 2D images and videos but by organising them, with the community's collaboration, in a 360° digital environment. More specifically, with the inhabitants' indications, the place is represented in a 360° virtual space, giving the users a virtually real experience (Ramirez & LaBarge, 2018) of visiting the settlement. Most importantly, the users will be able to virtually visit the specific place in the future when they will no longer be able to physically visit that space anymore (Figure 8.1).

Virtual reality (VR) technology

Audiovisual technology is all about simulations of reality. A definition of simulation would be 'anything which attempts to reproduce another thing in

Figure 8.1 A 360° image of the conjunction at the main entrance of Pontokomi village.

such a way that the simulation is relevantly like the simulated thing without being exactly like it' (Ramirez & LaBarge, 2018, p. 250). A film, for example, attempts to give the audience the 'experience of what it would actually be like' to witness a specific situation, in a particular place, during a specific time (Ramirez & LaBarge, 2018, p. 256). Apart from the apparent features they share with other audiovisual media and technology (e.g., films and computer environments), VR applications additionally offer users a potential for interactivity – similar to computer simulations (Ramirez & LaBarge, 2018, p. 257), or to digital communication technologies (Ostertag & Ortiz, 2013, p. 190), which allow the (formerly known as) audience to 'take a more active role' – altering the relationship between the speaker and the receiver (Rosen, 2008, & Bruns, 2010, cited in Ostertag & Ortiz, 2013, pp. 189–190). However, VR's innovation is the degree of perspectival fidelity (Ramirez & LaBarge, 2018) it offers, that none of the previous simulation technology had. For instance, in movie theatres, audiences enjoy the film while keeping a sense of the world around them. On the contrary, VR systems are designed to visually separate users from the (real) surrounding world, making them feel immersed in the virtual world they are experiencing (Ramirez & LaBarge, 2018, p. 252). Behavioural, physiological, neurological, or cognitive similarities between virtual and real experiences facilitate the VR users to experience the virtual simulation as real (Cummings & Bailenson, 2016). VR users feel present in a virtual environment, and they react at least to some extent bodily and emotionally, as if they were in a physical world (Parsons et al., 2017).

In correspondence with the use of all technological environments, the design and use of VR should be executed carefully, as – under certain circumstances – it could become unethical. A risk evaluation should consider all the agents, especially the creators, involved in developing and using the simulated virtual environment, as responsible for (not) maintaining or normalising socially unaccepted attitudes in the simulation. Finally, the structure and appearance of the virtual environment should consider the age, perception and wit of the potential users and respect their visual and cognitive limitations. In any case, VR should always be used thoughtfully.

Virtual reality therapies and interventions

VR applications could serve as the means, of the technological environment, where personalised emotion-based environments are developed for various kinds of therapy, such as dealing with anxiety and stress (e.g., employee stress, in Heyse et al., 2020). Specifically, unlike traditional in-person relaxation therapies, a VR application can facilitate relaxation, without the need for a qualified trainer and relevant infrastructure, and also less costly, with only prerequisites an internet connection and a head-mounted display (Heyse et al., 2020). Another kind of trauma treatment intervention through technology is developing and using information communication technologies (ICTs), such as VR games, to empower collaborative therapeutic communities and affect social awareness and action. For instance, Tian et al. (2014) worked with chronic disease patients to develop narratives about their personal traumas concerning their illness, intending to raise societal awareness.

Although there is a vast amount of literature about cultural trauma, there are not many studies about digitally mediating cultural trauma, neither during the process of constructing it (Ostertag & Ortiz, 2013, p. 193) nor for its repair. Researchers claim that therapeutic communities established with the support of ICT can overpass society's failure to manage traumatic events and experiences (Tian et al., 2014). As Heyse et al. (2020) prove, there are plenty of studies supporting the effectiveness of VR-based therapy in clinical settings, as compared to the effectiveness of traditional (*in-vivo*) therapies. Most of the studies mentioned by Heyse et al. (2020) are about developing a virtual environment with the user's collaboration and decisions. Then, the users experience a virtual presence in the personalised virtual environment developed with their input. In other words, developers prepare some digital virtual data and according to the user's selections on the choices offered, the virtual environment is rendered. Then the users see and evaluate the personalised virtual environment and provide researchers with feedback about their thoughts and feelings after the virtual experience.

The case study

The initial case study is about Pontokomi, a refugees' village in South-Eastern Europe, in Western Greece, whose inhabitants' ancestors had arrived there from Asia Minor and the Caucasus a century ago. The present inhabitants are now being forced to leave their houses and relocate their families and their lives to another area close by, due to the lignite mine's needs, outside the settlement. They have lived in this condition of uncertainty for the past seven years, with continuous protractions of the deadline to leave. As has happened with other settlements of the region since the 1970s, the houses will be demolished, because the land has to be mined for the lignite in the subsoil to be used in electric power production. This means that within a few years, the place will no longer exist as it is today, and no one will be able to physically visit the settlement in its current form. The infrastructure in the new territory where the community was supposed to move has not been finished yet, so the citizens are moving to other cities. As a consequence, the cohesion of the community dissolves. This disturbance of the continuity of life (Fried, 1967), along with the loss of the homeland and the bonds with the place and the people there, might cause feelings of mental instability and insecurity, especially to the older community members. Nevertheless, some other members are perceiving this as a chance to move to a bigger city, but this is not the focus of our study (Figure 8.2).

A multi-layered ethnographic study with the people of this community is conducted in order to answer the first research question about the members' emerging feelings due to their upcoming relocation. Although the initial idea was to capture still images of only some parts of the settlement (indicatively, some specific family houses), through the interaction with the members of the community, the plan gradually transformed into a bigger, multi-layered project, currently entitled 'Pontokomi project: the decisive moment'.

Figure 8.2 The lignite mine near the settlement of Pontokomi. Another village used to be here some decades ago.

Digitally mediating cultural trauma 111

Through unofficial meetings with the community's members, and time spent together with them, Eleni Pnevmatikou was able to note out the needs that emerged, in terms of what the participants want from their history in the settlement to be remembered and how. Besides, as Labov claimed back in 1972, the goal is that the researcher finds a way to observe and understand the participant, without her noticing she is being observed and participating in research. So, Pnevmatikou spent a lot of time, staying for continuous days in the community, reaching a point when the community was inviting her to important collective events.

Simultaneously, through semi-structured interviews, specific spots of the settlement were selected, such as the main entrance of the village (see Figure 8.1), the church, the cemetery, the primary school and the three main cafes of the village. Then, all those spots were digitally captured, with a camera and a video camera. Later, a 360° camera was used to capture all the roads of the settlement inside a moving vehicle, and in 360° still photos the conjunctions and the signs with the road names, and again the primary school, the church and the cemetery. The 2D material was organised and presented in an online digital map of the settlement (using Google's My Map application) and in the short (4-minute) teaser video of a feature documentary that was released online. A longer version of the teaser (around 12 minutes) was screened during a traditional cultural gathering of the community, at the school's yard, with approximately 400 attendants. The 360° audiovisual material will be presented in a virtual environment, which will then be tested as a healing means for the settlement's inhabitants' negative feelings. We argue that the ability to revisit the destroyed settlement at a later point in time, even virtually, will facilitate the participants to cope with their negative feelings about the situation. So far, even by knowing that the researcher will be present at a collective event to capture the moments with her camera, and certainly after watching parts of the edited audiovisual material, they all express their gratitude to the researcher.

However, gaining the people's trust was not a given from the beginning. After the researcher's continuous visits in the field, always along with her video camera, and numerous unofficial meetings with the people in the settlement, there was a point when they were even inviting her to capture on camera several collective important for the community events, in order for them to be preserved in time. In parallel, after some public screenings of a short video about Pnevmatikou's work within the community, more people expressed their interest in getting interviewed and taking part in the bigger project. Overall, more than 50% of the interviewed individuals, mainly above the age of 60, have already expressed that they are experiencing negative feelings due to this displacement of their community. Some even relate their current displacement to their ancestors', naming it 'a second immigration'. Some others, the older ones, even wish that they die before they have to move, so that they don't have to leave their roots, their house or even their parents' bones. Nevertheless, as expected, not all the community members perceive and interpret this relocation as unfavourable. Some see it as a way to escape from the unhealthy environment and move to a bigger city with more opportunities for their kids.

This chapter proposes a virtual environment intervention in dealing with the (compressed) cultural trauma of a displaced community, by visually capturing the community's place, in the state its people want to remember it before it is irreversibly destroyed. The primary purpose of the intervention will be the mental empowerment of the individuals who experience their community's relocation in a negative way. Through the semi-structured interviews and several informal meetings, community members, current and former inhabitants of the settlement, have already indicated the specific points of interest and even the way (angle) they should be captured and the order they should be presented. Now the technical part of developing the virtual simulation of the settlement follows. Currently, the 360° audiovisual material is being processed and edited in order to be included in the virtual environment. The virtual result will be demonstrated to the participants, who will evaluate the extent to which their virtual experience met their expectations of what they want from their place to be remembered.

In parallel, semi-structured interviews in the beginning and after the development of the virtual environment will give voice to the inhabitants of the settlement, and time and space to express their thoughts and feelings, organised in a narration for an active listener. Their narratives were expected to be complex and scattered. We assume that the process of narrating the history (the individuals' and the community's as a whole) and organising the narrative of the contemporary displacement can have a positive impact on the individual's feelings and perspective on such mobility. After all, we claim that knowing that their homeland will be captured and (re)presented in a virtual environment and that they will have the opportunity to revisit it, even though virtually, in the future when they will not be able to physically do so – as the actual place will no longer exist – might reduce the negative feelings of nostalgia and sadness, and help restore the cultural bonds, the togetherness, among the members of the community.

Conclusion

The disruption of life's continuity (Fried, 1967) could potentially cause negative consequences on the individual's as well as the community's identity. In order to design and conduct an intervention for digitally mediating a (compressed) cultural trauma, it is essential to understand first the uniqueness of each case and the way each event is perceived and interpreted by the individuals and the community as a total. Such a crisis, which arises from the loss of place, threatening the collective identity of the residents, could be socially processed and long-term become a (cultural) trauma. Recently, scholars stressed the importance of working *with* rather than *on* people (Heron &

Reason, 2006) who experienced catastrophic events as an approach to help individuals repair their trauma (Demertzis & Eyerman, 2020). This chapter proposed a digitally mediated trauma healing practice through a virtual environment that will be organised with the collaboration of the community that has the characteristics of potentially experiencing trauma. Although the VR platform has not been developed and evaluated yet, we expect that working together with the Pontokomians to construct a virtual mapping of the settlement of Pontokomi – with emphasis on the places that have been connected to their collective identity – will help them cope with their negative feelings and evolved trauma. This approach, although promising, should be applied carefully considering the ethical issues that might arise.

Note

1 This chapter is part of an ongoing PhD thesis research, an ethnographic case study, entitled 'Cultural Trauma and Displacement: The Use of Virtual Reality Applications in the Case of the Community of Pontokomi', by Eleni Pnevmatikou, at the Panteion University of Athens. Angeliki Gazi is the Supervisor Professor. On this day, the collected audiovisual material for the virtual environment is being organised and prepared to be included in the VR platform that is being developed.

References

Alexander, J. (2002). On the social construction of moral universals: The 'Holocaust' from war crime to trauma drama. *European Journal of Social Theory*, 5(1), 5–85.
Alexander, J. (2004). Toward a theory of cultural trauma. In J. Alexander, R. Eyerman, B. Giesen, N. Smelser, & P. Sztompka (Eds.), *Cultural trauma and collective identity* (pp. 1–30). Berkeley: University of California Press.
Alexander, J. (2012). *Trauma: A social theory*. Cambridge, Malden: Polity Press.
Banks, M. (2008). *Using visual data in qualitative research*. SAGE Publications Ltd. https://doi.org/10.4135/9780857020260.
Berberich, C. (2019). Introduction: The Holocaust in contemporary culture. *Holocaust Studies*, 25(1–2), 1–11.
Bhandari, K. (2017). 6. Travelling at special times: The Nepali diaspora's yearning for belongingness. In S. Marschall (Ed.), *Tourism and memories of home. migrants, displaced people, exiles and diasporic communities* (pp. 113–131). Channel View Publications. http://www.multilingual-matters.com/display.asp?k=9781845416027
Bruns, A. (2010). From reader to writer: Citizen journalism as news produsage. In J. Hunsinger, L. Klastrup, & M. Allen (Eds.), *International handbook of internet research* (pp. 119–133). New York: Springer.
Cummings, J. J., & Bailenson, J. N. (2016). How immersive is enough? A meta-analysis of the effect of immersive technology on user presence. *Media Psychology*, 19(2), 272–309.
David, E. (2008). Cultural trauma, memory, and gendered collective action: The case of women of the storm following hurricane Katrina. *NWSA Journal*, 20(3), 136–162.
Demertzis, N. & Eyerman, R. (2020). Covid-19 as cultural trauma. *American Journal of Cultural Sociology*, 8, 428–450.

Erikson, K. T. (1995). Notes on trauma and community. In C. Caruth (Ed.), *Trauma: Explorations in memory* (pp. 183–199). Baltimore, MD: Johns Hopkins University Press.
Eyerman, R. (2013). Social theory and trauma. *Acta Sociologica*, 56(1), 41–53.
Eyerman, R. (2015). *Is this America? Katrina as cultural trauma*. Austin: University of Texas Press.
Fried, M. (1967). Grieving for a lost home: Psychological costs of relocation. In J. Q. Wilson (Ed.), *Urban renewall: The record and the controversy* (pp. 359–379). Cambridge and London: The M.I.T. Press.
Giannoulaki, C., & Polychroni, K. (2020). Refugees in Lesvos: Grief and identity. *Oedipus*, 21, 80–108. [in Greek: Γιαννουλάκη, Χ., Πολυχρόνη, Κ. (2020). Πρόσφυγες στη Λέσβο: Πένθος και ταυτότητα. *Οιδίπους* 21, pp. 80–108].
Halbwachs M. (1952 [1925]). *Les cadres sociaux de la mémoire*. Paris: Librairie Félix Alcan.
Halbwachs, M. (1992). *On collective memory*. Chicago: University of Chicago Press.
Hanif, S., Ullah, I. (2018). War trauma, collective memory, and cultural productions in conflict zones: Kashmir in Focus. *SAGE Open*, 8(3), 1–10.
Hannam, K. & Yankovska, G. (2017). 3. You can't go home again – Only visit: Memory, trauma and tourism at Chernobyl. In S. Marschall (Ed.), *Tourism and memories of home. migrants, displaced people, exiles and diasporic communities* (pp. 53–68). Bristol, Blue Ridge Summit: Channel View Publications. https://doi.org/10.21832/9781845416041-005
Heron, J. & Reason, P. (2006). The practice of co-operative inquiry: Research "with" rather than "on" people. In P. Reason & H. Bradbury (Eds.), *Handbook of action research* (pp. 144–154). Thousand Oaks: SAGE Publications.
Heyse, J., Torres Vega, M., De Jonge, T., De Backere, F., & De Turck, F. (2020). A personalised emotion-based model for relaxation in virtual reality. *Applied Sciences*, 10(17), 6124.
Kidron, C. (2013). Being there together: Dark family tourism and the emotive experience of co-presence in the holocaust past. *Annals of Tourism Research*, 41, 175–194.
Koh, E. (2021). The healing of historical collective trauma. *Genocide Studies and Prevention: An International Journal*, 15(1), 115–133.
Labov, W, (1972). *Sociolinguistic patterns*. Oxford: Blackwell.
Laplante, L. J. (2007). The Peruvian truth commission's historical memory project: Empowering truth-tellers to confront truth deniers. *Journal of Human Rights*, 6(4), 433–452.
Levi-Strauss, C. (1962). *La pensée sauvage*. Paris: Plon.
Meyrowitz, J. (1985). *No sense of place: The impact of electronic media on social behaviour*. Oxford: Oxford University Press.
Moores, S. (2012). *Media, place & mobility*. London: Palgrave Macmillan.
Onwuachi-Willig, A. (2016). The trauma of the routine: Lessons on cultural trauma from the Emmett Till verdict. *Sociological Theory*, 34(4), 335–357.
Ostertag, S. & Ortiz, D. (2013). The battle over meaning: Digitally mediated processes of cultural trauma and repair in the wake of hurricane Katrina. *American Journal of Cultural Sociology*, 1, 186–220.
Parsons, T. D., Gaggioli, A., & Riva, G. (2017). Virtual reality for research in social neuroscience. *Brain Sciences*, 7(4), 42.

Ramirez, E. J., & LaBarge, S. (2018). Real moral problems in the use of virtual reality. *Ethics and Information Technology, 20,* 249–263.
Rosen, J. (2008). Afterword: The people formerly known as the audience. In N. Carpentier and B. De Cleen (Eds.) *Participation and media production* (pp. 163–166). Cambridge Scholars Press. DOI: 10.18574/nyu/9780814763025.003.0005
Santayana, G. (1905). *The Life of Reason.* New York City: Scribner.
Smelser, N. J. (2004) Psychological trauma and cultural trauma. In J. C. Alexander, R. Eyerman, B. Giesen, N. J. Smelser, & P. Sztompka (Eds.), *Cultural trauma and collective identity* (pp. 31–59). Berkeley: University of California Press.
Stamm, B. H., Stamm, H. E., Hudnall, A. C., & Higson-Smith, C. (2004). Considering a theory of cultural trauma and loss. *Journal of Loss and Trauma, 9*(1), 89–111.
Tata-Arsel, L. (2014). *With persecution in the soul.* Kedros [in Greek Τατά Αρσέλ, Λ. (2014). *Με το Διωγμό στην Ψυχή.* Κέδρος].
Tian, K., Sautter, P., Fisher, D., Fischbach, S., Luna-Nevarez, C., Boberg, K., Kroger, J., & Vann, R. (2014). Transforming health care: Empowering therapeutic communities through technology-enhanced narratives, *Journal of Consumer Research, 41*(2), 237–260.
Tilley, C. (1994). *A phenomenology of landscape: Places, paths and monuments.* Oxford-Providence: Berg.
Tuan, Y.-F. (1977). *Space and place: The perspective of experience.* Minneapolis: University of Minnesota Press.
Tuan, Y.-F. (1979). Space and place: Humanistic perspective. In S. Gale & G. Ollson (Eds.), *Philosophy in geography.* Theory and Decision Library (vol. 20, pp. 387–427). Dordrecht: Springer. https://doi.org/10.1007/978-94-009-9394-5_19
Wild, J. (1963). *Existence and the world of freedom.* Englewood Cliffs, NJ: Prentice-Hall Inc.
Yankovska, G., & Hannam, K. (2014). Dark and toxic tourism in the Chernobyl exclusion zone. *Current issues in Tourism, 17*(10), 929–939.

9 'Alone together'
Reconnecting death stranding's broken sense of sociality

Onur Sesigür

Death Stranding (DS) is a video game produced by Kojima Productions in 2019, which deals with isolation, togetherness, connectivity and collaboration in a post-apocalyptic world. We play the story of Sam Porter Bridges, a delivery person who is responsible for connecting survivors in an alternate USA. The apocalypse-torn country is surrendered to 'timefalls', pours of rain that speed up the passage of time and age people alongside Beach Things (BTs), those who could not leave the mortal world and roam the post-apocalyptic landscapes. Avoiding such dangers, we deliver cargo and connect delivery locations to a network, all the while carrying an artificial womb filled with artificial amniotic fluid immersing a Bridge Baby (BB). A BB is a baby trapped between the world of the living and the beach, who can sense the existence of BTs and is used as a living early warning system attached with an artificial umbilical cord to his chest.

The game world possesses an arguably confusing amount of narrative tools worked in as mechanics and around 12 hours' worth of cutscenes providing narrative depth. When it is viewed through the lens of Sherry Turkle's *Alone Together: Why We Expect More from Technology and Less from Each Other* (2011), in terms of digital communication, connectivity, togetherness and loneliness, an analysis of the social and technological narrative of DS provides a new perspective to our increasingly mediatised and individualised daily lives.

In order to construct this perspective, this chapter utilises notions such as 'being alone together' and the concept of 'tethered self' (ibid.) to unload narratives and allegories DS harbours, to make sense of our[1] contemporary sociality that is aggressively being framed by communication technologies, as well as the growing impact of networks, media and mediatised human interaction on our collective reality. Certain verbal story components in DS such as *strand, porter, tether, umbilical cord, network* and *bridge* and certain applications of wordplay, pointing to communication and connectivity, provide instances to discuss Turkle's approach to togetherness in the era of digital communication.

DOI: 10.4324/9781003389972-11

'Tethered self' and alone together

Alone Together is presented in two parts. Throughout the second part titled *Networked: In Intimacy, New Solitudes*, how the sociality we strive to live through communication technologies and networks pushes us to loneliness is discussed in length and detail. Turkle argues that the 'new' socialities of digital cultures claiming to substitute for 'old' ones, have recently become 'simply better' rather than 'better than nothing' (Turkle, 2011, p. 207). In order to understand our existence in an alone–together culture, she proposes the concept of 'tethered self'.

The word 'tether' provides a thematic connection between Turkle's work and DS. Being tethered, in a traditional sense, means that something or someone is physically tied, limiting their movement. In contemporary digital parlance, 'tethering' defines a wireless connection, through which a device or person by extension, is tied not physically but somewhat metaphorically. The uses of allegories of rope, strand, tether, road or bridge are narrative devices to understand the connection. Telling stories of connectivity and sociality through such tools is something DS and Turkle's work have in common. Even the name of the game, *Death Stranding*, is an obvious utilisation of this similarity. A curious wordplay that invites us to think about connection and togetherness is presented to the players, in one of the many lengthy cut-scenes throughout our gameplay. One of the characters in DS, Amelie, contemplates the word:

> It's a funny word "strand" … A "strand" is part of a rope or band. While "stranding" means being washed up on the shore. And being "stranded" is when you can't go home.
> (Kojima Productions, 2019)

Turkle claims 'tethered, we are not to deny the body and its pleasures but to put our bodies somewhere beautiful while we work' (Turkle, 2011, p. 165). In these places, tethered selves magically create a future different from the one they see coming out of a past they never knew. In the future, they have the opportunity to spend time with each other and their families (Turkle, 2011, p. 265). In this future, the habitat of selves is mediatized realities of imaginations of a new time and space.

However, connectivity causes certain problems as well. These new realities which are products of individualism bring problems regarding sociality. Turkle states that online life creates a large space for individual experiments, yet it can be difficult to escape the new social demands it creates. People expect to be able to reach their friends. The social contract made available by technology demands a constant presence. In return, the tethered self takes the security and support provided by this social contract for granted (Turkle,

2011, p. 174). This support gets us used to the joy of never being alone. However, according to Turkle:

> Feeling a bit *stranded* used to be considered a part of adolescence, and one that developed inner resources. Now it is something that the network makes it possible to bypass. Teenagers say that they want to keep their cell phones close, and once it is with you, you can always "find someone".
>
> (emphasis added, Turkle, 2011, p. 243)

She continues to say that, without devices, we feel 'naked' and the 'naked tethered self' feels threatened. Connection may soothe anxieties but it also creates its own problems (Turkle, 2011, p. 248).

The world of DS provides the player with connection in the form of 'Chiral Network', a communication and data transfer system that allows those who are connected to be and act together in an alone-together fashion. Apart from our parcel delivery missions, one of our key missions is to connect as many bunkers and Knot Cities[2] to the Chiral Network and reform UCA (United Cities of America). While we are roaming around the world to make deliveries, to make up for the physical component of connectivity the Chiral Network fails to provide, we may stray out of the coverage zone. When we are not connected to the network, in addition to losing connection to the key non-player characters, we also lose the ability to build roads, postboxes, generators, etc. It is curious how the loss of connection to the Chiral Network results in not only the loss of in-game connectivity but also inter-player connectivity. Furthermore, when we are out of the coverage zone, we find ourselves bereft of vital information such as our map access and weather report, which we use to stay away from timefalls and BTs. The loss of connection causes not only communication problems but also very real material ones. The tranquil atmosphere we can experience while travelling alone transforms into an uncertain and anxious one. The game alerts and directs us inside the coverage area using striking sounds and visuals, which adds to the sensation of panic, caused by loss of connection. The loss of connection for a tethered self, which defines themself through the connection to the network, brings existential problems as well as physical ones. Alone and isolated, we are in danger.

Social isolation and technology

In order to provide a further theoretical basis for the breaking off and the subsequent lack of connection in the world of DS, one may lean on the literature on loneliness and social isolation as a prolific starting point to discuss sociality, connectivity and lack thereof.

The desire and impulse to be connected to other people is a well-known phenomenon. Giles Slade drives our attention to the discovery of mirror neurons in the 1980s and stemming studies, proposing that humans are in a constant search for connection with other humans. Additionally, he claims that we are neurologically programmed to seek not just any connection but only genuine ones (2012, Breadcrumbs: Incunabula, para. 21). Furthermore, it is known that in an evolutionary manner, those who managed to stay together and cooperate had better chances to survive, flourish and reproduce (Gardner, Griffin & West, 2016). We are the children of those who cooperated, those who communicated and those who sought genuine connections. It is not far-fetched to view loneliness as a dynamic that imbues sociality into our behavioural patterns. According to Cacioppo and Patrick, loneliness is a 'stimulus to get humans to pay more attention to their social connections, and to reach out toward others, to renew frayed or broken bonds' (2008, p. 7). In a sense, loneliness can be seen as having an evolutionary function as a punishment, a negative reinforcement. As we reinforce our connections to others, the negative reinforcement of loneliness disappears. The spaces left behind can be filled with beneficial physical and abstract factors that are only available through genuine connections (2008, p. 18).

It appears DS's creator, Kojima, attaches a particular importance to loneliness as well. In his interviews, he mentions that the main goal of the game is to form connections (PlayStation, 2019; PlayStation France, 2019). He explains his fundamental motivation towards designing DS in a video interview as such:

> I'm very prone to loneliness. I think there are similar people around the world, especially gamers. Even though they're having fun with others outside when they're alone playing video games in their living room they don't feel like they fit into society or their community. So when those people play this game they realise people like them exist all over the world. Knowing that even though I'm lonely, there are other people like me makes you feel at ease.
>
> (BBC Newsbeat, 2019)

If loneliness and lack of connection in DS is a partial and aestheticised allegory of today's conditions, as partially stated by Kojima, one can speculate on the factors that lead to the looming apocalyptic events of the real world. Considering the game is set in an alternate version of the USA, and the narratives are formed in the frames culturally attributed to the USA, a certain publication could provide a basis for this specific discussion: Philip Slater's *The Pursuit of Loneliness*, written in 1970 when the efforts towards creating counterculture (the so-called hippie movement) staggered the nation, prophesying the collapse of society as a whole due to growing isolation. According to Slater, three essential needs, community, engagement and dependency, were being suppressed by 'a commitment to individualism' (1990, 'III. Dependence and Independence', para. 20).

In times of COVID-19, while writing this chapter, concepts such as acting together and thinking of others as well as loneliness and selfishness weigh heavily on my mind. It is also intriguing how nations that are set in neoliberal systems based on individuality began to employ certain social statist applications to remedy the problems caused by a global catastrophe.

Individualisation, competition and cooperation

Encountering discussions of constructed binaries reproducing the dichotomies of sociality and individualisation, security and freedom are not uncommon in academic conversations as well as contemporary politics and everyday life. It is often seen as if it is a spectrum between poet John Donne's 'no [one's] an island' and existentialist philosophy claiming people are ultimately alone (Biordi & Nicholson, 2013).

Slater explains how the structure of human societies that require responsibility and solidarity got diminished and outright rejected through private homes, vehicles, gardens and the service industry in the USA (Slater, 1990, 'I. Community and Competition', para. 12). While Giles Slade reminds us how this situation of needs being met exclusively in an individual manner is preferred by manufacturers and marketers since individuals consume more than communities. Families or communities can share cars, laundry machines, televisions, computers... However, according to Slade, today's carefully enculturated consumer sharing is nothing more than an intervention in personal space (Slade, 2012, Immortality and free will, para. 3).

If one thinks about the post-apocalyptic world DS throws us in, it can be clearly seen that sharing is preferred to individual consumption and this choice of sharing is encouraged and rewarded by the game mechanics. Roads, bridges, post boxes, power generators, shelters, ladders and climbing ropes we as seemingly disparate players build to overcome obstacles can be used by other players to overcome the same obstacles. Moreover, motorcycles, trucks and any other vehicle or tool that could ease our voyage can be shared through communicable lockers in post boxes or in Knot Cities. This can be understood as a conscious secession from individuality or efforts of catastrophe-torn people to reinstate their sense of security. Whatever Hideo Kojima saw when he looked at lonely people like him, led him to depict this disconnection as a post-apocalyptic nightmare scenario.

No matter what the cause of this disconnection may be, it can be stated that DS is a game that encourages the player to cooperate rather than to compete. Even though it is not a usual cooperative game where multiple players are in direct communication and they move towards the same goal together, DS guides players to act together through narratives and game mechanics. The main difference between DS and MMO (Massively Multiplayer Online) games, such as *World of Warcraft*, is the deliberately designed communication restrictions. As will be discussed in detail later in this chapter, players do not see or hear each other in a familiar sense, but the game constantly reminds them that there are others, experiencing the same adventure. In this sense, DS can be considered an MSO (Massively Single Player) game, where players experience the game alone together. MSO games allow content sharing between players while not facilitating in-game interaction (Stenros, Paavilainen, & Mäyrä, 2009). It is possible to think that such games offer a space for sociality for players suffering from loneliness, who would also like to stay away from often too competitive and sometimes toxic interactions (online bullying, harassment, etc.) in MMOs. It would not be wrong to assume that a diluted form of connection, which does not allow negativity or anti-social behaviour could easily be more preferable to some of today's individuals living mediatised lives. What is more, DS is a non-zero-sum game, one player winning the game does not require others to lose. This provides an opportunity to act together without the need for a hostile sub-text (Stenros, Paavilainen, & Mäyrä, 2011). Kojima confirms this was an intentional design choice:

> The attacks and violence seen online these days are out of control. So I designed this for people to take a step back and by connecting, relearn how to be kind to others.
> (BBC Newsbeat, 2019)

Slater is inclined to think that competitive behaviour that can reach hostile levels is related to the pursuit of further privacy. We come together to share less and less and we see those 'coming togethers' as chores or ordeals more and more (Slater, 1990, 'I. Community and Competition', para. 13). Yet, historically, collectivism is the natural state of people and communities. Slater reminds us of this somewhat forgotten fact possibly due to getting used to living in increasingly individualistic societies (Slater, 1990, 'I. Community and Competition', para. 1).

According to evolutionary biologist Martin Nowak, one of the most significant properties of evolution is its ability to foster solidarity in a competitive world (as cited in Cacioppo & Patrick, 2008, p. 62). Cacioppo and Patrick further Nowak's statement to add that homo sapiens have a more prominent story of social solidarity than other hominid apes (Cacioppo & Patrick, 2008, p. 63). They also state that in the current state of human evolution, 'individual success was now driven by the ability to transcend selfishness and act on behalf of others. The selfish gene had given rise to a social brain and a different kind of social animal' (Cacioppo & Patrick, 2008, p. 72).

This line of thinking sensitises us to not see individuality and sociality as a deep binary. Nevertheless, these two concepts could be efficient tools for understanding human experience as well as the universe beyond humanity. However, individualism as an ideology is a different story. According to Slater,

> The problem with individualism is not that it is immoral but that it is incorrect. The universe does not consist of a lot of unrelated particles but is an interconnected whole. Pretending that our fortunes are

independent of each other may be perfectly ethical, but it's also perfectly stupid. Individualistic thinking is unflagging in the production of false dichotomies, such as "conformity vs. independence," "altruism vs. egoism," "inner-directed vs. other-directed," and so on, all of which are built upon the absurd assumption that the individual can be considered separately from the environment of which he or she is a part.
(Slater, 1990, 'I. Community and Competition', para. 17)

Or as President Bridget Strand of DS puts it while imploring Sam to take on the mission to connect what is left of the USA, 'alone, we have no future'.

However, the game is not so headfirst about pushing players together. DS does not support communication via voice, video or chat between players. The direct communicational connectedness we can experience on various levels of video games is not provided as an affordance, congruous with the post-apocalyptic atmosphere of the game. As a single-player game, the suitability of DS to discuss togetherness can be questioned. However, the fact that a game is played alone does not mean it has no social component (Stenros, Paavilainen, & Mäyrä, 2009). In mediatised worlds, 'social games', social media platforms, gameplay videos, live streams, game wikis, software such as Discord that can be used in the background to voice-chat while gaming and the vast reach of game culture, all game experiences can be considered to have a sociality potential.

Nevertheless, DS affords some significant indirect communicational connectedness opportunities. All the equipment, vehicles and physical infrastructure we need to survive and make deliveries are sharable in different ways. In some cases, they can be collaboratively built, with players providing what materials they have to accumulate the necessary amount, which is sometimes not feasible for one player to collect on their own. A delivery mission scenario could come in handy to better explain how these dynamics operate.

Sam accepts a mission to deliver a parcel from Knot City A to Bunker B. He has to complete this mission in spite of the rough terrain, timefalls, BTs and MULEs.[3] In order to journey in safety, Sam needs a ladder to climb hills or pass rivers, a climbing rope to rappel down cliffs, spare boots in case his boots get worn out, a gun to fight BTs and ammunition. In addition to these, he has to carry a portable 3D printer and the necessary raw materials to build bridges, post boxes and power generators. Moreover, he would be better off with a motorcycle or a truck if he needs to deliver large pieces of cargo he cannot carry on his back or if he is going on a long trip. Finally, he would need construction materials such as metal, ceramics and Chiral matter for stationary printers that automatically build pieces of pre-planned roads between Knot cities and bunkers. This would provide a safer and faster route for his return as well for his and other porters' future missions. All these equipment and materials, all the roads and bridges, all printers, all postboxes constructed by players as well all lockers in Knot cities are sharable. This makes connectedness possible and essential for DS players through various mechanics of collaboration.

'Alone together'   123

Not so surprisingly, this collaboration requires effort. That is, a player needs to connect a certain part of the area to the Chiral network in order to make use of the collaborative functions of the game. Collaboration necessitates connectedness and further connectedness necessitates collaboration. The main reward of this effort is the physical and arguably mental safety the connectedness provides. However, a further reward and encouragement mechanism also exists: the 'likes'.

Society rewards sociality

Let's discuss the likes and social reward mechanisms in DS with an example. Imagine we constructed a bridge on a river en route to a delivery location. It can be used by another player if they have put the effort to connect that specific area to the network. After using the bridge, they can show their appreciation by liking the bridge. These likes accumulate and are shown to any who has access to the bridge. The more useful the bridge, the more likes it generates. Furthermore, the game itself presents 'like rewards' to players in certain circumstances. For example, every time another player passes through a road we built or provided some of the materials needed, we earn such automatic like rewards. Similarly, whenever you find a parcel another player dropped in the wild or left at a postbox, preferring not to complete the mission, and deliver the parcel on their behalf, you are rewarded with, again, likes. These likes we earn accumulate in a pool called 'Bridge Links' and as the pool gets filled, the game further rewards us with perks such as higher carrying capacity. The Bridge Links that we construct by interacting with an object built by another player are listed under a submenu, easily available. Among these links, we can make a 'Strand Contact' with another player of our choice. Buildings, infrastructure and vehicles built by Strand Contracted players appear more frequently in our DS world; in a sense, we start to share our game world with them. In essence, if we holistically view the game mechanics, most of the in-game communication is defined by shared objects, missions and affordances, and strengthened by multiple like mechanisms.

In addition, there are signs and waymarks that facilitate communication among players. They are categorised into five groups depending on their colours, the icons and special signs on them. Red, indicates caution signs to warn about dangers, blue, signifies direction, distance, views, etc., orange, for delivery of raw materials or equipment, blue lightbulb signs suggest such delivery instead of ask or demand (an interesting distinction in my opinion), and finally various emoji signs that raise Sam's or BB's morale, give a speed boost to vehicles, ask that others do not litter or drive at certain places, signs that simply have smiling, angry, tired faces on them and of course the sign that functions as a 'like for like' declaration. Access to these signs depends on our connection to the Chiral Network and the strength of our Bridge Links. Again, in order to make use of these aspects of interplayer communication we have to invest in in-game sociality. The outcome of utilising and strengthening these connections is the promise of a deeper game experience as well as support for making further connections. Investment in sociality is rewarded by further sociality.

The fact that the majority of interplayer communication is limited by specifically functional mechanics that highlights togetherness, eliminates the possibility of online bullying and harmful feedback. The only personal information we can access regarding other players is their nicknames we can see on buildings, signs or on the Bridge Links sub-menu. Thus, it can be argued that a high level of anonymity is provided (or arguably enforced) by the game. However, in my experience, this does not discourage players from connecting with others. Social and collaborative motivations regarding being in solidarity can co-exist with personal and competitive motivations to become the high scorer in the Bridge Links list. For, as Turkle argues, anonymity does not protect us from emotional investment (Turkle, 2011, p. 235).

Conversely, returning to the issue of toxicity, anonymity can play an encouraging or a veiling role in communication (Lapidot-Lefler & Barak, 2012). Considered together with the likes and how they function in DS, parallelism becomes apparent with the affordances and consequences of everyday social media practices. However, there is one particular aspect of DS and other similar MSOs that could be used to differentiate them from social media use: a common goal. In MMOs, it has been shown that toxicity appears in correlation with competitive performance (Neto, Yokoyama & Becker, 2017). Since in MSOs, the players are all putting effort towards their own individual journey on a common route and the route, the story of the game is strictly directed, it can be argued that players have less reason and less freedom to portray detrimental behaviour towards others. Furthermore, the game mechanics does not afford back-and-forth communication, which makes trolling for the sake of annoying others neither rewarding nor really possible. Thus, one's emotional investment, be it anonymous or not, is somewhat more protected than on regular social media platforms.

Behind this emotional investment, resides *performance* as a perspective to understand both games as a concept and essentially all sociality and communication. For instance, Ducheneaut et al. investigate the place of in-game performance in sociality through alone–together practices of *World of Warcraft* players (Ducheneaut et al., 2006). Furthermore, Stenros, Paavilainen, and Mäyrä confirm that performing for an audience could be a significant factor in such games (Stenros, Paavilainen, & Mäyrä, 2009).

It can be argued that the limited, thus focused and perhaps elevated sociality that is offered by DS has the potential to remedy the loss of connection and loneliness pointed out by Hideo Kojima. Nevertheless, it could be overreaching to claim that this method of sociality creates a fully functional community in its traditional meaning. Communities are spaces where people feel safe enough to deal with others and the whole community at its best and worst. We feel the support of others in a community and in response, we are responsible for facing feedback from other agents of the community.

According to Turkle, if we are in a position where we accept this support yet can avoid negative feedback, what we experience may have certain social aspects but is not really a community (Turkle, 2011, p. 238). In this sense, a connectivity where negative feedback is made impossible in order to facilitate more constructive communication, notwithstanding its social and cultural significance, is far from being a functional real-life substitute for community. We are together when we are connected to the network, but our expectations from each other diminish so that we still feel alone. Furthermore, this notion bears the risk of deducing sociality to seeing other people only as objects that can be reached, where we are only interested in the beneficial, relaxing or fun parts of these objects (Turkle, 2011, p. 154).

Conclusion

In many respects, both narratively and mechanically, DS is a noteworthy cultural output, to think about how deeply our mediatised worlds and interactions frame how we live our daily lives and who we are. One of the main motivations behind this chapter is how the COVID-19 pandemic, which broke out just a couple of months after the release of DS, made visible the reality and urgency of this process.

The fact that the post-apocalyptic world DS imagines could be such a potent allegory of our day and age's isolation as well as the communicational efforts in response, sensitises one to think we may not have yet fully understood the consequences of consenting to exciting opportunities of communication technologies. As these consequences include altering our sense of self and relationship with others in our societies, we will inescapably empirically experience the outcomes of our efforts to live always together, always alone. There seems to be no easy way around this, but our needs reside increasingly real and significant. As Cacioppo and Patrick remind us, depending on how well we manage our need for human connection, alone or together, we will win everything or lose it all (Cacioppo & Patrick, 2008, p. 269).

As a note, I think it is fitting to mention the quote from Kobe Abe's story 'Nawa', used by DS as an epigraph:

> '"The Rope" and "The Stick", together, are one of humankind's oldest "tools". "The Stick" is for keeping evil away; "The Rope" is for pulling good toward us; these are the first friends the human race invented. Wherever you find humans, "The Rope" and "The Stick" also exist.'
> (as cited in Death Stranding, 2019)

If we are to see technology not as a system of tools and skills but as the endless purification process of these tools and skills to dominate nature, it is only natural for us to arrive at the ultimate goal of such defined technology: reaching a state of existence completely outside of nature (Slade, 2012, Introduction, para. 8). If we decide to avoid this destination, we have to remember that we have to constantly contemplate and discuss the new forms of relationships that technology serves society and culture as well as yet to fully understand outcomes of these relationships such as being alone together. Both Turkle and Slade feel the need to mention Henry David Thoreau, who strived to question, understand and redefine the value of his time's sociality, away from our modern (and post-modern) distractions. As a final homage to Turkle, it is fitting to end this chapter with her final words for *Alone Together*.

> When Thoreau considered 'where I live and what I live for' he tied together location and values. Where we live doesn't just change how we live; it informs who we become. Most recently, technology promises us lives on the screen. What values, Thoreau would ask, follow from this new location? Immersed in simulation, where do we live, and what do we live for?
>
> (Turkle, 2011, p. 277)

If indeed, where one lives informs who they become, it could be inevitable to completely resist the transformation of sociality facilitated by contemporary communication technologies. Nevertheless, forming and sustaining human connections, doing and being together remains a vital goal in an increasingly individualised and mediatised world. Trying to understand mediatised conditions of togetherness and sociality, particularly through works of popular culture that operate in these very conditions, such as video games, provides a 'meta' perspective that can inform the discussion regarding, where we live and what we live for.

Notes

1 The pronoun 'we', used throughout this chapter was preferred as an inclusive subject, for all who, on varying levels, experience mediatisation of their social world.
2 A curious choice of expression for shelter cities in the United Cities of America, a diminished, post-apocalyptic version of the USA.
3 MULEs are former porters who developed what came to be known as 'drone syndrome' due to prolonged exposure to a fictional element, Chiralium, that accumulates as a result of timefalls. MULEs have an irrational obsession with any sort of cargo, which drives them to steal and amass parcels in their makeshift camps.

References

BBC Newsbeat. (2019, November 4). Death Stranding: Inside Kojima Productions | Newsbeat Documentaries. Retrieved from https://youtu.be/kjUpYlKs0nM

Biordi, D. L., & Nicholson, N. R. (2013). Social Isolation. In I. M. Lubkin & D. P. Larsen (Eds.), *Chronic Illness* (pp. 97–132). Burlington, MA: Jones & Bartlett Learning.

Cacioppo, J. T., & Patrick, W. (2008). *Loneliness: Human Nature and the Need for Social Connection*. New York & London: W. W. Norton & Company.

Ducheneaut, N., Nicholas, Y., Nickell, E., & Moore, J. R. (2006). "Alone Together?" Exploring the Social Dynamics of Massively Multiplayer Online Games. *CHI 2006 Proceedings*. 407–416. New York: ACM.

Gardner, A., Griffin, A. S., & West, S. A. (2016). Theory of Cooperation. *Encyclopedia of Life Sciences*, 1–8. doi: 10.1002/9780470015902.a0021910.pub2

Kojima Productions. (2019). *Death Stranding*. Sony Interactive Entertainment [Video game].

Lapidot-Lefler, N. & Barak, A. (2012). Effects of Anonymity, Invisibility, and Lack of Eye-Contact on Toxic Online Disinhibition. *Computers in Human Behavior*, 28(12), 434–444.

Neto, J. A. M., Yokoyama, K. M. & Becker, K. (2017). Studying Toxic Behavior Influence and Player Chat in an Online Video Game. *WI '17: Proceedings of the International Conference on Web Intelligence*, 26–33. doi: 10.1145/3106426.3106452

PlayStation. (2019, November 7). Countdown to Death Stranding. Retrieved from https://youtu.be/4TsLNmDj2VA

PlayStation France. (2019, November 9). Death Stranding | Interview with Hideo Kojima in PlayZONE - EN subtitles. Retrieved from https://youtu.be/juSvznijg3g

Slade, G. (2012). *The Big Disconnect: The Story of Technology and Loneliness*. New York: Prometheus Books.

Slater, P. (1990). *The Pursuit of Loneliness: American Culture at the Breaking Point*. Boston, MA: Beacon Press.

Stenros, J., Paavilainen, J., & Mäyrä, F. (2009). The Many Faces of Sociability and Social Play in Games. *MindTrek '09: Proceedings of the 13th International MindTrek Conference: Everyday Life in the Ubiquitous Era*, 82–89. Tampere Finland: Association for Computing Machinery.

Stenros, J., Paavilainen, J., & Mäyrä, F. (2011). Social Interaction in Games. *International Journal of Arts and Technology*, 4(3), 342–358.

Turkle, S. (2011). *Alone Together: Why We Expect More from Technology and Less from Each Other*. New York: Basic Books.

10 Twitch Developers as a 'company-led community'

Sarper Durmuş

Digital platforms have mastered the ability to turn human activities into potential sources of surplus value. Twitch, a live-streaming platform, has perfected the ability to increase these human activities on the platform through new extensions and features. The Twitch extensions are 'live apps that interact with the stream, as a panel on a channel, or with chat' (*Twitch Extensions 101*, 2017) basically adding different visual or interactive layers to a video livestream. These extensions are developed by third-party developers and managed by Twitch.

Twitch Developers is a space where amateur third-party developers and complementor companies come together to socialize around developing these new features and tools to be deployed to further the platform's commercial agenda. It is a community of developers that come together in live-streamed events, hackathons, and an official forum and a Discord channel. They collaborate on projects, share information, and comment on each other's work. This chapter takes Twitch Developers as a research site to investigate a community that is attached to a tech 'giant', Amazon. All the material posted by Twitch or Twitch employees on official channels constitutes points of interest to conduct the analysis.

Complementors that develop Twitch extensions are motivated by vocational promises of competency development and career advancement and by a sense of connection and camaraderie. Like in other platforms, Twitch can use its powerful position to leverage, control, and commodify these people's ambitions. By negotiating these wants and needs through its own filter of commodification, Twitch was able to usher various actors into something that can be called *deep engagement* (Durmuş, 2021). What moves deep engagement is simply the platform's appetite for profit. Deep engagement is a mode of collaboration and cooperation that, along with surplus data generation, points out a deep commitment on behalf of the actors involved. The platform benefits from this high level of engagement in terms of content, improving its services, and interlinking products and data with its parent company, Amazon.

While marketers portray 'community-led companies' as the cutting-edge approach to growing businesses (Elder, 2021), business studies have been

DOI: 10.4324/9781003389972-12

interested in online brand communities for some time (Wong & Lee, 2021). Conversely, this chapter wishes to contribute to a critical understanding of firm-initiated communities in terms of platformization, labour and political economy by taking Twitch Developers as a *company-led community*.

Literature review: exploring collaborative dynamics on the internet

The concept of collaboration on the internet and its implications have been explored at length, incorporating ideas such as gift economy, commons-based-peer production, convergence culture, interactivity, immaterial labour, platform work, and monetization. Due to the diverse work, platforms, and contexts involved, scholars have vacillated between positive and negative assessments of these contributions. Early studies of the electronic frontier and online communities focused on the gift economy as a key characteristic (Barbrook, 1998; Kollock, 1998; Rheingold, 2000), reflecting the left-leaning, decentralized culture of the 1960s Bay Area (Saxenian, 1996) and the subsequent anarchist hacker and free software movements (Levy, 1984). These movements promoted the idea of making code public and exchanging it among community members without copyright restrictions. Bergquist and Ljungberg (2001) argued that the gifting culture in various online communities is a mix of collectivism and individualism, which creates an alternative to private property, fosters creativity, and bridges social differences, but also gives rise to various asymmetric power relations.

The early utopic visions of the internet persisted even after the dot-com bubble and the rise of profit-driven social networking sites like Facebook. Benkler (2006) introduced the term 'commons-based peer production', which describes the ability of globally distributed individuals to collaborate on complex tasks over the internet. He argued that uploading pictures and videos to sites like YouTube and Flickr is an example of participating in the gift economy, which is characterized by a desire to contribute to collective actions and efforts for the benefit of the public good. However, others have argued that content creators will move to a market that pays them, abandoning the gift economy.

Berdou conducted an analysis of Free/Libre Open Source Software and argued for a more nuanced understanding of gift culture, particularly with regard to the relationship between voluntary communities and firms. She argued that these collective efforts are more complex than a simple contest between the profit-seeking of capitalism and the accumulation of social capital and benefiting from the collective effort of gift culture (2010, p. 2). While Mauss's classic work on gift-giving practices laid the foundation for discussing collaborative efforts on the early internet, it has also been co-opted by digital capitalism. Today, everyday actions like signing up for a 'free' online service or sharing content on digital platforms illustrate this point.

According to scholars such as Henry Jenkins (2008) and Clay Shirky (2009), citizens have become content creators as well as consumers of media products, thereby challenging the traditional media's control over information dissemination. This idea of a democratized public sphere has been embraced by mainstream media, with *Time Magazine* even choosing 'You' as their person of the year in 2006. However, this optimism has been criticized for claims of 'produsage' (Bruns, 2007) – only a small percentage of viewers participate in content creation, and the transformation of leisure time into free labour has been documented. Some scholars have argued that participants in 'altruistic' content creation are motivated by the desire to be part of something bigger than themselves or 'seeking 15 minutes of fame' (Lahey, 2016, p. 642). Jenkins has since become more cautious in his optimism, acknowledging the give-and-take between the top–down business and the bottom–up consumption.

The perspective of business and management studies is focused on examining the field of management and organizational practices and encompasses research that explores how different companies interact with one another within the platforms they own. For instance, Wen and Zhu's (2019) case study of Google's app store found that when the platform owner threatened to enter the services offered by the complementor companies, popular app developers increased their efforts on the affected apps. The authors attribute this behaviour to the complementor companies' desire to be acquired by Google. However, they suggest that such value-capture threats may decrease innovation and increase prices for the affected apps. While application ecosystems generally create value for both the platform owner and other associated actors (Zhu, 2019), there are risks involved in building complementary products or services for a platform owned by a for-profit corporation, as illustrated by high-profile cases such as the European Union's record-high fine against Google for using its market leader position to benefit its own price-comparison service. Third-party developers rely on various resources offered by platform owners, such as software development kits (SDKs), application program interfaces (APIs), marketing and advertising, technical help, and forums, which are all crucial to the application development process (Ghazawneh & Mansour, 2015, p. 13).

Complementors, who offer their services without receiving any financial compensation, are motivated by various factors such as demonstrating their mastery and expertise to fellow developers, adhering to open-source community norms that encourage members to share their code, and the sheer enjoyment of software development (Shah, 2006). Research has shown that complementors are driven to create innovative applications even when they are not paid. However, not all of these applications may achieve (Rudmark, 2013; Russpatrick, 2020) commercial success, due to various factors such as targeting niche audiences or users' reluctance to pay for additional services (Rudmark, 2013, p. 6). In addition, there are generally two types of peer production communities: those initiated and managed by companies, and those initiated and maintained by communities. The governance structures of these two differ, with companies controlling the former, while the latter is controlled through distributed authority.

A 'community' of third-party software developers: Twitch Developers

Twitch Developers[1] is one of the crucial places to make sense of Twitch as it is an integral part of the platform's affordances and design. It is an official Twitch site where third-party developers can launch new extensions. Game developers can also use Twitch Developers to connect their games to Twitch. According to an introductory video into extension development

> extensions add interactive features to key areas within the Twitch viewing experience such as in the video player itself or below the player in the panel. They are created by developers like *you* and are made available to all streamers.
>
> (Twitch Extensions 101, 2017)

Some of the extension categories that Twitch showcases are viewer engagement, loyalty and recognition, and polling and voting.

Most of the streamers on the platform make use of these extensions which result in what some call networked broadcasting (Taylor, 2018) as it includes live game stats, countdowns, audience feedback, mini games, etc. Other researchers have chronicled that streamers try out, employ, and improve various ways that they can monetize and gamify their streams (Bingham, 2017; Johnson & Woodcock, 2019). While doing this they make use of third-party apps. For instance, there are many services for collecting donations through complementors and several other tools developed for gamifying live streams.

To create a Twitch extension, one does not require deep knowledge of coding as they are webpages that can be coded on HTML. The documentation is ample and covers newbies to advanced developers to entice newcomers in different skill levels. This relatively easy entry into extension development not only motivates would-be coders but also fans of certain streamers to develop extensions for the specific needs of their preferred channels.

A third-party Twitch extension could be created by a small or large game company, a complementor company, or an individual. Twitch shared a quarterly developer survey performed before Developer Day 2020 on their website (*Twitch Developer Day 2020*, 2020). According to this, 73% of third-party developers who develop extensions for Twitch work alone, 16% work for a business with two to nine employees, 6% work for a company with 10–49 employees, and the remainder small portion work for a company with more than 50 employees. In addition to the website, Twitch Developers have their own social media presence, which contains introduction videos, comprehensive instructions, advice, and coding samples. This community also have their own Discord channel and GitHub website where coders can communicate about the newest code.

Additionally, Twitch Developers has a dedicated Twitch channel where they frequently live broadcast information about new extensions, partnerships, and new API and SDK releases that third-party developers use to create their extensions. These broadcasts feature Twitch staff members who have grown to be recognizable to outside developers. They refer to the third-party developers as the 'dev community' and work to maintain their involvement. Currently working for Twitch are some former third-party developers. James Sun, a senior product manager in charge of the Channel Points system, used the alias Revlo to create his own loyalty-based extensions. Larger businesses that create various live-streaming-based services for streamers and gaming companies may also hire independent Twitch developers.

This example demonstrates the possibility of being hired by Twitch or another company when a third-party developer showcases this kind of deep engagement with Twitch. Many people learn to code and create their first tools at Twitch Developers. Thus, it has a community service component that facilitates young people's entry into coding through documentation, videos, and community support. Fans of certain channels have been known to create extensions tailored to the needs of that channel. While the advantages of many people receiving vocational training are not to be overlooked, there are some concerns that need to be brought up regarding how Twitch is influencing would-be and more experienced developers.

Method

By conducting a thematic and hermeneutic analysis of online material posted by Twitch, Twitch employees, and third-party developers affiliated with Twitch Developers this study tries to unearth how this company employs its platform powers. These secondary sources are documentation, blog posts, and Twitch streams that are officially produced by Twitch. Additional data come from the Discord and the GitHub channels of Twitch Developers as established shared spaces. The analysis aims to unpack Twitch's discursive construction of an imagined community of developers, that in the words of Twitch's Developer Advocacy Lead, 'build some of the most interactive, innovative experiences for anyone's community' (*Twitch Channel Points Hackathon*, 2021).

The hermeneutic circle is related to the understanding of the text by interpreting its parts. The idea implies that to comprehend an intricate entity, it is necessary to examine preconceived notions regarding its individual components. By constantly shifting focus between these components and the entity as a whole, an understanding can be achieved (Gadamer, 1977, p. 67). The sorted-out material is ordered, explained, and interpreted several times to evaluate the meaning. This reinterpretation of parts leads to a revised understanding of the whole.

In order to analyse data posted in different forms on separate platforms a qualitative analysis software was used. Blog and social media posts and a live-streamed Twitch Developers event's transcript were coded using MAX-QDA. A combination approach was used to develop a set of codes. Firstly, a draft codebook was developed by relying on the literature review. An inductive coding was also implemented during the coding process, creating more codes. This latter, ground-up method is needed to make sense of this collection of data that comes in text and multimedia formats. After the first round, the qualitative codes have been organized into categories and sub-categories. A few additional rounds have been completed by sifting through the data.

A variety of justifications are used in the logic of selection. First, in terms of platforms, I looked at Twitch Developers' official Twitter, Discord, and Medium blog posts, paying close attention to those that dealt with extension development. The data span the months of December 2018 and December 2020. The former date denotes the start of the data collection period, whereas the latter date allows for the inclusion of a pandemic period that is linked to an increase in platform engagement because of stay-at-home orders.

Analysis: 'I think you guys should be vocal about it'

Twitch hosts the Twitch Developer Day every year to show off new tools for producing Twitch applications by third-party developers. During this event, Twitch presents a yearly gathering of its most popular developers, employees, and extensions. The video with the most views on Twitch Developer's channel as of March 2023 is 'Twitch Developer Day 2020 // November 13, 2020', which has received more than 520K views. Developer Day 2020's popularity could be explained by the COVID-19 pandemic because Twitch's popularity skyrocketed in the second half of 2020 (*Twitch Statistics & Charts*, n.d.), whereas the other videos in the channel did not surpass 10K views. The transcript of that livestream, which lasted five hours, 16 minutes, was 38,800 words long. Analysis of this particular event provided useful insights into the platform power of Twitch because it is a highly orchestrated event that exclusively revolves around the third-party coders who create various Twitch apps rather than streamers.

The emphasis on engagement and interactivity is the most frequent code whether coming from social media or from the Developer Day 2020 livestream. Twitch employees, in their addresses to third-party developers, often mention how valuable their feedback, contributions, comments, and proposals are. One Twitch employee, after thanking the developers who participated in beta testing of a new service, proclaims as follows:

> We heard your feedback, and we built events up for you. Head over to the dev site and [...] dig into everything that events offers. Use it and tell us how to make it better. Tell us what you like. Tell us what you hate, we're listening.

Another Twitch employee flatters the community to tap into the collective creativity which is tied to a purported collective intentionality:

> I'm sure there are plenty of other ideas and categories that we haven't even thought about, so we're really really excited to hear what you have

to say and see the awesome products that we can partner together and build as a community.

John Searle, the proponent of collective intentionality, discusses the collaborative efforts of both human and animal groups in achieving shared objectives. He asserts that converting a 'we-intention' into an individual 'I-intention' or vice versa (reducing an 'I-intention' to a 'we-intention') is not feasible. So whenever a staff member talks about how excited they are to hear about the third-party developers' ideas and how without these ideas their product can't meet the full potential, they refer to an imagined collective intentionality that can be explained by Searle's phrase: 'I believe that you believe that I believe that you believe ...' (Searle, 1997). Therefore, this construction of collective intentionality serves as the binder of a community that builds things together.

The concept of a collaborative community that collaboratively creates things emphasizes the significance of engagement and interactivity on various levels. Firstly, as illustrated in the above-mentioned example, this community serves as a reminder for third-party developers to explore, test, and offer feedback on various functionalities of Twitch in order to ensure the smooth operation of these systems. Secondly, Twitch employees instruct third-party developers to develop features that enhance engagement and interactivity. These metrics are advantageous for digital platforms as they serve as evidence of success (Srnicek, 2016). It is not surprising, therefore, that during Developer Day 2020, another member of Twitch's staff concludes a session with the following expression: 'You know that's what it's all about! Cool. Well, we love interactivity and engagement. Thank you so much for joining us today.'

Another theme was related to *signalling of community* and *emphasizing of the greatness of individual developers*. While the quotes above highlight the importance of interaction with one another, this theme is associated with feelings of camaraderie, sharing information, and doing good for the community:

> Just want to say congratulations and thank you so much for all you do for our community, it's really an inspiration to see not only all that you've created, but all the ways you help the community create *more* as well. (emphasis added)

When presenting the Developer Day 2020 event, Twitch staff members highlight how much the Twitch community depends on the individual developers by praising them for their dedication and 'how great they are'. In an interview, a third-party developer who joined the Twitch Ambassadors Program demonstrates this idea: 'I build not just for the people who use it, but for the entire community' (*Twitch Welcomes Our First Developer to the Ambassador Program*, 2020). According to MaxQDA's code relations matrix, codes relating to individuality *(showcasing of independent third-party developers, the challenges of working alone)* are frequently linked to the passages coded as *community*.

Products/codes is an additional category that has emerged. This category includes presentations of various APIs created by Twitch staff members. An API is a group of tools and services created by the owners of the platform to allow other software developers or businesses to create new applications or services that will function with or enhance the capabilities of the platform. Twitch staff members frequently mention that they 'are extremely excited to announce new products' or 'have a lot of very cool new products and improvements that [they]'ve been working on' during the Developer Day live stream. In addition to the subcodes for *new products* and *updates*, the third subcode is *future improvements*, where the staff discusses what is projected to occur in the future. This last subcode is particularly interesting because, by indicating that new features will be available, the staff is essentially telling complementors to continue creating apps and extensions for Twitch.

An official blog post about a third-party extension starts like this: 'Not every Twitch Extension is made by a whole team of people. Sometimes, like in the case of Sounds Alerts, all it takes is one person looking to improve the Twitch experience' (*Sound Alerts: A Twitch Bits-in-Extensions Success Story*, 2018). The blog entry describes how a 'hobbyist developer' and gamer created the concept for Sound Alerts, a 'Bits-enabled' extension that lets viewers play sounds during Twitch livestreams. The virtual currency used on Twitch, called 'bits', is mainly used for tipping, or 'cheering', the streamers. Twitch receives a portion of each bit used. The company promotes this extension because, for them, it is a good monetization strategy connected to audiences' wish for engagement. Twitch's blog article about the Sound Alerts extension serves as proof that extensions produce the best results for the platform. By encouraging extension development among its millions of users, Twitch can crowdsource innovation in extension development with little financial compensation. Because there are so many extensions, the Twitch experience is continually changing for both viewers and streamers who can make use of new extensions. Even though they state that their objective is to 'help streamers and developers generate revenue on Twitch' (Twitch, 2019). Twitch especially benefits from enhancements that are connected to bits because it is a straightforward commodification of Twitch's affordances.

In Twitch, third-party developers certainly have the opportunity to advance both the engagement and narrative of new media while also improving their coding abilities. However, their labour is shaped, groomed, and geared toward commodified practices that are primarily advantageous to the platform. As a whole, Twitch Developers is a tightly regulated 'community' where Twitch profits from having complete authority. Having said that, coders can also suggest changes to the framework for writing code or bring up other problems via forums or social media channels. However, the advantages of the site outweigh users' or developers' intense engagement with it. For example, according to the Twitch Developer Services Agreement, extension makers are not allowed to 'Transfer profile content to any ad network, data broker, or other advertising or monetization-related service'. To use the collected data for marketing or improvement of a product, third-party developers are urged to enter into a distinct arrangement with Twitch (*Twitch. Tv - Developer Agreement*, 2020). While the prioritization of users' privacy is certainly a positive development, it should be noted that Twitch currently engages in widespread data collection and aims to maintain exclusive control over this practice.

While companies have benefited from virtual communities that voluntarily create content related to certain brands (Zhao et al., 2012), Twitch Developers goes beyond being a typical online brand community which, according to Wong and Lee (2021), is considered an effective method for fostering business and brand growth. The developers associated with Twitch Developers are both fans of Twitch in a general sense and have the characteristics of specialized online gift-giving communities. Here, perhaps similarly to online brand communities, Twitch shapes the collective effort of developers by various discursive cues like *feedback* or *community*. The aspect of the necessity for feedback is reminded during Developer Day live streams in phrases like 'I think you guys should be vocal about it' in relation to which video games are more suitable to develop in-game Twitch extensions. In terms of community and doing together, Twitch employees underline a certain togetherness in achieving success as when they announce the milestone of a thousand extensions:

> Kudos to all our extension developers who continued to plug away at building extensions because this is a really, really awesome achievement and you all should pat yourselves on the back because we definitely celebrated for you and with you.

These examples indicate to a company-led community where meaningful or impactful bottom-up decision-making process remains slim.

When considering the benefits that Twitch and Amazon derive from these activities, it can be summarized as follows: For Twitch to thrive as a successful business, it requires a large viewership for its live streams, as well as engaged users who generate surplus data that can be utilized by its parent company. These data are then leased to advertisers and used to enhance and expand Twitch's services. In the case of Twitch, while users seek to express themselves and find entertainment, complementors developing Twitch extensions and video game developers aim to grow their own businesses. This dynamic places Twitch in a unique position to leverage, control, and commodify these diverse ambitions. The actors involved in 'deep engagement' on the platform have different expectations and needs. However, what they receive in return for their deep commitment often pales in comparison to what the platform capitalists gain. Consequently, Twitch, as a leading live-streaming platform, has the ability to gather information encompassing all aspects of the gaming industry. Through deep engagement, Twitch acquires even greater knowledge about games and users' in-game behaviours, which can be combined with data from other sources such as Amazon's other initiatives.

Conclusion

During the Q&A session at Twitch Developer Day, a front–end engineer at Twitch is asked if there are plans to allow a newly announced functionality to go through the API. He says that 'With our *limited resources* on the team, we'd like to make sure that we see things get adopted before we invest time in building the APIs for them'. So, the full-time Twitch employee laments their lack of resources in front of a group of precarious third-party developers and encourages them to stay engaged so the company can learn about the features that will stick around on the platform.

Twitch Developers utilizes the early internet's gift culture, where developers gain social capital and believe that contributing to the collective effort will benefit everyone on the platform. However, only a very small number of third-party developers' apps can generate income or are acquired or hired by Twitch. However, there is no evidence that these developers are any different from those who participate in open-source projects for the joy of sharing and writing code without pay. Thematic analysis reveals a governance structure that is administered by the firm despite references to buzzwords like community, engagement, or feedback that attempt to create the image of a more bottom–up peer-production community. Yet, this is a community of coders that was started and maintained by a company. Therefore, it can be called a company-led community.

Twitch provides the APIs that allow third-party developers to create extensions and enhance the platform's interactive experience with a wide range of features. Compared to other live-streaming platforms like YouTube or Facebook Live, Twitch has a relatively more busy third-party development community. Due to its dominant position in the market, Twitch aims to encourage developers to build extensions that generate surplus data, benefiting from economies of scale through its extensive reach within the gaming ecosystem.

The digital platforms have become adept at leveraging human activities to generate surplus value, and Twitch has excelled at amplifying such activities on its platform through new extensions and features developed by a diverse group of developers, many of whom are not directly employed by Twitch. These third-party developers and complementor companies often operate on an uncertain footing, trying to market their services to other parties or directly to Twitch. In this context, Twitch Developers serves as a community where novice to expert software developers collaborate to create new tools and features that support the platform's commercial goals.

Note

1 https://dev.twitch.tv

References

Barbrook, R. (1998). The Hi-Tech Gift Economy. *First Monday, 3(12)*. doi: 10.5210/fm.v3i12.631

Benkler, Y. (2006). *The Wealth of Networks: How Social Production Transforms Markets and Freedom.* New Haven, CT: Yale University Press.

Berdou, E. (2010). *Organization in Open Source Communities: At the Crossroads of the Gift and Market Economies.* Taylor & Francis Group. http://ebookcentral.proquest.com/lib/bilgi-ebooks/detail.action?docID=592964

Bergquist, M., & Ljungberg, J. (2001). The Power of Gifts: Organizing Social Relationships in Open Source Communities. *Information Systems Journal, 11*(4), 305–320. doi: 10.1046/j.1365-2575.2001.00111.x

Bingham, C. (2017). *An Ethnography of Twitch Streamers: Negotiating Professionalism in New Media Content Creation* [Oklahoma]. https://shareok.org/handle/11244/50709

Bruns, A. (2007). Produsage. *Proceedings of the 6th ACM SIGCHI Conference on Creativity & Cognition*, 99–106. doi: 10.1145/1254960.1254975

Durmuş, S. (2021). *Commodification of Agency: Surplus Value Creation in Twitch.* [Doctoral thesis], Istanbul Bilgi University.

Elder, D. (2021, May 18). Community-Led Growth: The Key to Acquisition and Retention? *Tribe Blog.* https://tribe.so/blog/community-led-growth/

Gadamer, H. G. (1977). *Philosophical Hermeneutics* (D. E. Linge, Trans. Ed.). Berkeley: University of California Press.

Ghazawneh, A., & Mansour, O. (2015). *Value Creation in Digital Application Marketplaces: A Developers' Perspective.* Thirty Sixth International Conference on Information Systems, Fort Wort, Texas. http://urn.kb.se/resolve?urn=urn:nbn:se:hj:diva-37988

Jenkins, H. (2008). *Convergence Culture: Where Old and New Media Collide* (Revised edition). New York: NYU Press.

Johnson, M. R., & Woodcock, J. (2019). "And Today's Top Donator is": How Live Streamers on Twitch.tv Monetize and Gamify Their Broadcasts: *Social Media + Society*. doi: 10.1177/2056305119881694

Kollock, P. (1998). The economies of online cooperation: Gifts and Public Goods in Cyberspace. In M. A. Smith & P. Kollock (Eds), *Communities in Cyberspace* (pp. 229–248). London: Routledge. doi: 10.4324/9780203194959-20

Lahey, M. (2016). The Framing of Value Television, User-Generated Content, and Interactive Involvement. *Convergence: The International Journal of Research into New Media Technologies, 22*(6), 633–646. doi: 10.1177/1354856514563903

Levy, S. (1984). *Hackers: Heroes of the Computer Revolution* (1st edition). Anchor Press/Doubleday. http://www.gbv.de/dms/bowker/toc/9780385191951.pdf

Rheingold, H. (2000). *The Virtual Community: Homesteading on the Electronic Frontier* (Revised ed. edition). Cambridge: The MIT Press.
Rudmark, D. (2013). The Practices of Unpaid Third-Party Developers – Implications for API Design. *AMCIS 2013 Proceedings.* https://aisel.aisnet.org/amcis2013/EndUserIS/GeneralPresentations/3
Russpatrick, S. (2020). Understanding Platform Ecosystems for Development: Enabling Innovation in Digital Global Public Goods Software Platforms. *IFIP Advances in Information and Communication Technology, 601,* 148–162. Scopus. doi: 10.1007/978-3-030-64697-4_12
Saxenian, A. (1996). *Regional Advantage: Culture and Competition in Silicon Valley and Route 128, With a New Preface by the Author.* Cambridge, MA: Harvard University Press.
Searle, J. R. (1997). *The Construction of Social Reality* (Illustrated edition). Free Press.
Shah, S. K. (2006). Motivation, Governance, and the Viability of Hybrid Forms in Open Source Software Development. *Management Science, 52*(7), 1000–1014. https://www.jstor.org/stable/20110576
Shirky, C. (2009). *Here Comes Everybody: The Power of Organizing without Organizations* (Reprint edition). New York: Penguin Books.
Sound Alerts: A Twitch Bits-in-Extensions Success Story (2018, August 27). Twitch Blog. https://blog.twitch.tv/en/2018/08/27/sound-alerts-a-bits-in-extensions-success-story-f464eb1c59d5/
Srnicek, N. (2016). *Platform Capitalism* (1st edition). Cambridge; Malden, MA: Polity.
Taylor, T. L. (2018). *Watch Me Play: Twitch and the Rise of Game Live Streaming.* Princeton, NJ: Princeton University Press.
Twitch. (2019, April 2). *Creating Monetization Opportunities for Developers and Streamers.* Twitch Blog. https://blog.twitch.tv/creating-monetization-opportunities-for-developers-and-streamers-771d13060f19
Twitch Channel Points Hackathon // Announcing the Winners. (2021, April). https://www.twitch.tv/videos/989734606
Twitch Developer Day 2020 (2020, November 13). https://www.twitch.tv/videos/801641556
Twitch Extensions 101 (2017). https://www.twitch.tv/videos/239080621?t=0h0m47s
Twitch Statistics & Charts (n.d.). TwitchTracker. Retrieved June 23, 2023, from https://twitchtracker.com/statistics
Twitch Welcomes Our First Developer to the Ambassador Program: AlphaDuplo! (2020, February 14). Twitch Blog. https://blog.twitch.tv/en/2020/02/14/twitch-welcomes-our-first-developer-to-the-ambassador-program-alphaduplo/
Twitch.tv—Developer Agreement (2020). Twitch.Tv. https://www.twitch.tv/p/legal/developer-agreement/
Wen, W., & Zhu, F. (2019). Threat of Platform-Owner Entry and Complementor Responses: Evidence from the Mobile App Market. *Strategic Management Journal, 40*(9), 1336–1367. doi: 10.1002/smj.3031
Wong, A., & Lee, M. (2021). Building Engagement in Online Brand Communities: The Effects of Socially Beneficial Initiatives on Collective Social Capital. *Journal of Retailing and Consumer Services, 65,* 102866. doi: 10.1016/j.jretconser.2021.102866

Zhao, L., Lu, Y., Wang, B., Chau, P. Y. K., & Zhang, L. (2012). Cultivating the Sense of Belonging and Motivating User Participation in Virtual Communities: A Social Capital Perspective. *International Journal of Information Management*, *32*(6), pp. 574–588. doi: 10.1016/j.ijinfomgt.2012.02.006

Zhu, F. (2019). Friends or Foes? Examining Platform Owners' Entry into Complementors' Spaces. *Journal of Economics & Management Strategy*, *28*(1), 23–28. doi: 10.1111/jems.12303

Part III
Acting together

11 From a political protest to an art exhibition

Collaboration and dialogue through artistic research

Işıl Eğrikavuk

From personal to theoretical

Performance as an art form requires collaboration and interaction in its nature with colleagues, technicians, organizers, actors, non-actors, and curators. As an artist with a master degree in performance art, I have an interest in and have explored over the course of years various forms of collaborations, engagement and dialogue with different individuals and groups, such as artists, non-artists, musicians, writers, a chef, a TV talk show host, an Iraqi doctor working on cancer treatment in the United States, Turkish coal mine workers in Germany or small shop owners such as a barber, a real estate owner in the Tophane district of Istanbul. More importantly, I have developed many projects and performances with my students over the years. My main interest of being and doing together lies in the community arts practices, in which artists work in collaboration with different segments of society, 'become catalysts for change', and 'reposition the self as citizen-activists' (Lacy, 1995, p. 8). Such practices of art involving communities are often referred to as new genre of public art (Lacy, 1995), littoral art (Kester, 1999), or dialogical art (Kester, 2005) and consist of collaboration between the artist(s) and communities in the process of engagement with various social issues. This chapter draws from my PhD research titled 'From A Political Protest to an Art Exhibition: Building Interconnectedness through Dialogue Based Art', which I completed in 2021 at Istanbul Bilgi University. I will specifically address the methodology I used during my research, which is a collaborative and participatory artistic process, where I explored the possibilities of co-creation.

In May 2013, something ground-breaking happened in Turkey, which is referred to as the Gezi Park protests in the media. The uprising started with a small crowd of protesters' coming together as a reaction towards the government's announcement of the destruction of Istanbul's centrally located Gezi Park. However, 'what began as a simple environmentalist protest grew rapidly and spread across the country as a result of police brutality faced by the small group of activists' (Batuman, 2015, p. 1). In a few days, thousands of people started gathering in Gezi Park and Taksim Square, the historically symbolic

DOI: 10.4324/9781003389972-14

location of protests and collective resistances. It is important to note that, the Gezi Park protest was more than a mere opposition to the destruction of a single park but rather a reflection of the growing reactions against the government policies radically transforming the processes that orchestrate the production and use of urban space (Kuyumlu, 2013). I participated in the protests as a citizen in practising my democratic rights. As an artist, I could observe the significance of the protests as a space facilitating inclusive artistic expression. Through my involvement and experience in the Gezi Park protests, I became more aware of emerging patterns about the role of creative expression and performativity within the recent protest movements around the globe, practised through performances, slogans, graffiti, songs and various other forms of communication.

Taking my inspiration from the creativity of Gezi Park protests and their collaborative nature, I initiated an artistic research project, *Komşuda Pişer, Bize de Düşer* (Maybe We Will Benefit from Our Neighbour's Good Fortune) in 2017, in which I worked with six art and environmental collectives in Turkey. In observing the certain qualities of recent political protests around the globe and in my home country Turkey, in this chapter, I reflect on the potential of community art practices and the significance of collaborative and artistic research for transformative knowledge production. My intention is not to present yet another socio-political analysis of the protests, but rather to observe and point to certain intersections between the protests and my ongoing research of community arts. As an artist, I also acknowledge that the engagement of community arts is not anew; I do not intend to draw a historical analysis, but rather see how the engagement of the social and creative is evolving through the recent protests, finding new forms of expressions, and reaching a non-art audience. I am intentionally writing and reflecting on my own experiences and artistic research in an attempt to exemplify how much the personal is critical in creating knowledge. As Sarah Ahmed says, I believe 'personal is theoretical' (Ahmed, 2017, p. 10). Existing literature and theoretical knowledge along with my own reflections and my collaborators' input diversify academic knowledge production mechanisms by bridging knowing with feeling.

Community arts and dialogue-based practices

My research in community art practices derives from the Brazilian philosopher and educator Paulo Freire's seminal work of *Pedagogy of the Oppressed* (1970) which defines the role of educators not as those delivering the information that turns the students into 'passive entities' (Freire, 1970, p. 76) but as those transform the pedagogical process through a reflexive and critical dialogue. By applying Freire's ideas on education through current contemporary art practices, art historian Grant Kester introduces the concept of 'dialogical aesthetics', as 'a discursive aesthetic based on the possibility of a dialogical relationship that breaks down the conventional distinction between artist, artwork and audience' (Kester, 1999, p. 4). This definition differs from the aesthetics defined by German philosopher Alexander Baumgarten in the 18th century as the 'study of sensory experiences' (Nanay, 2019, p. 2). Kester focuses on the function of dialogue as a discursive encounter between the artists and the subject, serving both as a process and the outcome of the work. Thus, the aesthetic experience lies in the discursive process among the partakers of a work, rather than a sensory experience one has upon viewing an artwork. Critical dialogue as the core of an artwork constitutes a significant part of Kester's theorization for two reasons. First, instead of focusing on the outcome as an object, Kester offers a model where the dialogical encounter between the participants in a work becomes the nucleus of the aesthetic experience. Secondly, by creating a dialogue between artists and different communities, he argues that artists can 'speak and imagine beyond the limits of fixed identities and official discourse' (Kester, 2004, p. 2). Through listening to and learning from each other's experiences, each participant can objectively reflect on the self. Thus, Kester suggests the fixed roles and identities attained by both the artists and the involved participants can be challenged and transformed through this process.

As much as I theoretically argue that a dialogical process is key in leading to a personal and social transformation, I also question the implication of these theories when applied to practice. In *Social Works: Performing Art Supporting Publics*, Shannon Jackson (2011) analyses socially engaged works in contemporary art practices and performance, highlighting the increasing role of the 'performative' and 'social' in recent art practices. Through the examples from the practices of contemporary artists such as Wochenklausur, Shannon Flaherty, and Santiago Sierra, Jackson asks the question of 'do such social practices break institutional boundaries or set the scene for the recuperation of sociality by a service economy hungry for de-materialized crowds?' (Jackson, 2011, p. 44). Jackson's question is valid in inviting both artists and institutions to think deeper into the making and displaying of sincere motivations for socially engaged practices. In *Truth Is Concrete: A Handbook for Artistic Strategies in Real Politics* (2015), curator Florian Malzacher refers to all kinds of new or renewed alliances between art and activism as 'artivism'. Such terminology foresees imagining the use of artistic tools and skills for activist purposes and for creating self-empowerment for its author(s) and engaged participants (Malzacher, 2015, p. 14). One of the qualities of artivist works is referred to as 'being many'.

> When the many emerge and start to engage in the constituent process of becoming a 'we', terrible and wonderful things can happen. The wonderful part is that, at such moments, the most important things can be reinvented: care, dignity, and the power to change our lives collectively, as recently in the squares and parks of Madrid, Cairo, New York, Athens, Istanbul.
>
> (Peters, 2015, p. 131)

Some of the artistic strategies listed under this category are carnivals, dancing, puppet demonstrations, coauthorship, and choirs.

Performativity in global protests

Gezi Park protests shared similar characteristics in artistic and cultural expressions of other global protest movements from Occupy Wall Street in New York in 2011, to the Arab Spring in Egypt (Egyptian Revolution) in 2011, and the Umbrella Movement in Hong Kong in 2014. These protests often became the platforms for various segments of society with different ideological views, positions, or identities to come together, express themselves, and recognize one another. By critiquing the lack of attention given to the role of arts and performances in political activism and social movements, the edited collection of *Aesthetics of Protest: Visual Culture and Communication* (McGarry et al., 2020), addresses the creative and communicative qualities of protests such as images, symbols, graffiti, art, and choreography across the world use them in order to communicate their ideas. These acts of 'new performativity' were translocal and transnational (Verstraete, 2016), bringing together transnational influences together with local nuance. For example, the 'human microphone chorus' of Occupy Wall Street, in which protesters repeat aloud what the speaker says was similar to the 'Complaint Choir Project'[1], in which participants write songs and sing together. Or the neighbourhood forums that were an essential part of the Gezi Park protests, were also quite significant in Occupy Wall Street as well. Another example of transnational performativity is seen in guerrilla gardening projects, such as that of British artist Richard Reynolds, who is the founder of www.guerrillagardening.org in 2004 in London, spaces in London. Reynolds joined the Occupy Wall Street protests in Zuccotti Park in 2011 by giving a workshop in which he commented on this experience in his blog: 'Here, for the first time I see guerrilla gardening used in a protest whose heart is far from a gardener's in a way that is not at the mercy of plants. It makes practical use of the energy and optimism within a crowd that has multiple objectives to change a society' (Reynolds, 2012).

These creative protest movements can be observed as similar to the principles of community art practices in their emphasis on not only being collaborative but also on being performative, generating critical dialogue and involving heterogeneous communities. The performative nature of the protests blurs the division between reality and representation by placing everyone in the role of the performer (Schechner, 2003). The examples of performances involved collective cooking, eating, and food sharing among the protestors or participatory events such as creating an open library for everyone, a free-speech station, a mock-marriage hall, free health-service halls, spaces for dancing, and music and performances. In one of the most iconic performances of the protests, known as the Standing Man in the media, hundreds of people stood together motionless in Taksim Square for many hours. The critical dialogue principle of community art was also apparent during the Gezi Park protests. The dialogical process was especially visible in the neighbourhood forums, where people from different views and positions take the stage one after another, expressing themselves and hearing the others. What intrigued me in this dialogical process was it is not being limited to a certain group, but embracing heterogeneous groups of people in Turkey, including 'feminists, queer activists, factory workers and leftists, observant Muslims, middle-class secularists and underserved ethnic and religious minorities' (Potuoğlu-Cook, 2015, p. 1) against the conservative, authoritarian, and hetero/patriarchal capitalism of the AKP government. During the protests, the park became a place where people 'from very different walks of life, from different political leanings, ethnic backgrounds, socio-economic groups, lifestyle choices and so on came together' (Aksoy, 2017, p. 20). Some defined this heterogeneity as something 'that had not existed before' (McGarry et al., 2020, p.16), referring to these diverse and agonistic groups (Mouffe, 2007) of people coming together and crafting something new against existing ideologies. This agonistic quality of the protests, along with performativity, critical dialogue and capacity for bringing different segments of the society together were the key qualities defining artistic research as a participatory and collaborative process with six art collectives leading to Komşuda Pişer, Bize de Düşer art exhibition.

Artistic research

The interest to not only place practice within the research process but to lead research through practice has led to new strategies initiated by artists and researchers known 'as creative practice as research, performance as research, research through practice, studio research, practice as research or practice-led research' (Haseman, 2006, p. 100). The practice-based research methodologies are often defined as 'a combination of artistic practice and theoretical approach while aiming at the production of knowledge' (Hannula, 2004, p. 70). Yet, this process of knowledge production differed from traditional forms of knowledge in natural sciences and humanities. Artistic research opens the concept of generalization into question as 'truth happens in a singular and interpretative mode instead of in a general and exact mode' (Nevannlina, 2004, p. 83). As Nevannlina points out, it constitutes 'a-knowledge, where the "a" can be freely seen either as an article or as a privative particle, or both' (Nevannlina, 2004, p. 83). Hannula, Suoranta and Vaden define 'democracy of experiences and methodological diversity' as two significant criteria underlying the need for artistic research. The democracy of experiences means that there is no longer a hierarchical degree among the sciences or the prioritized status of any one science over the other, especially science over the arts. The methodological diversity comes from the concept of 'methodological abundance', by philosopher Paul Feyerabend, who defends against a single philosophy of scientific viewpoint, saying that the world is too diverse to be reduced to a single method. In his seminal work, *Against Method* (1975), Feyerabend defines the essence of science as 'an essentially anarchic enterprise where theoretical anarchism is more humanitarian and more likely to encourage progress than its law-and-order alternatives' (1975, p. 5). Diversifying and growing practices and literature in artistic research during the last two decades have expanded the forms of knowledge production in line with the claim by Feyerabend for more room for methodological diversity in academia.

In addition to democracy of experiences and methodological diversity as significant criteria for my research, I consider the inclusion of others in the process as collaborators as a significant criterion. This, I believe is important as the core of my research explores the potential of co-creation and how to attain it in a setting of the arts. Therefore, the 'collaborative and participatory case study' approach constitutes the core of my research as a methodological approach in which one tries in one way or another to influence the research object and include people other than researchers in the research (Hannula et al., 2005, p. 88). In this form of research, the significance lies in solving a common problem through 'the active influence of the researcher, and not only her external observations on the events' (Hannula et al, 2005, p. 90).

Participatory and collaborative art exhibition of *Komşuda Pişer, Bize de Düşer*

It is important to note that when I started my research in 2017, the political atmosphere in Turkey was very different from the days of the Gezi Park protests. Cases of silencing were now numerous, not only in academia but also in the arts through 'growing censorship and cancellations of exhibitions' (Akkermans, 2016). With a question about the motivations and experiences involved in working as and being an art collective in such a politically restricted environment, I approached several different collectives working in Turkey. During my research process with the collectives, I followed a dialogue-based approach, in which I put emphasis on developing personal relationships with each collective member. I met members of each artist collective regularly, either in bi-weekly personal or Skype meetings and discussed their ideas on the process of the exhibition. I also documented some of these conversations. I was surprised to find out that most collectives had come together as a result of emotional needs to share feelings and support each other rather than with a straightforward aim to produce art together. The work that came out of that seemed only to have followed their shared patterns of emotions. They expressed a need for sharing, being heard, understood, and accepted. This common need for close friendship, for being heard, and for sharing feelings and emotions was a key finding for me during our conversations.

Reflecting similarities with the collaborative and heterogeneous nature of the protests, I worked with six artistic and environmental collectives in Turkey, using a collaborative and participatory artistic research methodology. These collectives were: dadans (contemporary dance-performance art), HAH (participatory art practices), Pelesiyer (sculpture/installation), artık-işler (video), birbuçuk (a collective of academics and cultural sector professionals, working on the intersection of art and ecology), and Istanbul Permaculture Collective.

My dialogues with the collectives inspired me to also turn to theories about the role of art and creativity in relationship to the capacity of transforming emotions. Eslen-Ziya et al. (2019) underline the transformative power of the collective and creative actions during the Gezi Park protests, from anger to hope and solidarity as the protest evolved through these creative rituals: 'Sharing food, cleaning the park, creating a library and organising yoga or praying together were all participatory activities that enabled one to one contact and strengthened the Gezi Spirit' (Eslen-Ziya et al., 2019, p. 5). The emotional solidarity within the collectives and the potential to transform not only their own emotions but also those of the art audiences they could reach were significant aspects for me to reflect on. In an atmosphere of extreme censorship and control, these emotional solidarities can serve as instigators of critical dialogue within society, by holding the potential for larger emotional change in hearing, understanding, and trusting each other. With that idea, I approached the collectives again, asking them if and how, through their work. In line with Keller (1968), the conformed kinships among people who had no identical backgrounds or lifestyles together (Keller, 1968). Just like the Gezi protests had triggered a new set of relationships across very different communities and identities and brought them together in solidarity, how could we, as artists, challenge the existing relationships in our society and initiate new models through our work? Thus came our exhibition entitled *Maybe We Will Benefit from Our Neighbour's Good Fortune*.

The saying 'Maybe, we will benefit from our neighbour's good fortune' (Komşuda Pişer, Bize de Düşer) in Turkish involves a slight double entendre; it means the positive circumstances and good fortunes of those around us will also hold for us, yet at the same time it signifies the state of exploiting and creating opportunities from these good fortunes. We thought that this old saying, referring very much to the changing dynamics of neighbourhoods in big cities, was something that captured our thinking during our dialogues. What made the Gezi Park protests so unique was that they had brought many different kinds of people under its roof as if they were neighbours. Building on such coming together, we set an exhibition framework that would extend the understanding of heterogeneous neighbourliness that emerged during the Gezi Park protests.

Having found the framework for the exhibition, I went back to our critical dialogues and asked each of the collectives how they experience and interpret neighbourliness and neighbourly relationships in their daily life. *dadans*, a collective founded by three women performance artists, from Turkey, focusing mainly on dance and performance was quite critical of neighbourliness in Istanbul 'I always saw the neighbour as an ideal structure, but in fact, that is not so. When we say neighbour, there are all sorts of things that emerge from underneath it, there comes out gossip, social pressure, you name it...' (dadans, personal communication, June 2017). *HAH*, the collective of five artists with interdisciplinary work in site-specific installations, publications, and dialogues was critical of the neighbourliness that is often interpreted today. 'The phenomenon of being neighbours is presently approached from a romantic and somewhat orientalist perspective... Actually, it is everyone we have contact with in everyday life, everyone we touch or not, everyone whose wind we swallow' (HAH, personal communication, June 2017). *Pelesiyer*, a collective of four artists who are mainly working with forms of sculpture based in Ankara, interpreted neighbourhoods not just as people living physically next to each other but also as neighbour geographies. 'I don't perceive the neighbour merely as the person living next door, I mean, I perceive it as the relationship between neighbouring countries' (Pelesiyer, personal communication, July 2017).

Moving in the light of the responses, I also asked each collective about the ways they could initiate new forms of relations or kinships to challenge existing, ideal, or romantic approaches towards neighbourliness. Just like the way the Gezi protests had triggered a new set of relationships across very different communities and identities and brought them together in solidarity, how could we, as artists, challenge the existing relationships in our society and initiate new models through our work? How could art become instrumental in opening up new dialogues or challenging the existing ones? How could we include others in our work?

With the other three collectives, namely, with birbuçuk, Artıkişler Collective, and Istanbul Permaculture Collective, I also had dialogues. Because these collectives' works were not geared towards producing objects or physical forms, but rather dialogue-based or time-based events, we decided to organize events, workshops, or talks oriented around dialogues. For example, with birbuçuk, who organizes talks on issues of art and ecology, we decided to organize a meeting by inviting local food cooperatives and bringing them together with artists working on the topics of ecology.

Our exhibition took place in September 2017 at the Halka Art Project in Istanbul. Through installation, food-based work, performance, workshops, and round table discussions, we searched for ways to communicate and widen the principal qualities of the protests and their extended forms, such as neighbourhood forums, to audiences and participants.

Here, I invite the reader to consider the whole exhibition process itself, not just the final outcome, defining our work. Through our dialogical process, I tried opening up both the collectives' and my own fixed positions and ideas by posing questions and reflecting on their answers. From my teaching experience of over ten years, I was already aware of how one's work and their ideas on that work could shift through a productive discussion.

Impacts of our research

Participatory and collaborative artistic research for me is the most representative and powerful tool to engage others in co-creating. Artistic research, at its core, is aimed towards finding 'a-knowledge', in which truth happens 'in a singular and interpretative way' (Nevannlina, 2004, p. 83). Our exhibition took place once and then, and if I were to repeat the same process again, even with the same collectives, the outcome would most likely be different. What interpretations can I make through this singular a-knowledge I have achieved? What interpretations can I draw from the exhibition other than the images of works produced? As Brad Haseman (2006) asks, 'how can presentational forms be understood as research? What makes a dance, a novel, a contemporary performance, the outcome of research?' (Haseman, 2006, p. 5).

In underlining it once more that practice-based research 'does not force upon an audience a single finalized perspective, but instead offers a provocative "picture" which preserves complexity and multiplicity, retaining some degree of openness and ambiguity' (Douglas & Carless, 2013, p. 57).

As an initial interpretation, the collective art models in Turkey not only serve as a platform for a shared artistic vision but also meet a major need for emotional solidarity with others, especially at times of social and political pressures and constraints. I identify this need specifically as expressing oneself, feeling heard, feeling accepted, connected, and safe. As some artists have expressed in our interviews, the fast-changing political climate and rising cases of censorship against freedom of thought in Turkey leave many people (in this case artists) lonely, and frustrated where collectivity provides a safe atmosphere to meet the emotional needs:

> Collectives produce spaces and relationships to breathe, to belong, to survive, to struggle and to hold on to life with the warmth of solidarity within the endless labour exploitation of capitalism, which isolates individuals, impoverishes them in every sense, or within the conditions of living based on property.
> (Artıkişler Collective, personal communication, April 2020)

> When we are together, we can create a 'normal' time. Time without tensions, hatred or ugliness of politics. That time period is an independent

> zone for us. We spoil each other to talk about something nice, it's a huge luxury to talk about beauty, dreams…simple things. The world is burning, we always feel responsible, we feel desperate, while we are together, we make that isolated bubble which we can breathe in.
> (HAH, personal communication, March 2020)

My second interpretation is that once the collective members connect and meet their own emotional needs, such as expressing themselves freely and being heard, they also extend this connection to art audiences by producing participatory and dialogue-based works involving others. In an environment where freedom of speech is limited, dialogue-based artworks serve as platforms, dialogue-based art practices can therefore become safe zones both for the artists and other people from different segments of society to express themselves, hear one another, and connect with each other.

> Change cannot happen, if we stay in the same group. For us, to overcome that, that's why we do interactive stuff. Catching little instances. In our last performance, we didn't perform as the three of us but we invited people to move the circle with us. We also decided to open up to other cities. Like we went to Adana. It opened our eyes when we did something in Çanakkale for example. There are less events there, so people are really involved. We had a discussion. It was so enriching. Here everyone has prejudices. We want to go to Artvin too.
> (dadans, personal communication, March 2020)

'I learned here the importance of togetherness. It's a chance. We really can team together and share everything' (Bahar Güneş, Halka Art Project, personal communication, March 2020).

My third interpretation is that dialogue-based art holds the potential to connect people and thus transform society. In our final meeting, the artist collectives expressed that our research process and the exhibition had solidified their collective identity, made them feel recognized and encouraged them to produce more participatory works in their future process. I contend that these dialogue-based art holds the potential to connect people and thus transform the society.

Finally, critical dialogue and the dialogical approach in my research first started between myself and the collectives, which then through the works produced in the process wider communication with the community was facilitated. I see my role an instigator of this process. I was glad to hear from the collectives that my openness helped them trust me and the project throughout the process which has also instigated more trust in myself about my work and its potential impacts.

The same principles and working methodology of our small-scale collaborative and participatory artistic research can be applied in larger contexts

Figure 11.1 Group image from our exhibition, together with the participant artists. September 2017. Photo: Işıl Eğrikavuk

within the arts, as long as the emotional aspects are systematically recognized. More dialogue-based approaches within the arts are needed, especially at this moment and now, which requires a re-thinking of roles, positions, and methodologies of art and art making, and embracing the potential that comes from a dialogue-based approach (Figure 11.1).

Note

1 http://www.complaintschoir.org/ Last access: 05 May 2020.

References

Ahmed, S. (2017). *Living a feminist life*. Durham: Duke University Press.
Akkermans, A. (2016, May 17). *Turkish Government Censors Video Projection and Youth Biennial Artworks*. https://hyperallergic.com/297665/turkish-government-censors-video-projection-and-youth-biennial-artworks/
Aksoy, A. (2017). What Emerged in the Gezi Park Occupation in Istanbul? In O. Hemer & H. Persson (Eds.), *In the Aftermath of Gezi: From Social Movement to Social Change?* (pp. 17–34). Cham: Springer International Publishing.
Batuman, B. (2015). Everywhere Is Taksim. *Journal of Urban History*, 41(5), 881–907. doi: 10.1177/0096144214566966

Douglas, K., & Carless, D. (2013). An Invitation to Performative Research. *Methodological Innovations Online*, 8(1), 53–64. doi: 10.4256/mio.2013.0004

Eslen-Ziya, H., & Mcgarry, A., & Jenzen, O., & Erhart, I., & Korkut, U. (2019). From Anger to Solidarity: The Emotional Echo-Chamber of Gezi Park Protests. *Emotion, Space and Society*, 33, 100632. doi: 10.1016/j.emospa.2019.100632

Feyerabend, P. K. (1975). *Against Method*. London: Verso.

Freire, P. (1970). *Pedagogy of the Oppressed*. New York: Bloomsbury Academic.

Hannula, M. (2004). River Low, Mountain High : Contextualizing Artistic Research. In A. W. Balkema & H. Slager (Eds.), *Artistic research* (pp. 70–79). Amsterdam: Rodopi.

Hannula, M., Suoranta, J., & Vadén, T. (2005). *Artistic Research: Theories, Methods and Practices*. Helsinki: Academy of Fine Arts.

Haseman, B. (2006). A Manifesto for Performative Research. *Media International Australia incorporating Culture and Policy*, no. 118, 98–106. doi: 10.1177/1329878x0611800113

Jackson, S. (2011). *Social Works: Performing Art, Supporting Publics*. New York: Routledge.

Keller, S. I. (1968). *The Urban Neighbourhood, a Sociological Perspective*. New York: Random House.

Kester, G. (1999). *Dialogical Aesthetics: A Critical Framework for Littoral Art, Grant Kester*. https://www.variant.org.uk/9texts/KesterSupplement.html

Kester, G. H. (2004). *Conversation Pieces: Community and Communication in Modern Art*. Berkeley: University of California Press.

Kester, G. (2005). *Conversation Pieces: The Role of Dialogue in Socially-Engaged Art*. In Z. Kocur & S. Leung (Eds.), *Theory in Contemporary Art Since 1985* (pp. 153–166). Chichester: Wiley-Blackwell. http://www.publicart.usf.edu/CAM/exhibitions/2008_8_Torolab/Readings/Conversation_PiecesGKester.pdf

Kuyumlu, M. (2013, June 25). *Reclaiming the right to the city: Reflections on the urban uprisings in Turkey*. Retrieved October 30, 2020, from https://www.tandfonline.com/doi/full/10.1080/13604813.2013.815450

Lacy, S. (1995). *Mapping the Terrain: New Genre Public Art*. Seattle, WA: Bay Press.

McGarry, A., & Erhart, I., & Eslen-Ziya, H., & Jenzen, O., & Korkut, U. (2020). *The Aesthetics of Global Protest: Visual Culture and Communication*. Amsterdam: Amsterdam University Press.

Mouffe, C. (2007, Summer). ART&RESEARCH. Retrieved November 03, 2020, from https://chisineu.files.wordpress.com/2012/07/biblioteca_mouffe_artistic-activism.pdf

Nanay, B. (2019). *Aesthetics: A Very Short Introduction*. Oxford: Oxford University Press.

Nevannlina, t. (2004). Is Artistic Research a Meaningful Concept? In A. W. Balkema & H. Slager (Eds.), *Artistic Research* (pp. 80–83). Amsterdam: Rodopi.

Malzacher, F., Faucheret, A., Kaup-Hasler, V., Kirsch, K., Peternell, A. R., & Rainer, J. (Eds.). (2015). *Truth Is Concrete: A Handbook for Artistic Strategies in Real Politics*. Berlin: Sternberg Press.

Peters, S. (2015). Being Many. In F. Malzacher, A. Faucheret, V. Kaup-Hasler, K. Kirsch, A. R. Peternell, & J. Rainer (Eds.), *Truth is Concrete: A Handbook for Artistic Strategies in Real Politics* (pp. 129–131). Berlin: Sternberg Press.

Potuoğlu-Cook, Ö. (2015). Hope with Qualms: A Feminist Analysis of the 2013 Gezi Protests. https://journals.sagepub.com/doi/full/10.1057/fr.2014.56

Reynolds, R. (2012). *Guerrilla Gardening*. The Guerrilla Gardening Homepage. http://www.guerrillagardening.org/ggblog33.html

Schechner, R. (2003). *Performance Studies: An Introduction*. London: Routledge.

12 Resonance in intercultural encounters

Mapping a critical perspective on communication in pluralised societies

Theresa Klinglmayr

Current challenges of living together in pluralised societies shaped by processes of globalisation and immigration require new perspectives on the part of intercultural communication studies. Given the 'super-diversity' (Vertovec, 2007) of our current living together, the dichotomous notion of distinct and behaviour-determining (mostly national) cultures that have significantly shaped the tradition of intercultural communication studies is no longer unrestrictedly tenable, if it ever was. In this chapter, I will discuss an approach to intercultural resonance that holds descriptive as well as normative potentials. In its more descriptive dimension, resonance addresses interactional dynamics at the micro-level of communication. As a normative concept, resonance allows for difference-sensitive forms of collectivity at a societal macro-level that go beyond traditional notions of *interculturality* and *integration*. Within this scope, it is not possible to reconstruct the debates around multiculturalism and interculturalism (see, e.g., Barrett, 2013; Meer & Modood, 2012). However, it is important to note that the idea of integration, as 'the incorporation of minority cultural groups into mainstream society through a two-way interaction process' (Barrett, 2013, p. 26), connected to the paradigm of interculturalism, has gained widespread approval in the public discourse of European countries. At the same time, critics of the term observe an essentialist notion of one-sided adaptation processes (Perchinig, 2012) as well as a 'problematization of migrant others' (Schinkel, 2018, p. 2), or more specifically, of 'their culture'.

Intercultural communication, a field with its normative foundations with the aim of mutual understanding between people who perceive each other as 'different', could contribute substantially to these societal issues by addressing current public debates around cultural diversity and integration from a critical stance. However, as Giuliana Ferri notes, 'intercultural communication still relies on neat classifications of cultural difference and unquestioned definitions of otherness while some of the most complex and contested challenges gripping contemporary multicultural societies are left unexamined' (Ferri, 2018, p. 6). Despite the frequent observation of a *critical turn* in intercultural communication studies, postpositivist, neo-essentialist approaches, relying on seemingly objective national and mutually distinct 'large cultures',

DOI: 10.4324/9781003389972-15

are still common within theory and methodology in the field (Holliday & MacDonald, 2020, p. 621). Many research agendas are shaped by what Fred Dervin calls a '*differentialist bias*', a strong focus on differences while neglecting commonalities, accompanied by 'an overreliance on culture and language' as analysis categories (Dervin, 2017, pp. 63–64). One conceptual problem that arises is the isolation of situations defined as 'intercultural' by presupposing a significant (cultural) difference between the individuals involved and by assuming that this difference is the most important aspect of that situation (Scollon & Scollon, 1996, p. 267). Given the worldwide dynamics of 'ethnoscapes', a term coined by Arjun Appadurai (1990) to describe the global and shifting movements of people, there is a need to acknowledge the increasingly hybrid cultural affiliations and identity negotiations that are (re-)produced, undermined and transformed not only by migrants but also by people who consider themselves as members of a so-called 'majority society'. Building on this critique, I suggest that the paradigm of interculturalism and the respective concept of communication need to be broadened in favour of a more extensive approach to intercultural understanding that goes beyond one-sided demands for integration or acculturation and that addresses complex sociocultural realities. To do so, I first discuss the main objections formulated by critical and feminist scholars when it comes to theorising 'the intercultural'. In the next step, I advocate for a processual, power-sensitive perspective that focuses on the potential for *resonance* emerging from manifold experiences of sociocultural difference. Based on this understanding, I outline why the widely promoted concepts of *intercultural competence* and *dialogue* have limitations when addressing contemporary issues in highly diverse societies. As an additional perspective, a resonance-inspired approach offers a normative perspective for living and acting together in pluralised societies that understands collectivity less in terms of homogeneous cultures and more in relation to manifold experiences of difference.

Making strangers: powerful discourses of intercultural communication

The theoretical perspective outlined here follows critical approaches that understand intercultural communication as a co-constructed, power-related, intersectional and subject-constituting social practice (see, e.g., Dervin, 2011; Ferri, 2018; Holliday & MacDonald, 2020; Martin & Nakayama, 1999; Scollon & Scollon, 1996). Within the scope of this chapter, it is only possible to highlight a few key insights of this research strand and the respective consequences for an approach to intercultural resonance. According to Tom Nakayama, intercultural communication is a genuinely political and practice-oriented research area (Collier et al., 2001, pp. 222–224). Those who enter the field find themselves within a 'risky terrain' that 'deals with other cultures and peoples and has the potential to have tremendous impact on how people might think about, understand, deal with, and make policy regarding these other cultural groups' (Collier et al., 2001, p. 222). In contemporary societies, not only are these effects relevant to everyday action but the very assumption of 'other cultural groups' needs to be questioned as such. Individuals find themselves within heterogeneous sociocultural formations shaped by national, cultural and societal affiliations, by discourses of culture as well as by social practices on the micro-level. This entanglement of heterogeneous elements requires us to reflect on what *intercultural* means in a pluralised society, how it is represented in discourses and how it emerges in the everyday experiences of different people. In contemporary societies, I argue, the intercultural sphere is shaped by discourses of 'integration' that have the tendency to reproduce a holistic and homogenising notion of cultures and to assume linear processes of immigrants' adaptation into the host society. This criticism also applies when alternative concepts such as *cross-cultural* or *transcultural* are used to describe societal phenomena with political implications. Very often, the respective discourse revolves around an essentialist notion of separate, homogeneous cultures and their 'clashes', which is a limited assumption that represents lived realities in an under-complex way. In view of such powerful discourses, communication needs to be considered as a reality-constituting force that 'involves the creating, constitution, and intertwining of situated meanings, social practices, structures, discourses, and the nondiscursive' (Halualani & Nakayama, 2010, p. 7). Culture, then, is 'a larger social formation constituted by communicative meaning-making practices' (Halualani & Nakayama, 2010, p. 7). As a consequence, intercultural communication goes beyond the process suggested by classical definitions of (mostly interpersonal and face-to-face) communication between individuals with different origins in terms of culture, nations and languages (e.g., Arasaratnam, 2015; Gudykunst, 2002). Even though these studies, many of them having their origins in interpersonal communication theories, offer explanations for cultural differences in communication practices, they often rely on positivist viewpoints and binary representations of cultural differences (Chuang, 2003, p. 25). Here, the legacy of Edward T. Hall and Geert Hofstede continues to have an impact, especially when it comes to the notion of cultural patterns such as high/low context cultures, uncertainty avoidance, power distance and the individualism/collectivism dichotomy (Chuang, 2003, p. 25).

Within the 'postpositivist paradigm' (Holliday & MacDonald, 2020, p. 634), the key criterion for defining a situation as *intercultural* is cultural difference: Whereas '[m]onocultural communication is *similarity-based*', as Milton Bennett states, 'intercultural communication is *difference-based*' and thus an 'essentially *unnatural*' process (Bennett, 2013, p. 5). However, in today's societies, these 'unnatural' forms of communication are becoming more and more the 'normality' of living together, although not in all areas and not for all groups of people in the same way. By this, I do not claim that all communication is per se intercultural. My concern is to adopt a phenomenological perspective on forms of communication that are shaped by an (inter-)

subjective experience of cultural difference. This experienced difference is not a given reality, but the result of preliminary social relations that produce different others as 'strangers' through processes of inclusion and exclusion (Ahmed, 2000, p. 5). It is because of the hidden nature of this discursive construction, as Sara Ahmed argues, that subjects appear to others as already 'known' human beings that can be described by certain character traits even before encountering them (Ahmed, 2000, p. 5). These different others are always already 'misplaced' bodies (Ahmed, 2000, p. 55) in the sense that 'they' inhabit places considered as 'our' homeland:

> 'Others become strangers (the ones who are distant), and "other cultures" become "strange cultures" (the ones who are distant), only through coming *too close to home*, that is, through the proximity of the encounter or "facing" itself'. (Ahmed, 2000, p. 12)

This notion is especially true for contemporary societies, where migrants are discursively constructed and perceived as strangers through *encounters* not only in the sense of face-to-face meetings but of a co-presence of human or nonhuman elements that are mediated by different other encounters, faces, bodies, places and temporalities (Ahmed, 2000, p. 7). Focussing on the encounter itself means trying to capture 'the wildness of variables in cultural lives' (Alexander et al., 2014, p. 73) that surface within 'the *-inter*, or the immanent and processual space of the intercultural' (Ferri, 2018, p. 74). Instead of building on assumptions of separate and homogeneous cultures and individuals acting as their representatives, intercultural encounters have a reality-constituting and subject-forming function: 'entering the inter', as Aimee Carrillo Rowe describes it, allows us to capture 'a process of becoming that is constituted *between* subjects, who, in engaging the inter are, in turn, reconstituted through their exchange' (Rowe, 2010, p. 216). By focusing more on the *inter* than on the *cultural*, the processual, dynamic character of intercultural communication is put at the centre of theoretical thinking (Ferri, 2018). This intermediate sphere is not some equalising space where differences are 'celebrated', but a highly ambiguous, contradictory one:

> The inter points to a process vexed with contradictions: a generative site of learning and yet one that can never be mastered; the spectre of difference that haunts, even as it invites us to interrogate the privilege of alleged sameness; a space most productively approached with humility and a *yearning* for an/other that inspires us to move to and through a space where we are not the expert.
> (Rowe, 2010, p. 216)

The encounter is not a 'level playing field' but it is infused with power relations and takes place within structures of privilege and marginality (Rowe, 2010, p. 216). In this regard, 'theories of the encounter/between' (Alexander et al., 2014, p. 74) necessarily need to include embodied aspects of difference, namely, the attribution of cultural otherness to certain bodies and the consequences for the lived realities of the people concerned (Alexander et al., 2014, p. 74). Interculturality is not merely a discursive construct but refers to concrete perceptions of other bodies and therefore must be examined from an intersectional perspective that 'requires taking into account the combination and interrelation of elements such as language, social status, gender and so forth' (Dervin, 2017, p. 64). Culture, then, is always intertwined with power, which is why Halualani and Nakayama, referring to Stuart Hall (1985), describe it as 'an assemblage of meanings and representations that are vested with or are reified and spoken via different power interests, most notably by dominant structures [...] and cultural groups themselves' (Halualani & Nakayama, 2010, p. 7). Similarly, communication is not 'some equalising, neutral channel of expression', but consists of meaning-making practices of articulation which are constitutive of culture (Halualani & Nakayama, 2010, p. 7). Therefore, it would be short-sighted to examine interactions between members of different cultures without considering the unequal resources and social positions that they have. Starting from these assumptions, I propose in the following section a first outline of an approach to *intercultural resonance* that tries to capture those dynamics that have hitherto been in a marginalised position within intercultural scholarship.

Dynamics of resonance: capturing relational modes in intercultural encounters

Building on the notion of intercultural communication as a power-infused and (often) unpredictable social practice, I argue for an extensive approach to address issues that arise in situations infused with experienced differences. In view of the previous argumentation that intercultural encounters are heterogeneous, multifaceted and intersectional, it seems justified to ask whether something like interculturality can exist at all. In other words, what are the key defining features of intercultural communication? In contemporary societies, experiences of difference are so manifold that a distinct separation of *intra*cultural and *inter*cultural can hardly be maintained. Instead of striving for a clear definition, I adopt a phenomenological perspective according to which those situations are called intercultural which are infused with (inter-)subjective experiences of sociocultural difference. Such a definition includes encounters that cannot be considered as per se *cultural*, but that are shaped by an entanglement of individual, relational, situational, discursive and structural elements. The main interest lies not in cultural differences as such, but rather in how individuals perceive each other as different and how the concept of culture arises in social actions (Scollon & Scollon, 2001, p. 545). Based on these assumptions, I aim to outline the first steps towards an approach to *intercultural resonance* inspired by recent critical theory (Rosa, 2019), affect studies (Mühlhoff, 2019) and social-phenomenological approaches (Miller, 2015).

Resonance, a term coming from physics, serves as a theoretical metaphor for specific relational qualities of encounters, whereby it has two main analytical functions: For descriptive and interaction-focused purposes, resonance captures 'a type of relational dynamics of affecting and being affected' (Mühlhoff, 2019, p. 189). In a more normative sense, resonance refers to encounters and relationships that are experienced in a positive and meaningful way, whereby the respective evaluation must be made by the involved individuals (Rosa, 2019). The concept offers potential for intercultural communication because it allows going beyond rationalist notions of mutual understanding, gaining competence or fostering dialogue. A resonance perspective builds on the assumption that individuals are affected by others even before they consciously enter an intercultural situation. Additionally, it includes both rational, understanding-oriented as well as affective-emotive, bodily aspects of communication. Resonance, in the sense of Hartmut Rosa's approach to critical theory, describes 'a kind of relationship to the world' (Rosa, 2019, p. 174) that is strongly based on processes of affect and emotion as well as on the recognition of difference. Inspired by this framework, *intercultural resonance* can be described as both fleeting and temporal as well as longer-term 'responsive relationship[s]' (Rosa, 2019, p. 174), thus opposed to mere 'echo' relationships, that emerge within encounters shaped by experienced sociocultural differences. Intercultural resonance includes processes of being affected by different others, establishing emotional connections and experiencing transformative moments (Rosa, 2019, p. 174). As such, intercultural resonance, in a broad sense, can be defined as an experience of being heard and being affected by different others. It is decisive here that 'resonance [...] precisely does *not* mean harmony or consonance, but rather refers to a process of *responding, moving, touching*' (Rosa, 2019, p. 219). Such a perspective on relational dynamics, I argue, can be applied to interculturality as ways of living and acting together in diverse societies not only on the micro-level of interactions but also on the macro-level of societal discourse.

On a *micro-level of interactions*, resonance presupposes a notion of interculturality as a situational dynamic that evolves in encounters 'premised on the absence of a knowledge that would allow one to control the encounter, to predict its outcome' (Ahmed, 2000, p. 8). Relational dynamics rather lie beyond the control of single individuals and are mostly unpredictable. Consequently, the status of the capable self is questioned, and greater agency is ascribed to the other who can affect the self. As Vincent Miller points out, '[r]esonance is *an experience created in the moment*, as a temporary, ad-hoc, or fleeting form of meaningful association' (Miller, 2015, 8.4). In affect studies, resonance is defined as 'a dynamically and inter-affectively co-constituted quality of being-in-relation' (Mühlhoff, 2019, p. 190) that emerges within 'instances of connection, motion, and amplification' (Paasonen, 2020, p. 50). Therefore, meeting different others has a surprising potential, since the conduct of speech and behaviour of the other cannot be anticipated. Thus, uncontrollability goes hand in hand with a focus on the bodily dimension of encounters. Resonance '*is embodied and experienced in physical co-presence*' (Miller, 2015, 8.4) and emerges between bodies that are entangled in affective constellations. Intercultural encounters necessarily involve the presence of bodies within 'affective arrangements' (Slaby, 2019), whereby different origins, properties and abilities are – often in a racialised manner – ascribed to those bodies. Therefore, the affective dynamics and felt emotions within an encounter are inextricably entangled with genuinely physical experiences of perceiving others. At the same time, language plays a crucial role 'in its capacity to affect and to be affected, through different speech acts or even single words, [it] establishes dynamics of affective resonance, in both consonant and dissonant ways' (Fleig & Scheve, 2020, p. 6). On the *macro-level* of societal discourse, intercultural resonance requires the recognition of different others, mainly on the side of members of a so-called majority or dominant culture. Recognition, here, does not refer to an unconditional acceptance of *all* attitudes and ways of living, but to the concession that other subjects are equally multi-layered and contradictory human beings like oneself. What can be termed a 'dispositional resonance' (Rosa, 2019, p. 190) or an 'ability to not understand' (Gurevitch, 1989, p. 161) goes hand in hand with a willingness to let change happen – not only in interpersonal encounters but also on broader levels of living together. This transformative moment does not include the attempt to make the unfamiliar adaptable by, for example, gaining knowledge about specific cultures or behaviours, but rather refers to a basic openness for something and somebody one does not know (yet). Resonance relations depend on sociocultural and material conditions that Rosa (2019, p. 166) calls 'resonant spaces'. It is decisive here that these spaces are not based on the equality of all involved individuals but are shaped by certain situational, socioeconomic, political and historical contexts. Power dynamics and different subject positions define who is capable of speaking (in a very broad sense), who is heard, and who has the possibility to achieve resonance. Despite these individually heterogeneous preconditions, discourses of intercultural coexistence, in their specific manifestations within different societies, are powerful frameworks that shape intercultural encounters, be it face-to-face or within wider-range-mediated contexts. For example, discourses of integration influence the way how people, who are directly affected by these discourses and the respective polities, are expected to act within certain situations that are in turn shaped by structures of dominance between the so-called major society and immigrants. As a result, the phenomenologically oriented principle that the emergence of resonance is a matter of (inter-)subjective evaluation needs to be bound to the awareness that subjective experiences are highly heterogeneous and are based on different preconditions resulting from more or less privileged or disadvantaged subject positions. It is therefore problematic, as I try to outline in the next section, to assume that 'successful' communication across differences is solely a matter of the capable self that rationally acts *on* cultural others.

Acting *with* different others: beyond the competent self

Based on the perspective outlined in the previous sections, *resonance* is considered a specific *relational mode* in intercultural encounters on interpersonal as well as collective levels of living and acting together. Such a perspective aims to supplement current normative approaches to *intercultural competence (or learning)* and *intercultural dialogue*. While both concepts, as parts of a growing 'intercultural industry' (Ferri, 2014, p. 9), have provided important insights into key issues of intercultural communication, they also show limitations. *Intercultural competence* generally refers to '*effective* and *appropriate* behaviour and communication in intercultural situations' (Deardorff, 2011, p. 66) or, more recently, to '*improving human interactions across difference*' (Deardorff, 2020, p. 5). Competence models are based on the underlying assumption of a linear and goal-oriented learning process undergone by a rationally acting individual. In doing so, they ignore that intercultural learning is rarely a straightforward development, but rather a fragile, lifelong process marked by recurring failure. For example, a seemingly 'interculturally competent' individual who is convinced to hold extensive knowledge about 'a culture' still can hold deep prejudices against people ascribed to that culture. Conversely, listening to the personal story of a different other can affect someone emotionally even though there seemed to be no commonalities in the first place. Intercultural competence, when promoted 'as a miraculous technology' that helps people to respect other cultures and to be tolerant neglects the problem 'that intercultural phenomena [...] cannot always be grasped, controlled and/or explained' (Dervin, 2017, p. 67). Additionally, competence models within a postpositivist (Holliday & MacDonald, 2020, p. 621) or functionalist (Martin & Nakayama, 2010, p. 60) paradigm are often based on a 'neo-essentialist attribution of cultural difference to the other' who are perceived as mere objects, while the self as acting subject should be enabled to handle the strangeness of those others (Ferri, 2018, p. 8). For example, members of dominant cultures who can afford to go abroad as sojourners or travellers for a short time period usually have better access to and profit more from intercultural competence programs compared to those who lack similar resources (Cooks, 2001, p. 342). These 'asymmetric relations' (Cooks, 2001, p. 342) are reflected in discourses that consider immigrants culturally different and therefore in need of learning, which can contribute to an ethnocentric view of cultural superiority (Holliday & MacDonald, 2020, p. 626).

Intercultural dialogue refers to the 'open and respectful exchange of views between individuals and groups that have different cultural affiliations, on the basis of equality' (Barrett, 2013, p. 26). As a politically relevant concept, intercultural dialogue suggests the possibility of an equal, deliberative exchange of opinions between members of different cultures. While this may be a desirable ideal, the concept of dialogue is problematic due to its often depoliticised character (Phipps, 2014). Alison Phipps criticises that intercultural dialogue 'avoids any attempt to engage with political issues which are root causes of conflicts' and thereby becomes 'a servant of the status quo' that conceals power relations and exclusion faced by marginalised individuals and groups (Phipps, 2014, p. 111). From a postcolonial stance, Gayatri Chakravorty Spivak offers a pointed critique of the idealised imagination that accompanies dialogue approaches:

> [A] neutral communication situation of free dialogue [...] is not a situation that ever comes into being – there is no such thing. The desire for neutrality and dialogue, even as it should not be repressed, must always mark its own failure. The idea of neutral dialogue is an idea which denies history, denies structure, denies the positioning of subjects.
> (Spivak, 1990, p. 72)

Along with this neglect of unequal preconditions, the rhetoric of dialogue, despite striving for mutual understanding, has an underlying tendency to engage in a rhetoric of othering by ascribing distinctive characteristics to those people that should be reached by dialogic means. Even if there is an 'emphasis placed on transformation and dialogue over the simple acquisition of competence', it is still the other who is 'identified with a foreign language and culture' and whom 'we' should tolerate (Ferri, 2014, p. 13). Additionally, the framework conditions for intercultural dialogue are determined by a dominant culture that defines the setting, the prerequisites of participants and the desired goals of such a dialogue.

Although it is not possible to have an in-depth discussion here, it can be summarised that notions of competence and dialogue, while having contributed to a better understanding of the cultural dimension of social interactions, tend to fit into a framework that Ahmed (2007, p. 326) calls 'a managerial focus on diversity [that] works to individuate difference' and therefore run the risk of underestimating the complexity and multidimensionality of intercultural encounters. Not only do such concepts often neglect power issues that influence interaction but they also focus on a seemingly rationally acting self that needs to 'cope with' cultural otherness. It is the active self that *acts on* others, while those others are more in a passive role of *reacting*. In contrast, intercultural resonance emerges out of an *acting with* others who are mutually open to each other's perspectives. Thereby, instead of overemphasising the acquisition of knowledge about 'other cultures', the focus shifts to the importance of difference-based interactions themselves as well as to the agency of others. As a normative framework, I suggest describing the relational qualities of intercultural encounters along a *resonance-alienation-continuum*. As a relational mode, resonance – either in the form of consonance or dissonance – is opposed to *alienation*, which is characterised by indifference or hostility (repulsion) and therefore by the absence of communication (Rosa, 2019, p. 184; Jaeggi, 2014). Relations of resonance or alienation are not so much an issue of gaining competence or striving for dialogue but of emotional connections and situational dynamics. Resonance genuinely is about *listening* and *being heard* (in interpersonal communication as well as in public discourse), and as such it describes a dynamic that strongly depends on the power positions the involved individuals or groups hold.

Outlook and open questions

The aim of this chapter was to outline a critical perspective on intercultural communication that has descriptive as well as normative implications by using the concept of *resonance*. Building on feminist critique, it was argued that instead of reproducing essentialising and homogenising notions of culture, intercultural scholarship could benefit from emphasising the situational and affect-grounded dynamics of communication. As a consequence, models of intercultural competence and dialogue can be supplemented by a perspective that prioritises emotion over knowledge as well as *acting with* others over *acting on* others. A resonance approach aims to sharpen the focus on power issues by integrating micro- and macro-levels of intercultural communication, i.e., the context-dependent interactions and the broader societal discourses. Current political discourses of *integration* show a lack of resonance potential since they are based on a logic of cultural adaptation of 'others' towards the host society and thereby neglect the complexity of cultural affiliations within a society. Here, the question arises to which extent resonance experiences within interpersonal communication can have a subversive potential – an issue that needs to be examined by connecting research on micro- and macro-levels in detail. Despite the analytical potential the concept of resonance holds for intercultural communication, some questions need to be discussed in depth. First, the phenomenological approach to experiences of cultural difference adopted here raises the question which forms of communication in a diverse society are *not* intercultural ones. In other words, what are the key defining characteristics of interculturality? Additionally, it needs to be discussed how the normative dimension of resonance can be reconciled with its phenomenological claim. If resonance is perceived as something 'good' and desirable, we also need to ask who, under which circumstances, and for what purposes, defines the context-specific characteristics of resonance. As a first preliminary conclusion, the resonance framework offers the potential to examine intercultural communication as a form of acting together on different levels of society without reproducing cultural essentialism and homogenisation. Resonance enables us to think of interculturality starting from the encounter itself instead of presuming large and behaviour-determining cultures. Given these conditions, the concept is on the right track, to use the phrase of Joan W. Scott, to contribute to a 'theory that will let us think in terms of pluralities and diversities rather than of unities and universals' (Scott, 1988, p. 33) and thereby enrich the field of intercultural communication studies.

References

Ahmed, S. (2000). *Strange Encounters: Embodied Others in Post-Coloniality*. New York: Routledge.

Ahmed, S. (2007). The Language of Diversity. *Ethnic and Racial Studies*, 30(2), 235–256. doi: 10.1080/01419870601143927

Alexander, B. K., Arasaratnam, L. A., Flores, L., Leeds-Hurwitz, W., Mendoza, S. L., Oetzel, J., Osland, J., Tsuda, Y., & Halualani, J. Y. & R. (2014). Our Role as Intercultural Scholars, Practitioners, Activists, and Teachers in Addressing These Key Intercultural Urgencies, Issues, and Challenges. *Journal of International and Intercultural Communication*, 7(1), 68–99. doi: 10.1080/17513057.2014.869526

Appadurai, A. (1990). Disjuncture and Difference in the Global Cultural Economy. *Theory, Culture & Society*, 7(2), 295–310. doi: 10.1177/026327690007002017

Arasaratnam, L. A. (2015). Research in Intercultural Communication: Reviewing the Past Decade. *Journal of International and Intercultural Communication*, 8(4), 290–310. doi: 10.1080/17513057.2015.1087096

Barrett, M. (2013). Introduction – Interculturalism and Multiculturalism: Concepts and Controversies. In M. Barrett (Ed.), *Interculturalism and Multiculturalism: Similarities and Differences* (pp. 15–41). Strasbourg: Council of Europe Publishing.

Barrett, M. (Ed.) (2013). *Interculturalism and Multiculturalism: Similarities and Differences*. Strasbourg: Council of Europe Publishing.

Bennett, M. J. (2013). *Basic Concepts of Intercultural Communication: Paradigms, Principles and Practices* (2nd ed.). Boston & London: Intercultural Press.

Breninger, B., & Kaltenbacher, T. (Eds.) (2012). *Creating Cultural Synergies: Multidisciplinary Perspectives on Interculturality and Interreligiosity*. Cambridge: Cambridge Scholars Publishing.

Chuang, R. (2003). A Postmodern Critique of Cross-Cultural and Intercultural Communication Research: Contesting Essentialism, Positivist Dualism, and Eurocentricity. In W. J. Starosta, & G.-M. Chen (Eds.), *Ferment in the Intercultural Field: Axiology/Value/Praxis* (pp. 24–53). Thousand Oaks, CA: Sage.

Collier, M. J. (Ed.) (2001). *Transforming Communication About Culture: Critical New Directions*. Thousand Oaks, CA: Sage.

Collier, M. J., Hegde, R. S., Lee, W., Nakayama, T. K., & Yep, G. A. (2001). Dialogue on the Edges: Ferment in Communication and Culture. In M. J. Collier (Ed.), *Transforming Communication about Culture: Critical New Directions* (pp. 219–280). Thousand Oaks, CA: Thousand Oaks, CA: Sage.

Cooks, L. (2001). From Distance and Uncertainty to Research and Pedagogy in the Borderlands: Implications for the Future of Intercultural Communication. *Communication Theory*, 11(3), 339–351. doi: 10.1111/j.1468-2885.2001.tb00246.x

Dasli, M., & Díaz, R. (Eds.) (2017). *The Critical Turn in Language and Intercultural Communication Pedagogy: Theory, Research and Practice*. New York: Routledge.

Deardorff, D. K. (2011). Assessing Intercultural Competence. *New Directions for Institutional Research*, 149, 65–79. doi: 10.1002/ir.381

Deardorff, D. K. (2020). *Manual for Developing Intercultural Competencies: Story Circles*. London & New York: Routledge.

Dervin, F. (2011). A Plea for Change in Research on intercultural Discourses: A 'Liquid' Approach to the Study of the Acculturation of Chinese Students. *Journal of Multicultural Discourses*, 6(1), 37–52. doi: 10.1080/17447143.2010.532218

Dervin, F. (2017). Critical Turns in Language and Intercultural Communication Pedagogy: The Simple-Complex Continuum (*Simplexity*) as a New Perspective. In M.

Dasli & R. Díaz, (Eds.), *The Critical Turn in Language and Intercultural Communication Pedagogy: Theory, Research and Practice* (pp. 58–72). New York: Routledge.

Ferri, G. (2014). Ethical communication and intercultural responsibility: a philosophical perspective. *Language and Intercultural Communication*, 14(1), 7–23. doi: 10.1080/14708477.2013.866121

Ferri, G. (2018). *Intercultural Communication: Critical Approaches and Future Challenges*. Cham: Palgrave Macmillan.

Fleig, A., & Scheve, C. (2020). Introduction: Public spheres of resonance – constellations of affect and language. In A. Fleig, & C. Scheve (Eds.), *Public Spheres of Resonance: Constellations of Affect and Language* (pp. 1–16). London & New York: Routledge.

Fleig, A., & Scheve, C. (Eds.) (2020). *Public Spheres of Resonance: Constellations of Affect and Language*. London & New York: Routledge.

Gudykunst, W. B. (2002). Intercultural communication. In W. B. Gudykunst & B. Mody (Eds.), *Handbook of International and Intercultural Communication* (pp. 179–182). Thousand Oaks, CA: Sage.

Gurevitch, Z. D. (1989). The Power of Not Understanding: The Meeting of Conflicting Identities. *The Journal of Applied Behavioral Science*, 25(2), 161–173. doi: 10.1177/0021886389252006

Hall, S. (1985). Signification, Representation, Ideology: Althusser and the Post-Structuralists Debates. *Critical Studies in Mass Communication*, 2(2), 91–114. doi: 10.1080/15295038509360070

Halualani, R. T., & Nakayama, T. K. (2010). Critical Intercultural Communication Studies: At a Crossroads. In T. K. Nakayama, & R. T. Halualani (Eds.), *The Handbook of Critical Intercultural Communication* (pp. 1–16). Oxford: Wiley-Blackwell.

Holliday, A., & MacDonald, M. (2020). Researching the Intercultural: Intersubjectivity and the Problem with Postpositivism. *Applied Linguistics*, 41(5), 621–639. doi: 10.1093/ap-plin/amz006

Jaeggi, R. (2014). *Alienation*. New York: Columbia University Press.

Martin, J. M., & Nakayma, T. K. (1999). Thinking Dialectically About Culture and Communication. *Communication Theory*, 9(1), 1–25.

Martin, J. N., & Nakayama, T. K. (2010). Intercultural Communication and Dialectics Revisited. In T. Nakayama & R. T. Halualani (Eds.), *The Handbook of Critical Intercultural Communication* (pp. 59–839). Oxford: Wiley-Blackwell.

Meer, N., & Modood, T. (2012). How does Interculturalism Contrast with Multiculturalism? *Journal of Intercultural Studies*, 33(2), 175–196. doi: 10.1080/07256868.2011.618266

Miller, V. (2015). Resonance as a Social Phenomenon. *Sociological Research Online*, 20(2), 58–70. doi: 10.5153/sro.3557

Mühlhoff, R. (2019). Affective resonance. In J. Slaby, & C. Scheve (Eds.), *Affective Societies: Key Concepts* (pp. 189–199). London & New York: Routledge.

Nakayama, T. K., & Halualani, R. T. (Eds.) (2010). *The Handbook of Critical Intercultural Communication*. Oxford: Wiley-Blackwell.

Paasonen, S. (2020). Resonant Networks: On Affect and Social Media. In A. Fleig, & C. Scheve (Eds.), *Public Spheres of Resonance: Constellations of Affect and Language* (pp. 49–62). London & New York: Routledge.

Perchinig, B. (2012). The Construction of the "Third Country Other" in EU Integration Discourse. In B. Breninger, & T. Kaltenbacher (Eds.), *Creating Cultural*

Synergies: Multidisciplinary Perspectives on Interculturality and Interreligiosity (pp. 137–150). Cambridge: Cambridge Scholars Publishing.

Phipps, A. (2014): 'They Are Bombing Now': 'Intercultural Dialogue' in Times of Conflict. *Language and Intercultural Communication*, 14(1). doi: 10.1080/14708477.2013.866127

Rosa, H. (2019). *Resonance: A Sociology of Our Relationship to the World*. Cambridge: Polity Press.

Rowe, A. C. (2010). Entering the Inter: Power Lines in Intercultural Communication. In T. Nakayama, & R. T. Halualani (Eds.), *The Handbook of Critical Intercultural Communication* (pp. 216–226). Oxford: Wiley-Blackwell.

Schiffrin, D., Tannen, D., & Hamilton, H. E. (Eds.) (2001). *The Handbook of Discourse Analysis*. Oxford: Blackwell.

Schinkel, W. (2018). Against 'Immigrant Integration': For an End to Neocolonial Knowledge Production. *Comparative Migration Studies*, 31(6). doi: 10.1186/s40878-018-0095-1

Scollon, R., & Scollon, S. W. (1996). *Intercultural Communication: A Discourse Approach*. Oxford: Blackwell.

Scollon, R., & Scollon, S. W. (2001). Discourse and Intercultural Communication. In D. Schiffrin, D. Tannen, & H. E. Hamilton (Eds.), *The Handbook of Discourse Analysis* (pp. 538–547). Oxford: Blackwell.

Scott, J. W. (1988). Deconstructing Equality-Versus-Difference: Or, the Uses of Poststructuralist Theory for Feminism. *Feminist Studies*, 14(1), 33–50.

Slaby, J. (2019). Affective arrangement. In J. Slaby, & C. Scheve (Eds.), *Affective Societies: Key Concepts* (pp. 109–118). London & New York: Routledge.

Slaby, J., & Scheve, C. (Eds.) (2019). *Affective Societies: Key Concepts*. London & New York: Routledge.

Spivak, G. C. (1990). *The Post-Colonial Critic: Interviews, Strategies, Dialogues*. New York: Routledge.

Starosta, W. J., & Chen, G.-M. (Eds.) (2003). *Ferment in the Intercultural Field: Axiology/Value/Praxis*. Thousand Oaks, CA: Sage.

Vertovec, S. (2007). Super-diversity and Its Implications. *Ethnic and Racial Studies*, 30(6), 1024–1054. doi: 10.1080/01419870701599465

13 Acting together, reflecting together

Two ethnographic accounts of Jamaica's first 'pride event' in 2015

David Lowis and Simone Kimberly Harris

Introduction

'The Most Homophobic Place on Earth?': this is how *Time* magazine referred to Jamaica in 2006 (Padgett, 2006). To anyone not familiar with the country, this might seem surprising. Located in the Caribbean, this small island inhabited by around three million people is internationally well-known for its reggae music and the musician Bob Marley, its Rastafarian movement, the fastest Man in the World as well as for its mountainous scenery and beaches. Yet, Jamaica has been scrutinised by human rights organisations (Reynolds, 2014), LGBTQ organisations (J-FLAG et al., 2015), and international media (VICE, 2014) for social and legal discrimination against LGBTQ people. This discrimination has been especially visible following several widely publicised homicides – one such case being that of Dwayne Jones, a sixteen-year-old assigned male gender at birth who attended a party in women's clothes and was brutally murdered as a consequence (Reynolds, 2014). At the same time, there has been much academic debate about how to epistemologically move beyond a sole focus on homophobia in Jamaica and the Caribbean by centering the experiences of LGBTQ people themselves (Anderson & MacLeod, 2020). This chapter is one contribution to this endeavour, remembering and reflecting on a 2015 flash mob event that was widely branded as the first 'Gay Pride' event in Jamaica.

In 2015, this flash mob event which was part of a whole Pride Week was much publicised in international media, but less so in Jamaican and Caribbean media, resulting in narratives about it being constituted by external perspectives, mostly from the Global North. To an extent, global solidarity and joining the ranks of countries with Pride parades was the expressed purpose of the flash mob event. Yet, seven years later, we want to reframe the narratives around the flash mob event by providing two ethnographic accounts of it.

The idea for doing so sprang out of the authors of this chapter, Simone and David, who had both been present at the 2015 Pride, meeting again at an exhibition in Berlin in 2022. Simone is a Jamaican LGBTQ activist as well as an artist. She was the public 'Face of Pride' 2015, and one of the leading organisers and choreographers of the flash mob event. David is a researcher from Germany who conducted three months of ethnographic fieldwork with JFLAG, Jamaica's largest LGBTQ organisation, in the summer of 2015 in fulfilment of his undergraduate thesis. Meeting again in 2022 and reflecting on the brief moment in time that we shared in our personal histories, we wanted to try and think through the multiplicity of the 2015 flash mob together, as well as the impacts it has had and where it is now situated in the context of the current Jamaican, Caribbean, and global LGBTQ community.

Methodology

To remember the flash mob together, we each separately wrote an ethnographic account of it, based on our memory as well as, in David's case, field notes from 2015. We then read each other's accounts, and following this had multiple calls where we spoke about our shared recollections, discrepancies in how we perceived the event, as well as our evaluation of the flash mob in the context of our perspectives in 2022. This experimental methodology, situated within a body of work on the potentialities of shared memory and collaborative ethnography (Boyer & Marcus, 2020; Harris et al., 2011; Lassiter, 2008; May & Pattillo-McCoy, 2000; Stevenson, 2014), proved very productive for us. It allowed us to engage intensely with our understanding of the role the flash mob played in each of our development, and how we understand its relevance today. In particular, our ontological realities of being at home in Jamaica in Simone's case, and having been a brief guest in Jamaica in David's case served as a starting point to think through our material.

Ethnographers are constantly looking for ways through which to express and make visible the collaborative aspects of the practice of ethnography, in fact, the anthropologists Boyer and Marcus (2020) recently published a volume with different accounts of experimental collaborative ethnographic methodology. One tension at the heart of the question around ethnographic collaboration is one of equity: How can we develop products of ethnographic work that do not (re)assert the epistemological primacy of a single academic, setting out to study some unfamiliar group, place, or individual? While there have been exciting developments in the field of multimodal ethnography (Westmoreland, 2022), allowing the collaborative production of knowledge in various mediated formats, the question of how to take a similar approach in the context of academic writing remains.

As we began the process of developing this chapter, we wondered about this question, and about how to go about producing a shared written account of our ideas. We each had different experiences of Pride 2015, and simply merging them together in some way, or letting them sit side by side, removed from each other, did not feel like it would do justice to this. Instead, we wanted to recreate the dialogic process through which we had both been re-experiencing Pride 2015 and developing new ideas on the basis of our exchange. Consequently, we decided to structure this chapter much in the same way in which we had structured our collaborative process of recollection: Each of us sharing our memories of Pride 2015 individually, then laying out the ideas and discussions which had emerged from this sharing. Collective reflection, thinking through shared and non-shared experiences together, can be seen to 'hold an emancipatory potential because it provides opportunities to make visible social and cultural premises of a particular context that are often taken for granted' (Rantatalo & Karp, 2016, p. 710). We hope to make use of emancipatory potential with the help of our methodology.

In the following, we provide a short theoretical background, followed by the ethnographic accounts of Simone and David. Finally, we reflect together on the meanings and impacts of Pride 2015.

LGBTQ rights and identities – between Jamaica and a 'global community'

While homosexuality is not technically illegal in Jamaica, a colonial buggery law still prohibits anal intercourse as well as 'indecency between two men' (Long, n.d.). The law is rarely applied in practice but provides a legal basis for the anti-LGBTQ sentiments expressed by many Jamaican politicians, representatives of churches, and more generally on the island (Gilpin, 2016; Reynolds, 2014). While sexuality had long been muted in academic discussions about the Caribbean and was often subsumed within studies of gender and kinship, Sharpe and Pinto (2006) note in a review of the subject that this changed around the turn of the 21st century, with a whole volume on LGBTQ experiences in the Anglophone Caribbean being published in 2020 (Anderson & MacLeod, 2020). In her attempt at outlining something resembling a history of sexuality in the Caribbean, La Font (2001) notes that this very undertaking is necessarily fraught due to the lack of sustained historical documentation of slave sexuality. However, whilst in one of the only colonial reports available on the subject a group of enslaved peoples arriving in Barbados was described as 'Chaste [...] as any people under the Sun' (La Font, 2001), within colonial discourse the enslaved were soon denounced as morally deficient, especially with respect to sexuality. Exploitation specifically the sexual exploitation of enslaved women by the ruling elites was thereby justified. Afro-Jamaican enslaved peoples themselves viewed the ruling elites' well-documented sexual escapades as immoral, allowing them to assert their own moral superiority in the face of a lack of resources and power. A 'respectability politics' emerged from this complex, in which acting morally, especially in regard to sexuality, attained a high degree of importance. Once slavery was abolished, social mobility for the freed slaves depended to a large extent on 'moral character, respectability, and reputation' (La Font, 2001).

Questions of sexual (im)morality were key in justifications for the subordination of Afro-Jamaicans enslaved by the European elites, as well as in the foundation of the postcolonial Jamaican nation-state[1]. Heterosexuality is just as 'determined by the specificities of time, place, and culture, and thus by globalising forces' (Boellstorff, 2012, p. 179) as any other kind of sexuality, and the colonial project and its aftermath created a specific kind of heterosexuality in Jamaica centred on respectability. Discourses about LGBTQ people in Jamaica are set against the backdrop of the sexual mores which emerge out of this particular configuration of heterosexuality.

Anthropologist David Murray notes that scholars tend to reify the Caribbean as homophobic and violent, attributing to Caribbean nations a kind of exceptional homophobia as a 'pathological sociocultural trait' (2012, p. 5). However, analysing sexuality in the Caribbean always harbours a danger of 'reinscribing a discourse of negativity and hypersexuality onto the bodies of people who have been historically oversexualized through colonial and racist discourses' (Kempadoo, 2003, p. 62). If studies of sexuality can indeed be said to be always political, then theorising exceptional homophobia in Jamaica and the Caribbean is a problematic political move which at times resembles the old colonialist discourses about 'savage' sexuality, especially since the respective research is often carried out by academics from the Global North. The alternative to contributing to a discourse of exceptional homophobia in the Caribbean has often been to defer to 'culture', and to analyse 'local ethno-racial sexual identifications and practices that do not align neatly with Euro-American models of gender and sexuality' (Murray, 2012, p. 10). Yet, this kind of argument tends to reproduce the local/global dichotomy that Boellstorff (2005) has problematised. The cultural relativism often foundational to such accounts (Cooper, 2004; King, 2014) can also render a more critical stance towards the violence suffered by many LGBTQ people in the Caribbean difficult to articulate (Sharpe & Pinto, 2006). This is emblematic of wider tensions of situating sexuality, gender identity and the LGBTQ rights movement within global histories of colonialism, and global presents of coloniality (Boellstorff, 2012).

'Pride' as a banner has fast become one of the hallmarks of the international LGBTQ movement, with parades in cities around the world laying claim to the existence of the community itself and advocating for its societal acceptance. Modelled after the gay liberation marches in Chicago, San Francisco, and New York in 1970, Pride has since become a global cultural phenomenon, centred around celebratory parades which have become a site for the consolidation of the existence of an LGBTQ movement, tourism and economic development, as well as accusations of neo-colonialism and 'pinkwashing' (Greensmith & Giwa, 2013; Johnston, 2005; Krstić et al., 2020; Peterson et al., 2018). Pride parades have become signifiers (Enguix, 2009): cities and countries can polish their progressive credentials by playing host to them and accommodating them – or even larger gatherings such as 'World Pride' and 'Euro Pride' and LGBTQ communities in countries with less permissive legal and/or cultural norms regarding LGBTQ people have had widely publicised debates around whether to host Pride events, as well as an international backlash if there are incidents of violence at a parade or if a city makes the decision to stop having parades, such as the 2022 cancellation of

'EuroPride' in Belgrade, which laid in the open the political fault lines around LGBTQ rights in the country (Eror, 2022).[2]

It was within that particular tension that JFLAG, Jamaica's largest LGBTQ rights organisation, decided to organise a Pride Week, including a flash mob, in 2015. This was widely received by international media as 'Jamaica's First Pride' a label mostly embraced by JFLAG in spite of the fact that many events in prior years could well have fit under the 'Pride' umbrella. Rather than having a parade, which would have been politically contentious and prone to threats of violence, JFLAG decided on the Pride Week format, with the flash mob as its galvanising event aimed at celebrating visibility in the spirit of parades around the world. Other events, such as 'Sports Day' and a Pride Party, would round out the week. In the following two chapters, Simone and David relay their respective ethnographic accounts of the flash mob.

Ethnographic account of the flash mob: Simone's perspective

Recalling the Pride Jamaica Flash Mob, triggers feelings of exhilaration, intense anticipation, and memories of community solidarity. The flash mob was the first time I had experienced, in Jamaica, artistic modalities, specifically dance, being used as a tool for community engagement and public action. Seven years on, I am still exploring the formula that made the flash mob possible and how performance art, visibility, and our own ideas of 'community in action' intersect to create a sustainable impact in LGBTQ advocacy.

In 2015, I had been re-establishing myself in Jamaica, having lived in the USA for close to ten years. I did not want to hide my sexual identity to survive in Jamaica. At that time, JFLAG and Women's Empowerment for Change (WeCHANGE) were undertaking a series of LGBTQ advocacy training programmes, and I took the opportunity to get involved. In 2015, Kingston had reached a turning point in the struggle for LGBTQ equality, and I felt like I belonged to a movement that was ready to publicly fight for our rights as citizens. The possibility of removing Jamaica's anti-gay-legislation, challenging the stigma and discrimination that we faced was at the forefront of our minds. The gruesome murder of Dwayne Jones by a raging mob acting together required all of us to reflect on how we could harness our own energies as a community to confront the systems that were holding us hostage.

I recall early discussions about what would be branded as 'Jamaica's first Pride' in Kingston during the 'Emancipendence' period, August 1–7. The committee chose this period because it was thought that its historical significance was indicative of Jamaicans' ability to endure a harsh history while pushing back on the oppressive systems of that time. This resonated with me as a seventh-generation descendant of the Maroons and a member of the LGBTQ community. The Maroons fought the British for over 200 years to liberate us from slavery and I could not deny the feeling of excitement that grew inside me, we were, after all, in a war for equal rights as LGBTQ people.

We would be writing a new chapter in our histories and confronting the systems that sought to erase our existence.

I volunteered as a movement instructor at the Rainbow House, JFLAG's headquarters in Kingston. The dance studio was the dusty parking lot, but I quickly understood that this in itself was how, with limited resources, we could still create opportunities for safe spaces. These evening dance classes became the starting point of the flash mob. A few community members interested in exercise came together to move. This gathering was mirroring the optimism of the time allowing us to move through the trapped emotions of policing our bodies as LGBTQ persons in a society that demanded that we hide.

Very soon, the planning committee decided that a bold statement was needed for the opening day, 1 August 2015. We agreed that this would be a Flash mob. I would choreograph a dance routine that would be executed as a flash mob at the Redemption Song statue in the Emancipation Park in New Kingston. This bronze sculpture standing 11 feet tall features the bodies of a man and woman gazing to the skies symbolising their triumphant rise from the horrors of slavery. This would be our stage.

The flash mob's recruitment and rehearsals commenced almost immediately. We were more movers than dancers, but it was the process that was more important. – coming together as a community. I don't think we understood the potential impacts of what we were doing at the time, the process was satisfying, and the joy and connection felt like something revolutionary, that would finally free us from our colonial legacies.

I cannot recall every detail of planning for the flash mob, many things have faded with time, and I realise more and more that it is the emotions of the moment that I have retained for the past seven years. For example, from memory, I could not decipher whether the soundtrack to the flash mob was 'It's Carnival' or 'Fly' by Trinidadian soca artist Destra. And yet, as choreographer of the flash mob, I had chosen the song that inspired the moves that shaped our bodies in the space.

It was Soca, rather than Dancehall or Reggae that was the preferred genre for the flash mob soundtrack. The excitement we felt as a group was appropriately captured by the lyrics of Destra Garcia's 'It's Carnival'. As I listened to the lyrics, I could envision us as an army marching en masse down Hope Road, together, proclaiming our right to exist. This image grew more colourful with each passing day in all of our imaginations. The feeling was so electric in the lead-up to 1 August that even when we found ourselves in a Soca party and the song was played, we would perform the moves of the flash mob without fear, releasing our embodied memories of that moment of collective action. This song became a community anthem, a call to demonstrate our resilience as a community.

As the sun climbed over the horizon on the morning of 1 August 2015, it seemed that I was witnessing the dawning of my liberation as a queer Jamaican. The darkness of the night gave way to the warmth of the sun, and the anticipation of what was to come seemed to intensify the beauty of everything I saw on the short trip from my home to the Rainbow House. It appeared as if all things had aligned in our favour and our ancestors were urging us to act together. I was ready.

When the group arrived, we geared up in Pride paraphernalia provided by JFLAG. We were aware that the colours we wore would make us even more visible and that this would signal to any onlookers that we were members of the LGBTQ community. As the excitement grew, there were concerns from some corners, would everything go as planned? Would we be safe? JFLAG ensured that we were escorted by security agents, but this concern for our safety was something that had always followed us as queer people on the island. So, despite some concerns, we were ready.

I drove ahead of the bus, and I remember feeling very nervous as I parked at Emancipation Park. The location of the statues was in full view of the road, and we knew we had to go to work right away. We formed a circle around the Redemption Song statue, and I shouted '5, 6, 7, 8' and Destra's vocals shot up into the air; the rest was history. What we intended to be a five-minute flash mob lasted at least thirty minutes. My fear evaporated as adrenaline took hold. We repeated the routine around the statue while waving rainbow flags in glee. One of the most surprising moments came when a few cars that were driving by started to honk their horns and wave to us in a sign of solidarity. On the drive back to Rainbow House, some people hung outside the windows of the bus waving their pride flags and screaming happy pride!

Seven years on from this moment of acting together as a community I am asking myself: did it happen? Reliving this moment has pushed me to confront my feelings about the flash mob's impact beyond 1 August, did this message of demonstration of Pride – from Jamaica to the world reverberate the way we hoped it would?

Ethnographic account of the flash mob: David's perspective

I had arrived in Kingston a few weeks prior to the flash mob to work with JFLAG and conduct ethnographic research for my undergraduate thesis. It was partly the flash mob that had drawn my attention to Jamaica as a place to conduct research about LGBTQ people, mirroring the heightened international attention the flash mob afforded the Jamaican LGBTQ community. Working at the JFLAG office and preparing for Pride Week, which was to be kicked off by the flash mob, I was unsure what to expect. While JFLAG had branded the event under the global(ising) 'Pride' banner, they had chosen a flash mob as a more viable alternative to the parades that I had come to know from living in Germany and the UK. I had seen a group of people, headed by Simone, practising the dance for the flash mob, but despite being involved in the preparations, was unsure how it was going to go down.

On the day of the flash mob, I got to the JFLAG office at around 9 AM on a Saturday morning, about two weeks after I had arrived in Kingston.

As I walked into the front yard, loud music was playing from speakers that had been set up at one end of the lawn. Some people were dancing, others chatting, some just walking around busily, and a general feeling of excitement and anticipation was palpable. The office itself was packed with people walking about and yelling across the small rooms of the JFLAG office, and balloons and rainbow-coloured flags were all around. Rainbow-coloured shirts and feather boas were being handed out by JFLAG employees and the LED flashlights of smartphones and tablets were ubiquitous, ready to capture every moment for social media. A camera team for the American media company VICE was mingling with the participants, handing out release forms, attempting to get everyone's signature, just as Latoya, one of the event's organisers, strutted out of the office, wearing shutter shades and a rainbow Mohawk wig, signalling to everyone that it was time to leave. One by one, about forty of us crammed into a white bus, and we drove off.

Nikkia, who sat next to me on the bus, said out loud what I was thinking: 'We are about to make history!' We were going to stage the first-ever public LGBTQ pride event in Jamaica. The fact that we were going to put on this event on Emancipation Day, the Caribbean day celebrating the emancipation of slaves, in Emancipation Park in Kingston, was a deliberate nod to the slave liberation movement. In the back row, the camera team sat filming the chanting, shouting, and singing in the bus.

When the music turned on, we all got out of the bus, and instead of following the choreography that we had been practising, we all started dancing with whoever happened to be next to us, holding each other by the hands and laughing, as we sang along to Destra's 'It's Carnival'. We danced in a circle around the three-metre-high Redemption Song sculpture, comprised of the bodies of a naked black man and woman looking towards the sky, a monument celebrating the end of slavery. There were a few bystanders watching, but they were barely noticeable. The song ended quickly, and everyone started hugging each other and continued waving the flags around. And instead of going back to the bus and driving to the office as planned, someone turned the song on again. And for a second time, we danced around the fountain in Emancipation Park, even more ecstatic than before, and this time everyone took their mobile phones out, took pictures, and waved into the film crew's camera.

After this second performance, we took a group picture and then went back onto the bus. Some took their own cars and waved rainbow flags out the windows, and bus and car horns blew the entire way back. In the bus, people gave speeches; everyone was chanting, shouting that they were 'not slaves anymore' and 'a bit closer to freedom'. American pop singer Katy Perry's famous song 'I Kissed a Girl' started playing, and we all started singing the lyrics together. When the song was over, the bus driver put it on again. And again. And a fourth time. And we kept singing at the top of our voices. Only when we arrived back at the JFLAG office did the general feeling of excitement and ecstasy subside. People quietened down and got ready to leave. But not without someone shouting loudly when leaving the office that 'We have just made history!'

The flash mob event challenged the status quo in Kingston in which LGBTQ life was relegated to private spaces. A large group of LGBTQ people was thrust into the public sphere with the explicit aim of attracting attention. In the process, the event also aided in the creation of a community of Jamaican LGBTQ people. However, as Dave notes, '[o]ut of possibility come new forms of closure' (2011, p. 8). At the moment of consolidating a community, there will always be some excluded from this new venture. And in this case, those excluded seemed to be a remarkably large cohort. A group of around thirty to forty people attended the flash mob; of these people, an overwhelming majority were women, and many seemed to come from Kingston's upper middle class (although this observation has to be qualified, as it was impossible to speak to all people in attendance and their respective backgrounds). JFLAG's expressed mission was to represent the entire spectrum of LGBTQ people in Jamaica, and other events and outreach programmes conducted by JFLAG targeted a wide variety of groups of all genders and social classes – from self-identifying women and men to trans people, to homeless LGBTQ people. This cast a spotlight on the limited diversity of the group in attendance at the flash mob in terms of the community it actively sought to represent, summon up, and weld together. While the other, less public events that JFLAG had put on for Pride Week were well-frequented by diverse attendees, this was not the case with the flash mob. Perhaps just as important as recounting who was present at the flash mob, therefore, is the question of who was not there to partake in this foray into publicness and visibility, and why.

An easy assumption might be that it was a concern for safety that led some people, in particular men and lower-class Jamaicans, to stay away from the event. The potential dangers of being LGBTQ in Kingston increase exponentially once one is visibly LGBTQ in public, and fear of the potential implications of this did impact some people's decision not to attend. Jonathan, a gay student whom I met through the gay dating app Grindr, told me he would never consider going to the flash mob, or any other JFLAG event for that matter, for fear of being victimised as a result. I first met Jonathan in my first week in Kingston and met up with him a few times after that. He came from a not particularly privileged area of Ocho Rios, a tourist city in the north of Jamaica. Jonathan was always slightly on edge when talking about his, or anyone's, sexuality. In fact, when I first told him I was working with JFLAG, he suggested I should not tell anyone else, and to tell people I worked with a human rights agency instead, to avoid becoming the target of aggression. It was partly this fear that kept him away from the flash mob.

But fear was not the only reason people did not attend. I was surprised to see that many JFLAG employees and regulars whom I expected to attend the flash mob, including one of the coordinators of Pride week, did not. When I asked the employee about this afterwards, he replied that 'It is not my kind of thing'. This sentiment was echoed by Kristion, a JFLAG regular whom I met at a Pride Week art show that he had helped curate. Kristion was around my age, and I had seen him in the JFLAG office quite often. The evening of the art show, he approached me to ask what I thought about it. We soon started discussing the flash mob, which had happened a few days earlier. He told me he was not a fan of such events because they were too 'in your face' and overtly 'flamboyant'. He felt that the entirety of Kingston did not need to know about his 'persuasion'. Alongside concerns of not being able to attend due to making oneself vulnerable as a result, not wanting to attend due to the intense publicness and visibility of the event crystallised as a central concern for some people. The very visibility which marked the flash mob event, in particular, seemed, in fact, undesirable for a significant group of LGBTQ Jamaicans, who were consequently more engaged with less public events or spaces.

All the while, the flash mob event was essentialised and celebrated as 'Jamaica's First Pride' in the international news coverage, which I tracked for JFLAG (see Table 13.1 for more detail). Making front page news in international newspapers may have caused trepidation for some Jamaican LGBTQ people but produced a sense of historic importance for many others I spoke to, including among people who did not attend the flash mob.

Pride as a source of communal joy

Our initial and most prominent reaction to sharing the above accounts with each other was one of joy: Reading each other's ethnographic accounts of the flash mob proved very evocative for both of us and doing so made us remember, in our own ways, the joy, excitement, and momentousness we both felt in the summer of 2015 (Figure 13.1).

What struck us was the centrality that music takes in both of our accounts. The musical elements of the flash mob were what allowed us to feel connected to all of the participants. The music, combined with the act of dancing, in a place of such historical importance for Jamaica allowed us to feel and simultaneously express collective joy, referred to by anthropologists Victor and Edith Turner as 'communitas', or the 'sense felt by a plurality of people without boundaries' (Turner, 2012, p. 2). The fact that it was Trinidadian artist Destra Garcia whose music was playing, rather than a Jamaican artist, is telling: many Jamaican artists, particularly in the widely popular Dancehall genre, have used music to express anti-LGBTQ messages. Soca, short for the Soul of Calypso, originating in Trinidad and Tobago, in contrast, is a music genre most associated with Caribbean carnival and popular among many LGBTQ people in Jamaica. Only once we had re-entered the bus did the group put on a song more explicitly dealing with LGBTQ content in American pop singer Katy Perry's 'I kissed a girl'. The fact that the group

Acting together, reflecting together 179

Figure 13.1 Pride flash mob in Kingston, Jamaica, 2015.

re-played both the Destra Garcia and Katy Perry songs again and again retrospectively seems like an attempt to freeze this moment of collective joy in time, and to relive it over and over. This expression of collective joy, to us, was at the core of the experience of the flash mob event – and stands in contrast to media representations of LGBTQ life in Jamaica as solely marked by fear and experiences of homo-/transphobia.

The flash mob and the public sphere

Joy and momentousness were not the only emotions evoked in both of our accounts: Simone writes of nervousness and concern for safety. David, in the interviews he conducted at the time, reports a degree of hesitance and even rejection of the flash mob among gay men in particular. At stake, here, was a renegotiation of the place LGBTQ sexualities ought to take in the Jamaican public sphere. As geographer Nancy Duncan writes, '[p]ublic space is regulated by keeping it relatively free of passion or expressions of sexuality that are not naturalized or condoned [,] banishing from sight behaviours that are [considered] repugnant' (1996, p. 141). Pride parades, given their history as protest marches, are an attempt to renegotiate what kinds of sexuality are acceptable to be expressed in public. In this sense, they are a form of 'deconstructive spatial tactics' (Duncan, 1996, p. 138) – and Jamaican Pride 2015 is no exception here.

This desire to claim public spaces has been situated by many queer studies scholars as tied to a normative project rooted in the Global North. Openness about the self, as philosopher Michel Foucault discusses (1978), is a prescriptive tenet of Western engagement with sexuality. Confession became, throughout the Enlightenment period, ubiquitous and was no longer, as previously when administered through the church and connected to the practice of penance,

> a question simply of saying what was done-the sexual act-and how it was done; but of reconstructing, in and around the act, the thoughts that recapitulated it, the obsessions that accompanied it, the images, desires, modulations, and quality of the pleasure that animated it.
> (Foucault, 1978, p. 63)

To sexuality was attributed 'inexhaustible and polymorphous causal power' (Foucault, 1978, p. 65) for negative effects, which thus necessitated excavating it. This excavation ought not simply to be negotiated with oneself, but had to take place in an interaction, because 'the ways of sex were obscure' (Foucault, 1978, p. 66) and were latent. They had to be deciphered and interpreted in engagement with others. It is this prescriptive openness which comes to the fore in the concept of 'coming out of the closet'; telling others – one's friends, family, or even acquaintances – about one's sexuality. A practice that took off in the aftermath of the 1970s Gay Liberation movement (Weeks, 2015), it has developed in novel ways via the Internet, as demonstrated for example by Miller (2016) in his study of an Internet Coming Out Advice Forum, and through the agglomerative creation of LGBTQ identities and their advocacy.

Rosamond King (2014) argues that this normativity of openness and visibility does not pertain to the Caribbean: 'Instead of a mandate of constant revelation, in Cariglobal communities there is a mandate of discretion, which is not (always) the same as hiding' (King, 2014, p. 64). She employs the notion of el secreto abierto (the open secret), a term coined by queer Puerto Rican author Lawrence La Fountain-Stokes, to describe this Caribbean framework. According to her, while many Caribbean people may know that another person might be not heterosexual, this is never openly discussed. This awareness might come about 'through any combination of factors such as behaviours, speech, or dress' (King, 2014, p. 64), and requires collective action by the entirety of a community around an individual to keep the knowledge of their sexuality in this liminal space, of known, yet not acknowledged. Outside perspectives might see el secreto abierto as a manifestation of self-loathing, due to the ingrained social imperative that 'insists on the right and necessity to tell' (King, 2014, p. 65), whereas el secreto abierto 'insists on the necessity and right 'not to tell" (King, 2014, p. 65). In this reading, a public event displaying LGBTQ sexualities and gender identities such as the flash mob, then, can be seen as a threat to their tacitly accepted relegation to private spaces. Seen through this lens, Simone and David both understand the flash mob as a first foray into the public sphere – albeit not **too** public. Through choosing a flash mob rather than a parade and playing a song that was not LGBTQ specific, as well as through focusing on a larger Pride Week, all other events of which were held in private venues, JFLAG tested the waters as to whether 'publicness' was something they should aim to incorporate into their activism.

While this attempt was embraced wholly by international news outlets, Jamaican and Caribbean news media showed a more muted reaction, as demonstrated by the number of articles published on the flash mob shown in Table 13.1: News outlets in the United States published the most English language articles on the topic of Jamaican Pride 2015 by a far margin, with 37 online articles being published on the subject between June and August 2015. In Jamaica, by contrast, 12 articles on the topic were published in that same time frame; and in the rest of the Caribbean (without Jamaica), only 5 articles were published on the topic.

The articles published by Jamaican news outlets, as well as the comments under them, were largely critical of the flash mob. International news outlets, in contrast, were buoyant in their assessment of the flash mob. These outlets often sought to cast the flash mob as an instance of hope for worldwide 'progress' on LGBTQ rights. This mirrored the attitude many Jamaican

Table 13.1 Number of English language articles published by digital news outlets on the topic of Jamaican Pride 2015 between June and August 2015, differentiated by the news outlets' country of origin. Articles were identified in September 2015 using the search terms 'Pride' and 'Jamaica' on Google's 'News' function and then checked qualitatively for whether their central topic was Jamaican Pride 2015

Digital News Outlets Country of Origin	*Number of English Language Articles on Jamaican Pride Published by Digital News Outlets Situated in Respective Countries, June–August 2015*
Germany	1
Netherlands	1
Canada	2
New Zealand	2
Caribbean (without Jamaica)	5
United Kingdom	6
Jamaica	12
USA	37
Overall	66

LGBTQ activists had and still have towards Pride 2015. As Simone puts it: As a singular event in my lifetime, the 2015 Jamaica Pride and the Flash Mob at the Emancipation statue represented a galvanising of our collective desire to defiantly stand publicly and in unity as queer Jamaicans claiming space in the public sphere.

Pride 2015s legacy: Kingston's first and last flash mob

This is, perhaps, as good a place as any to note that 2015 saw both the first and as of 2022 last flash mob Pride event in Kingston. In the years following 2015, JFLAG followed up with continuing Pride Weeks, repeating events such as the Sports Day, yet eschewing the flash mob and not replacing it with any kind of event laying claim to the public sphere. The annual calendar of events has evolved into celebrations in rented private spaces, free from the eyes of the public. The flash mob which seemed momentous and perhaps like a turning of the tides at the time and still does now, as we noticed when reading each other's ethnographic accounts turned out to be a one-off event. This is even more remarkable when considering that, in October 2015, only a few months after the Kingston flash mob, another gay pride flash mob celebration took place in Jamaica. This event was organised by a Jamaican activist living abroad and was held in Montego Bay, a tourism hub in the North of the island, and received somewhat less news coverage. The Montego Bay flash mob continued in the following years, with a parade being held in 2018. In 2019, the event was shut down for security reasons. Seemingly, there has not been another Montego Bay Pride since then. The (im)possibilities of publicness and their negotiations have, seemingly, remained a central question in Jamaican LGBTQ rights discourse – but the Kingston flash mob has not proved to be an inflexion point in this debate.

Seven years on from this moment in Jamaican LGBTQ history, the flash mob lives on mostly in the shadows of the memories of a few. While at the 10th anniversary of the Caribbean Womens' Sexual and Diversity Conference in Barbados, which was attended by over 100 activists from across the region, Simone asked representatives from across the Caribbean, including Antigua, Barbados, Trinidad and Tobago, and Guyana, if they had heard about the Flash mob; no one could say that they had. Since 2015, there have been changes in legislation governing the freedoms of LGBTQ people in these countries, and with these changes have come pride parades in Barbados and Trinidad and Tobago. While other Caribbean nations are moving forward with public Pride parades, this has remained elusive in Jamaica.

A Pride Parade is perceived by many, including LGBTQ Jamaicans, as the 'gold standard' for publicness, and so perhaps, thirty black queer bodies dancing to the music of a Trini on Emancipation Day in celebration of Jamaica Pride may seem to be 'small tings', but in the context of Jamaica, the defiance roared. It represented a push towards to strike a blow to the systems that would have LGBTQ Jamaicans and their bodies relegated to the private prisons created by colonial norms. Through remembering the 2015 flash mob in this chapter together and reflecting on its implications and legacy, we hope to reignite conversations around solidarity and protest as well as contemporary activism and its role in a post-colonial space such as Jamaica and we situate our collective reflection as part of a process of ongoing collective action by the LGBTQ community in Jamaica.

Notes

1 As Boellstorff puts it, referring to postcolonial states more generally, 'Victorian sexual norms of domestic heterosexuality became identified as the 'authentic' sexualities of the postcolonial state, set against a West assumed to be a source of promiscuity and degeneracy' (2012, p. 177).
2 For an earlier, in-depth analysis of the political dimensions and implications of Pride in Serbia, see Bilić (2016).

References

Anderson, M., & MacLeod, E. (Eds.). (2020). *Beyond Homophobia: Centring LGBTQ Experiences in the Anglophone Caribbean*. Mona: The University of the West Indies Press.
Bilić, B. (2016). Europe♥ Gays? Europeanisation and Pride Parades in Serbia. In B. Bilić (Ed.), *LGBT Activism and Europeanisation in the Post-Yugoslav Space: On the Rainbow Way to Europe* (1st ed., pp. 117–153). London: Palgrave Macmillan.
Boellstorff, T. (2005). *The Gay Archipelago: Sexuality and Nation in Indonesia*. Princeton, NJ: Princeton University Press.
Boellstorff, T. (2012). Some Notes on New Frontiers of Sexuality and Gobalisation. In P. Aggleton, P. Boyce, H. Moore, & R. Parker (Eds.), *Understanding Global Sexualities: New Frontiers* (pp. 171–185). New York: Routledge.
Boyer, D., & Marcus, G. E. (Eds.). (2020). *Collaborative Anthropology Today: A Collection of Exceptions*. Ithaca, NY: Cornell University Press.
Bruce, K. M. (2013). LGBT Pride as a Cultural Protest Tactic in a Southern City. *Journal of Contemporary Ethnography*, 42(5), 608–635.
Cooper, C. (2004). *Sound Clash: Jamaican Dancehall Culture at Large*. New York: Palgrave Macmillan.
Dave, N. N. (2011). Activism as Ethical Practice: Queer Politics in Contemporary India. *Cultural Dynamics*, 23(1), 3–20.Duncan, N. (1996). Introduction: (Re)placings. In N. Duncan (Ed.), *BodySpace: Destabilizing Geographies of Gender and Sexuality* (pp. 1–12). New York: Routledge.
Enguix, B. (2009). Identities, Sexualities and Commemorations: Pride Parades, Public Space and Sexual Dissidence. *Anthropological Notebooks*, 15(2), 15–33.
Eror, A. (2022, September 14). 'It's a Win for Us': Serbia's Cancelled Europride Exposes Ongoing LGBTQ+ Struggle. The Guardian. https://www.theguardian.com/world/2022/sep/14/belgrade-serbia-cancelled-europride-exposes-ongoing-lgbtq-struggles
Foucault, M. (1978). *The History of Sexuality, vol. 1, An Introduction*, trans. Robert Hurley. New York: Pantheon.

Gilpin, J.-A. (2016). *No to Gays! - Adventists Urge Government to Keep God in Deliberations on Buggery Law*. Jamaica Gleaner.https://jamaica-gleaner.com/article/lead-stories/20160328/no-gays-adventists-urge-government-keep-god-deliberations-buggery-law

Greensmith, C., & Giwa, S. (2013). Challenging Settler Colonialism in Contemporary Queer Politics: Settler Homonationalism, Pride Toronto, and Two-Spirit Subjectivities. *American Indian Culture and Research Journal*, 37(2), 129–148.

Harris, C. B., Keil, P. G., Sutton, J., Barnier, A. J., & McIlwain, D. J. F. (2011). We Remember, We Forget: Collaborative Remembering in Older Couples. *Discourse Processes*, 48(4), 267–303.

J-FLAG et al. (2015). Human Rights Violations Against Lesbian, Gay, Bisexual, and Transgender (LGBT) People in Jamaica: A Shadow Report.

Johnston, L. (2005). *Queering Tourism: Paradoxical Performances of Gay Pride Parades*. New York: Routledge.

Kempadoo, K. (2003). Sexuality in the Caribbean: Theory and Research (With an Emphasis on the Anglophone Caribbean). *Social and Economic Studies*, 52(3), 59–88.

King, R. S. (2014). *Island Bodies: Transgressive Sexualities in the Caribbean Imagination*. Gainesville: University Press of Florida.

Krstić, A., Parry, K., & Aiello, G. (2020). Visualising the Politics of Appearance in Times of Democratisation: An Analysis of the 2010 Belgrade Pride Parade Television Coverage. *European Journal of Cultural Studies*, 23(2), 165–183.

La Font, S. (2001). Very Straight Sex: The Development of Sexual Mores in Jamaica. *Journal of Colonialism and Colonial History*, 2(3).

Lassiter, L. E. (2008). *The Chicago Guide to Collaborative Ethnography*. Chicago: University of Chicago Press.

Long, S. (n.d.). Jamaica LGBTI Resources. amera International. Retrieved from https://www.amerainternational.org/jamaica-lgbti-resources/

May, R. A. B., & Pattillo-McCoy, M. (2000). Do You See What I See? Examining a Collaborative Ethnography. *Qualitative Inquiry*, 6(1), 65–87.

Miller, B. (2016). A Computer-Mediated Escape from the Closet: Exploring Identity, Community, and Disinhibited Discussion on an Internet Coming Out Advice Forum. *Sexuality & Culture*, 20, 602–625.

Murray, D. (2012). *Flaming Souls: Homosexuality, Homophobia, and Social Change in Barbados*. Toronto: University of Toronto Press.

Padgett, T. (2006, April 12). *The Most Homophobic Place on Earth?* New York: TIME.

Peterson, A., Wahlström, M., & Wennerhag, M. (2018). 'Normalized' Pride? Pride Parade Participants in Six European Countries. *Sexualities*, 21(7), 1146–1169.

Rantatalo, O., & Karp, S. (2016). Collective Reflection in Practice: An Ethnographic Study of Swedish Police Training. *Reflective Practice*, 17(6), 708–723.

Reynolds, R. et al. (2014). *Not Safe at Home: Violence and Discrimination against LGBTQ People in Jamaica*. New York: Human Rights Watch.

Sharpe, J., & Pinto, S. (2006). The Sweetest Taboo: Studies of Caribbean Sexualities; A Review Essay. *Signs: Journal of Women in Culture and Society*, 32(1), 247–274.

Stevenson, A. (2014). We Came Here to Remember: Using Participatory Sensory Ethnography to Explore Memory as Emplaced, Embodied Practice. *Qualitative Research in Psychology*, 11(4), 335–349.

Turner, E. (2012). *Communitas*. New York: Palgrave Macmillan US.
VICE. (2014). *Young and Gay: Jamaica's Gully Queens*. New York: VICE.
Weeks, J. (2015). Gay Liberation and its Legacies. In *The Ashgate Research Companion to Lesbian and Gay Activism* (pp. 45–58). New York: Routledge.
Westmoreland, M. R. (2022). Multimodality: Reshaping Anthropology. *Annual Review of Anthropology, 51*, 173–194.

14 Reflections on teaching the ethics of digital communication technologies

Yusuf Yüksekdağ

Introduction

This chapter outlines the rationale behind a newly developed course titled 'Ethics in the Digital Age', which draws on materials covered in applied ethics and critical technology studies. The primary objective of this interdisciplinary course is to enhance media and communication students' understanding of digital communication technologies and platforms, with a particular emphasis on their ethical implications. The course employs a process and case-oriented ethical approach that aims to explore the socio-economic implications of datafication and data-driven digital platforms (Mejias & Couldry, 2019). Datafication, described as quantifying and transforming various social spaces, opens up many unpredictable issues about how the relationship between digital technologies and societies takes shape (Sadowski, 2019). That is why the course incorporates collaborative learning tools aiming at encouraging not only mutual engagement but also collective construction of the ethically charged issues within the course's context (Roschelle & Teasley, 1996; Sawyer & Obeid, 2017).

Instead of prioritizing predetermined ethical questions and perspectives, the course aims to cultivate a collaborative approach to ethical inquiry among its participants. By fostering a shared ethos of doing media ethics together, the course attempts to generate an inclusive learning environment where students can contribute their situated insights to the ethical questions posed by digital communication technologies and platforms. This approach recognizes the complexity and unpredictability of ethical issues related to datafication and acknowledges that there is no one-size-fits-all solution to the challenges posed by these technologies. Instead, the course encourages a process-oriented approach to ethical inquiry that emphasizes collaboration and reflexivity.

Integrating such an ethos into the course assignments aims to foster critical thinking and recognize the epistemological significance of participants' perspectives as contributions to the emerging field of the ethics of datafication (Gomez-Lanier, 2018). Although the learning outcomes of this approach have yet to be tested, the increasingly complex digital environments demand

DOI: 10.4324/9781003389972-17

learning methods that prioritize the development of collaborative, case-based thinking in the applied ethics classroom, rather than focusing solely on ethical theories (Peek, Peek & Horras, 1994).

In the first section of this chapter, the concept of datafication and its relevance for digital communication technologies are introduced, followed by questioning the relevance of theory and practice in doing applied ethics. After setting out some exemplary processes and discussion points that can be described as the ethics of datafication with a focus on socio-economic relations stemming from data-driven communication platforms, I briefly introduce the case-based design of the course that focuses on cases such as doxing, extreme speech, digital labouring, smart cities, and face/emotion recognition solutions.

Ethics of digital communication technologies

In this section, the prospects and challenges posed by the process of datafication embedded in digital communication technologies are highlighted and its implications for doing applied ethics have been put forward. This is followed by outlining the field of ethics of datafication or data relations that reflects resulting socio-economic processes (e.g., changing nature of privacy and identity, commodification, exploitation, and inclusion/exclusion practices) in the context of the pertinent and emerging case-based discussions (e.g., extreme speech, digital labour practices, smart city, and face/emotion recognition solutions). Note that the listed examples are case studies or topics that are discussed in the context of the course.

Digital communication technologies: revisiting the concept

To better understand the prospects and challenges presented by digital communication technologies, it is crucial to begin by considering their basic conceptualization. Digital communication technologies can be viewed in various ways, including as digital media platforms where communication, meaning-making, and sharing occur, such as X (Twitter), TikTok, or Tinder (Gómez-Urrutia & Tello-Navarro, 2020). They can also be seen as the digital devices we use, such as laptops, wearable goggles, or smartphones (Curran & Hesmondhalgh, 2019; Kuntsman & Miyake, 2019; Cover, 2023). Additionally, these technologies can be understood as the specific information and communications technologies, computing infrastructures, or wireless sensors and networks that enable digitalization and platformization efforts in the first place (Bibri, 2019). By understanding these conceptualizations, we can better explore the ethical implications of the process of datafication that is embedded in many digital communication technologies.

The scope of ethics of digital communication technologies encompasses all these aspects, focusing on digital environments, the devices, and the background structures on which they are built, as well as their implications for communication, information use, sharing, and governance. For instance, X (Twitter), as a prominent platform for information dissemination, cannot be considered independently of the mobile devices that facilitate its access, or the background technologies, such as personalized recommendations, that shape user interactions. These factors collectively relate to the manner in which users engage in meaning-making, highlighting the interplay between digital communication technologies and ethical considerations.

One might question, however, what exactly are the agents or cases that fall under the scope of digital communication technologies and whether it goes beyond orthodox examples such as X (Twitter) or TikTok. Following Nick Couldry (2019) and adapting a rather thin concept of media and communication technologies, I consider any type of digital space or platform where meanings are constructed, shared, and preserved across time and space as the subject matter of ethics of digital communication technologies. Such a thin conception of media and communication would no doubt extend the scope of digital communication technologies to a variety of platforms. Digital spaces or platforms varying from X (Twitter) to smart urban solutions and face/emotion recognition applications through which individuals make sense of either their urban surroundings or their emotional interactions or expectations are then considered as the very agents of such a contestation.

A little more conceptual scrutiny is needed here. Notably, Onora O'Neill (2021) questions the use of the term 'digital ethics' as if the use of digital technologies would necessarily imply similar issues. That is why she prefers to narrow down her discussion to the ethics of 'digital communication' (O'Neill, 2021, p. 8). I share a similar concern over conflating issues of different types such as artificial intelligence, blockchain technologies, Metaverse, robots, autonomous vehicles, and many other examples of buzzwords in the big tech and business world. Such a bandwagon approach would potentially prevent us from a well-considered and conscientious ethical analysis and at best merely popularize the issues at hand in the public realm. However, it raises the question of why achieving a narrower approach necessarily relies on this conceptual choice rather than beginning with specific cases and discussions. It is reasonable to narrow down one's scope to the ethical implications of 'using digital technologies to communicate with other' as O'Neill (2021) calls her project (p. 9). Disregarding platforms or technologies such as smart cities or face/emotion recognition solutions would then hold onto a very specific and transmission-based understanding of communication. Alternatively, communication has also been considered as a ritual, instead of functional information sharing, through which not-so-visible practices and processes such as meaning-making, social relations, and identity and community forming are to be explored (Holmes, 2005).

Instead of limiting the analysis to the text and meanings disseminated through digital platforms like X (Twitter), considering communication as a ritual practice that occurs through these platforms enables an examination of how individuals form connections, engage in social integration, and build communities within or through technological infrastructures (Couldry, 2004, p. 127; Holmes, 2005, p. 6). This approach would also broaden the range of ethical considerations, moving beyond a focus solely on the text or the act of sharing content. This aligns with viewing media platforms as relating to a diverse and dynamic range of practices, which would then imply not only analyzing the transmission and content but also scrutinizing the actions and behaviours of individuals 'in relation to media across a whole range of situations and contexts' (Couldry, 2004, p. 119). Considering digital communication technologies not only as content containers but also as a form of 'doing' and 'practice' emphasizes the importance of being open to diverse media-oriented practices through which users interact with and make sense of these technologies.

Overall, focusing on particular digital communication or media environments considering the specific platform; its structure, interface, the relevant devices, and the pertinent background technologies would be a fitting approach to discussing its potential prospects, benefits, and disruptions.

Digital communication technologies: prospects and challenges

Particular digital communication platforms accommodate unique prospects and challenges. It would be a very holistic and conflating approach to treat all digital communication platforms as if they pose similar issues. The idea that digital platforms offer unlimited opportunities would also fully disregard the human factor, the structural design and sharing limitations, and the profit-driven rationale that governs emerging data-driven technologies (Sadowski, 2020; Biloria, 2021; Gratch & Gratch, 2022, p. 71). Since the design of technologies is not value-neutral and might reflect the norms and values of their designers and their intended prospects, the function and features of particular platforms are shaped accordingly (Gratch & Gratch, 2022, p. 71; Waight et al., 2022). Digital communication technologies transform different aspects of our lives with their usefulness and efficiency in sharing information, forming social connections, or understanding the social environment better, yet as Facebook's infamous motto suggests, they also move fast and break things. While shaping the materialities in one way or another, many technologies remain in the background, making it a challenge to comprehend particularly how they disrupt certain activities or what kind of values or goods are at stake. Some even consider that we move towards the end of the process of digitalization where everything has become digital making the digital aspect transparent to the public eye (Müller, 2021). Regardless, more visible and pressing issues over privacy, surveillance, and censorship have received more attention in relation to X (Twitter) and Facebook.

The ethics of digital communication technologies, or digital ethics as it has been called, have been mostly established around issues such as privacy, free speech, and the ethical implications of sharing content on social media platforms (Beever, McDaniel, & Stanlick, 2020; Müller, 2021; O'Neill, 2021). Digital platforms like X (Twitter) have been appreciated for enriching the public sphere or at the least for empowering underprivileged groups to contest their representations (Tromble, 2018; Couldry, 2019). On the other hand, they also have happened to upset the communication between the sender and the receiver by providing novel opportunities to control, suppress or amplify what is being communicated and by whom (O'Neill, 2021, p. 7). It is reasonable for such disruptive forms of communication to be the primary subject of ethically-charged discussions as they hinder issues that are of relevance to long-standing ethical inquiries such as the moral responsibility of performing contestable speech acts.

While such questions are still of relevance, this approach is beset by certain barriers or limited in its scope. How big data technologies function, transform, limit, or suppress different spheres of social activities (e.g., dating, learning, labouring, and protesting) posits more than the concerns over privacy and free speech albeit them being foundational ones (O'Neill, 2021). While the ethical implications of the practice of sharing content on X (Twitter) or Instagram are of importance for particular issues such as extreme speech, shaming, trolling, and fake news, the fact that content sharing is done via digital technologies should also have a bearing on the discussion (Sullivan & Alfano, 2021). Otherwise, the discussion would collapse into the conventional ethics of communication. Critical technology scholarship has recently shown interest in the functioning of digital platforms and the underlying processes of datafication, hyperconnectivity, and algorithmization (Calvo, 2020; Bibri & Allam, 2022). If we are to target digital communication technologies from an ethical perspective, understanding the nature of such data-driven processes and their implications would be paramount even for rethinking more conventional issues as such.

Digital technologies, by their very nature, invite scrutiny regarding data collection practices and the utilization of big data sets that shape activities and opportunities within a given digital realm. This is not merely a matter of different activities being transformed into digital mediums that are best described by the term, digitalization (Bibri & Allam, 2022). The data-driven nature of digital communication platforms, characterized by the process of datafication, involves more than just the surface-level digitalization of activities. It encompasses the quantification of various activities and information, along with the utilization of processed data sets to manage and govern the relevant sphere in real time. All these developments exacerbated by the developing quantification technologies also lead to being able to treat the data as a very valuable commodity in the global digital marketplaces that enables the process of datafication to be expansive into different spheres and sectors (Sadowski, 2019; Müller, 2021).

Datafication and its discontents

Datafication, as a process, serves as a common denominator or, at the very least, a useful framework that alludes to numerous processes and issues prevalent in data-driven communication platforms. As much as particular prospects and issues revolving around specific digital communication platforms are of importance as mentioned, determining a well-situated backdrop has its merits to frame the discussion and be able to ask comparative questions about corresponding goods and values.

Datafication is a process by which everyday activities of life are turned into data points (Mejias & Couldry, 2019). As a term, it does not only point to the processes of how such individual data points in different spheres of lives (e.g., consumer preferences, recreational activities) are collected, used, and distributed as data streams but hints at the very acclimation of such practices in evaluating, designing, and managing socio-economic spaces. It rests on the prospect of understanding the world better providing a God's eye view of socio-economic processes and enabling algorithmic designations of those particular material instances (Kitchin, 2016). No doubt, even particular individual materialities are designed in this capacity. As Jathan Sadowski (2020) exemplifies, for data-driven and thus 'smart' toothbrushes, for instance, it is not only a matter of collecting tooth brushing patterns, but it extends to distribution of the data points on the brushing to other agents such as one's dentist and managing such activity by real-time digitally mediated suggestions or hygiene scores (p. 2). The proliferation of such examples hints at the assumption behind datafication that the technologies as such would inherently produce meaningful and objective sets of knowledge about that relevant phenomenon (Williamson, 2019). However, it is important to recognize that being 'smart' or technologically advanced does not automatically equate to being ethical. The knowledge and governance implemented through datafication are not inherently neutral or objective. They are shaped by human biases, power dynamics, and societal values that can influence the ethical implications of digital communication technologies. Given the private deployment of technological affordances, such processes are arguably utilized mainly for economic profit (Couldry & Mejias, 2019).

The effects of datafication on our understanding of privacy, how certain content or group presentations are amplified or suppressed, or the exploitation of data points that are collected via the process of datafication have been mainly discussed in the critical technology scholarship (Couldry, 2019; Couldry & Mejias, 2019). The emerging ethical accounts would benefit from such a framework (Bradshaw, 2020; Véliz, 2021). It is noteworthy that the recent *The Oxford Handbook of Digital Ethics* rarely accommodates a perspective on datafication while including rich discussions on a variety of issues such as online shaming, extreme speech, face/emotion recognition, and robots (Véliz, 2021).

There are many unforeseeable issues stemming from datafication but the embedded processes would be a starting point. While the private deployment of data-driven technologies makes processes such as quantification, commodification, and exploitation quite vivid, these processes do not necessarily imply a one-sided take on their effects. This is what ethics is about. It is a matter of balancing different goods and values stemming from such complex processes. At this stage, it is meritorious to briefly discuss what exactly is doing applied ethics before delving into the ethics of datafication approach in teaching the ethics of digital communication technologies.

Doing applied ethics: theory and practice

Before describing the specific approach to be taken in teaching the ethics of digital communication technologies, it is important to clarify what is meant by doing applied ethics and what its basic preliminaries are. Applied ethics, as a field of research, questions the important values at stake in specific cases and determines the rightness or wrongness of an action or policy. This argumentative and normative logic can be applied to different areas of life (Edmonds, 2019). As such, the field of applied ethics encompasses a variety of fields, including computer ethics, political ethics, environmental ethics, media ethics, and digital ethics, where researchers discuss the ethical implications of data-driven platforms governing various aspects of our lives, such as smart city applications (Calvo, 2020).

It should be noted that the discussions of ethical values or positions go beyond mere description and focus on the basis, meaning, and function of different values. For this purpose, ethical evaluations initially rely on conceptual clarification and the proper analysis of relevant values and claims (Collste, 2012). As well as conceptual clarity, applied ethics is also about discussing ethically charged issues and conflicting values in different cases. One of the exemplary methods is the 'reflective equilibrium' (Rawls, 2001). This method suggests a systematic analysis of ethical positions by starting with our moral intuitions, followed by ethical principles and background social and psychological theories, or vice versa. This back-and-forth method aims to bring everything into a state of harmony, using different but specific cases to approximate an articulate and well-considered ethical judgment. In applied ethics, existing theories may initially guide a discussion. However, it is also possible to apply a bottom–up approach in which individual intuitions and perceptions are primarily assessed.[1]

Especially when it comes to digital ethics, there is quite a struggle regarding the extent to which practical insights are to be included in normative discussions (Müller, 2021). The standard teaching practice in digital ethics is usually to provide one of the traditional theories and apply cases based on such theoretical dispositions varying from consequentialism, and Kantian ethics to virtue ethics (Paltiel et al., 2022). Notably, Deborah Johnson made an emphasis two decades ago referring to the discussions on whether computer ethics will in the end boil down to doing applied ethics in an ordinary fashion or will provide its theoretical insights (Bynum, 2001). Regardless of the theoretical position one can take, particularly focusing on the processes and issues at hand can act as a starting point.

It becomes somewhat disengaging to apply the general theoretical perspectives if conducted merely in a top–down fashion to emerging technologies for two distinct reasons. The first is that as the empirical turn in the contemporary philosophy of technology suggests there is merit in focusing on concrete and particular technologies disregarding transcendental takes for the sake of pinpointing emerging yet distinguishable processes and issues (Romele, 2021). Secondly, the perceptions or standpoints of prospective users and designers do matter deprived of generalizations about the function and intent of a technology. The recent post-phenomenological approach to digital technologies, in particular, places this concern at its core. Otherwise, the discussion may overlook how users experience and interact with these technologies, as well as the norms and values that emerge as a result (Verbeek, 2015). From the perspective of analytical normative ethics, this approach may not be considered normative because it does not necessarily propose principles or ethos to argue for and apply. Notwithstanding, the particularist focus and eagerness to benefit epistemologically from participant perspectives is an insightful rationale to apply in a digital ethics classroom setting while designating course assignments and exercises.

While competence in ethical theories is paramount to developing analytical abilities, it might also delimit students or pave the way for an understanding where the theory itself is prioritized over the practice. When this would be the case in one of the most practical strands of normative philosophy where intuitive considerations are of utmost importance, it brings the danger of not catching up with emerging technologies and their implications. There are also similar calls by a variety of applied ethics instructors in the scope of different fields (Dutmer, 2022).

Ethics of datafication: data relations approach

One of the critical approaches to take on the socio-economic implications of datafication and its embedded or resulting processes and social relations is the data relations approach put forward by Nick Couldry and Ulises Ali Mejias (2019). The concept of data relations has recently attracted some attention in critical technology and media scholarship yet it is still an emerging concept to be fully developed (Johanssen, 2021).

This particular approach to data-driven platforms borrows the Marxist notion of relations of production and explores how the datafication of everyday life implies and also justifies certain and mostly perverse and profit-driven socio-economically salient processes and relations (e.g., commodifying, exploitative) (Johanssen, 2021). The notion of 'data relations' posits an insightful approach to explore and formulate the ethical implications of data-driven and privately deployed communication platforms. In a pedagogical setting, this approach would enable (i) being perceptive of emerging yet concrete issues concerned with datafication, (ii) focusing on the processes such as commodification or exploitation and the pertinent cases, (iii) problematizing not merely the rights and material benefits but also social relations stemming from data-driven technologies, and

(iv) providing a space for participant and user perceptions. Lastly, while being critical enough of profit-driven platforms but not to the extent of being fully anti-tech and in order to leave a space for value balancing, a thinner conceptualization of data relations can be explored. To that end, I take 'data relations' not necessarily as justifying certain social relations as the term relations of production suggests, but merely as processes and relations stemming from data-driven platforms.

It is not in the scope of this chapter nor in line with its pedagogical and empirical approach to fully account for what kind of data relations or processes would be implied by different technological settings. Nonetheless, in what follows I will briefly delineate some potential processes or relations pertinent to the data-driven communication technologies covered in the course. These are informational privacy, commodification, exploitation, inclusion/exclusion practices, and identity.

Informational privacy is one of the processes to be explored in the context of datafication. The reason why I refer to privacy as a process is implied by how we can reflect on the concept, its scope and its perceived value in different digital contexts. Quantification and collection of data points from public environments such as CC-TV cameras or digital platforms such as Facebook challenge the traditional conceptualizations of informational privacy resting upon the private-public dichotomy (Mai, 2016).

Commodification is another process that might stem from data-driven platforms of any kind when quantified data points are transformed into marketable goods. It also paves the way for the process of exploitation when the revenues based on quantified daily activities and preferences are largely owned and commercialized by the platforms themselves (Sadowski, 2019).

In addition, data-driven platforms might accommodate different forms of inclusion/exclusion practices either via excluding the collection of certain individual or group activities or preferences or via instances of algorithmic bias or discrimination while governing that relevant digital space (Calvo, 2020). Furthermore, the formation of identity, particularly through bodily practices and memory-making, is not solely shaped within the context but also in relation to digital communication technologies (Gratch & Gratch, 2022; Kudina, 2022; Cover, 2023).

Teaching the ethics of datafication

Ethics in the Digital Age is a general elective BA-level course offered by the Department of Media at Istanbul Bilgi University to all university students. I offered and designed the course to be opened starting in the Fall semester of 2020. The course usually has 35–40 students. In this section, I will introduce the design and the case-based rationale of the course. This will be followed by some remarks on the ethos of doing applied ethics together with the course participants.

Course design and rationale

In the first half of this 14-week/3-hour term course, various ethical theories and approaches are introduced, such as utilitarianism, theories of justice and freedom, and communitarianism. Rather than the theoretical assumptions, the argumentative structures and the challenges faced by applying traditional theories are emphasized. This is followed by introducing the process of datafication and the resulting socio-economic processes briefly as mentioned before.

In the second half of the course, a case-based pedagogy is conducted. Case-based teaching practices are applicable to a variety of fields of study through which participants would engage in actual or potential practical dilemmas or problems (Biggs & Tang, 2007; Johnson et al., 2012). The application of case-based learning methods has been appreciated in research ethics, medical ethics, nursing ethics, and information ethics settings as it seems to enable more efficient engagement, reflection, and student contention (Lin et al., 2010; Dow et al., 2015; Tammeleht et al., 2019). As Tammeleht and others (2019) suggest, engaging with cases in an applied ethics classroom setting might help with having a better contextual and practice-based understanding while aiding with collaborative discussions (p. 3).

The use of practice and case-based thinking in teaching the ethics of digital communication technologies aligns with the approach described in the previous section. Digital communication technologies are not merely containers for content. They facilitate a wide range of media-oriented social practices (Couldry, 2004). Moreover, users' interactions with digital communication platforms can contribute to the development of ethical norms and judgments (Verbeek, 2015). As such, the classroom can serve as an experiential space for students to develop well-considered judgments about these issues.

The assignments in this course are grounded in an anti-functionalist perspective on media, which also emphasizes the importance of relying on user perspectives in identifying ethical issues and norms that arise from interacting with these technologies. By adopting this perspective and embracing diverse media-oriented practices, the course encourages using reflexive pedagogies in applied ethics classrooms (Stephansen, 2016, p. 29). As with qualitative research, which emphasizes the situatedness of researchers and the need for reflexivity in constructing knowledge, higher education classrooms must also consider the situatedness of students (Chow et al., 2011; Reid et al., 2018; von Unger, 2021). Future practitioners must be able to draw on their personal experiences and intuitions when grappling with ethically charged responses to various social problems they deem important. This way, the course pedagogies emphasize the participants' insight and situatedness in understanding and constructing the ethical implications of media-saturated environments.

Much attention is given to designing case-based discussion sessions in the course in different capacities that would enable students to engage with current and leading-edge issues relevant to digital communication technologies including doxing, digital labour, and smart cities. For instance, the process of informational privacy is explored in connection to the practice of doxing on X (Twitter), while commodification is discussed in connection with particular smart urban solutions such as smart street lighting systems.

In every case-based discussion, the socio-economic processes and relations enacted by datafication are emphasized for students to reflect on various goods they deem valuable emerging from various speculative designs and platforms. While more systematic problem-based learning approaches are to be explored, the course provides certain tools such as small-scale speculative design group discussions where students are asked to provide a data-driven solution to one of the real-life problems in groups followed by others reflecting on potential norms and values at stake. While students are selectively guided about the presence of a variety of stakeholders and values, such discussions are sometimes intentionally ambiguous and complex for students to experience 'unpredictable decision-making processes procedures' (Kim et al., 2006, p. 870). The instructor's guidance partially resembled the scaffolding technique where the learners are aided or nudged as the need arises to sustain goal orientation and to encourage them to explore their 'value standpoints without telling what is right or wrong' (Tammeleht et al., 2021, p. 230). Student perceptions are overall important as potential users and designers.

The course concludes with a two-piece structured case-based discussion session where student preferences, norms, and reasoning – and thus doing applied ethics together – are the guiding ethos of this iterative exercise.

Doing applied ethics together

Following and adapting Lucia E. Peek, George S. Peek, and Mary Horras's (1994) collaborative business ethics class exercise, the ethics bowls in the last two weeks of the course attempt to compel students to come to a well-considered argumentative position. The case and problem are determined through a survey two weeks before the exercise. If, for instance, the majority prefers extreme speech on X (Twitter), then at the beginning of the exercise, the students are provided with an example of an extreme speech and they are asked to provide different arguments about how to handle extreme speech on X (Twitter). Among the alternatives, three different arguments are selected based on another survey.

Alternative 1: X (Twitter) should delete the tweet and ban the user who posted this tweet.
Alternative 2: I believe that such tweets are harmful and wrong but we should deal with them by offering counterarguments and discussion.
Alternative 3: I believe that it is every person's right to free speech to exercise any form of speech whatsoever.

Later, students are divided into groups of three, and each student in the group is assigned a number ranging from 1 to 3. Each numbered participant receives a specific worksheet to work individually on the potential talking points about one of the alternative arguments. For instance, Worksheet 1 offers guiding questions regarding the concept of hate speech, its scope, prudential reasons for deleting a tweet, and the responsibilities of digital communication platforms. This is followed by the group discussion through which the students are asked to discuss the alternatives and rank them according to their preferences as a group by reaching a consensus. The process is iterated later with different groups.

Appraisal

The effectiveness of the ethics bowls and the course assignments is yet to be tested empirically. While course evaluations are typically considered exempt from research ethics review, it is more appropriate to limit the remarks to self-evaluation at this stage. The assignments attempt to rationalize the significance of emerging data relations and enhance the capacity to utilize a model for ethical decision-making (Dow et al., 2015). The student enthusiasm towards the relevance of these issues has been consistently apparent over the course of three different semesters, while the common theory heaviness in applied ethics classrooms has not been a point of contestation (Manninen, 2020).

Another aim is to appreciate the student input not only for designing the case-based learning activity itself but also for exploring potential values and goods to balance in an ethical decision-making process (Dow et al., 2015). Yet again, while the effects of situatedness in carrying out tasks and on the variance of ethical judgments should be tested, relying on student perspectives and norms has mostly resulted in high retention both in in-class participation and assignment completion. In an environment where the norms and ideas of the students have been given prominence, establishing and reproducing the feeling of being in a safe environment becomes significant.

Considering that the course is usually registered by media and communication studies students, acquiring such experiential and experimental tools might help them to adapt to new or unforeseeable issues they might face later as potential designers or content producers for digital communication technologies.

Concluding remarks

Digital communication technologies offer many opportunities yet it would be futile to think of them devoid of the materialities they are constructed upon and the socio-economic relations they might lead to. While they offer tremendous opportunities for communication, collaboration, and innovation, they also raise complex ethical issues that demand our attention. In particular, the datafication paradigm underlying many of these technologies has significant implications for privacy, surveillance, and social justice.

To address these ethical challenges, I have proposed a case-based pedagogy that emphasizes reflection and doing applied ethics together. By engaging with real-world cases and reflecting on their ethical judgments, students can develop the skills and knowledge necessary to navigate the ethical complexities of digital communication technologies. This approach is grounded in the anti-functionalist perspective of media and emphasizes the importance of incorporating user perspectives in the design and evaluation of digital technologies.

While there is no single way to offer an ethics course on digital communication technologies, I believe that this pedagogical approach can be useful in fostering ethical conscientiousness and self-reflective capabilities among potential designers and stakeholders. An interdisciplinary case-oriented course may even function as an integrated ethics license, which is essential to developing fair digital mediums. While this chapter does not sufficiently cover what would be implied by similar teaching practices, further conceptual and empirical exploration is warranted.

Note

1 This part is adapted from an earlier work (Yüksekdağ, 2019).

References

Beever, J., McDaniel, R., & Stanlick, N. A. (2020). *Understanding digital ethics: Cases and contexts*. New York: Routledge.

Bibri, S. E. (2019). The anatomy of the data-driven smart sustainable city: Instrumentation, datafication, computerization and related applications. *Journal of Big Data*, 6(59), 1–43. doi: 10.1186/s40537-019-0221-4

Bibri, S. E., & Allam, Z. (2022). The metaverse as a virtual form of data-driven smart cities: The ethics of the hyper-connectivity, datafication, algorithmization, and platformization of urban society. *Computational Urban Science*, 2(22), 1–22. doi: 10.1007/s43762-022-00050-1

Biggs, J., & Tang, C. (2007). *Teaching for quality learning at university*. Buckingham: SRHE and Open University Press.

Biloria, N. (2021). From smart to empathic cities. *Frontiers of Architectural Research*, 10, 3–16.

Bradshaw, J. L. (2020). Rhetorical exhaustion & the ethics of amplification. *Computers and Composition*, 56, 1–14. doi: 10.1016/j.compcom.2020.102568

Bynum, T. W. (2001). Computer ethics: Its birth and its future. *Ethics and Information Technology*, 3, 109–112.

Calvo, P. (2020). The ethics of Smart City (EoSC): Moral implications of hyperconnectivity, algorithmization and the datafication of urban digital society. *Ethics and Information Technology*, 22, 141–149.

Chow, A. Y. M., Lam, D. O. B. Leung, G. S. M., Wong, D. F. K., & Chan, B. F. P. (2011). Promoting reflexivity among social work students: The development and evaluation of a programme. *Social Work Education: The International Journal*, 30(2), 141–156.

Collste, G. (2012). Applied and professional Ethics. *Kemanusiaan*, 19(1), 17–33.

Couldry, N. (2004). Theorising media as practice. *Social Semiotics*, 14(2), 115–132.

Couldry, N. (2019). *Media: Why it matters*. Cambridge: Polity Press.
Couldry, N., & Mejias, U. A. (2019). *The costs of connection: How data is colonizing human life and appropriating it for capitalism*. Stanford, CA: Stanford University Press.
Cover, R. (2023). *Identity and digital communication: Concepts, theories, practices*. London: Routledge.
Curran, J., and Hesmondhalgh, D. (2019). *Media and society*. New York: Bloomsbury.
Dow, M., Boettcher, C., Diego, J., Karch, M., Todd-Diaz, A., & Woods, K. (2015). Case-based learning as pedagogy for teaching information ethics based on the Dervin sense-making methodology. *Journal of Education for Library and Information Science*, 56(2), 141–157.
Dutmer, E. (2022). A model for a practiced, global, liberatory virtue ethics curriculum. *Teaching Ethics*, 22(1), 39–67.
Edmonds, D. (2019). *Ethics and the contemporary world*. New York: Routledge.
Gomez-Lanier, L. (2018). Building collaboration in the flipped classroom: A case study. *International Journal for the Scholarship of Teaching and Learning*, 12(2), 1–9. doi: 10.20429/ijsotl.2018.120207
Gómez-Urrutia, V., & Tello-Navarro, F. (2020). Gender, love and the Internet: romantic online interactions in Chilean young people. *Journal of Youth Studies*, 24(6), 731–745.
Gratch, L. M., & Gratch A. (2022). *Digital performance in everyday life*. New York: Routledge.
Holmes, D. (2005). *Communication theory: Media, technology and society*. London: Sage Publications.
Johanssen, J. (2021). Data perversion: A psychoanalytic perspective on datafication. *Journal of Digital Social Research*, 3(1), 88–105.
Johnson, J. F., Bagdasarov, Z., Connelly, S., Harkrider, L., Devenport, L. D., Mumford, M. D., & Thiel, C. E. (2012). Case-Based ethics education: The impact of cause complexity and outcome favorability on ethicality. *Journal of Empirical Research on Human Research Ethics*, 7(3), 63–77.
Kim, S., Phillips, W. R., Pinsky, L., Brock, D., Phillips, K., and Keary, J. (2006). A conceptual framework for developing teaching cases: A review and synthesis of the literature across disciplines. *Medical Education*, 40(9), 867–876.
Kitchin, R. (2016). The ethics of smart cities and urban science. *Philosophical Transactions*, 374(2083), 1–15.
Kudina, O. (2022). Speak, memory: The postphenomenological analysis of memory-making in the age of algorithmically powered social networks. *Humanities and Social Sciences Communications*, 9(1), 1–7.
Kuntsman, A., & Miyake, E. (2019). The paradox and continuum of digital disengagement: Denaturalising digital sociality and technological connectivity. *Media, Culture & Society*, 41(6), 901–913.
Lin, C.-F., Lu, M.-S., Chung, C.-C., & Yang, C.-M. (2010). A comparison of problem-based learning and conventional teaching in nursing ethics education. *Nursing Ethics*, 17(3), 373–382.
Mai, J. (2016). Big data privacy: The datafication of personal information. *The Information Society: An International Journal*, 32(3), 192–199.
Manninen, T. (2020). Reflections on teaching philosophy of censorship. *Teaching Ethics*, 20(1–2), 127–138.
Mejias, U. A., & Couldry, N. (2019). Datafication. *Internet Policy Review*, 8(4), 1–10.

Müller, V. C. (2021). The history of digital ethics. In C. Véliz (Ed.), *The Oxford Handbook of digital ethics* (pp. 1–18). Oxford: Oxford University Press. doi: 10.1093/oxfordhb/9780198857815.013.1

O'Neill, O. (2021). *A philosopher looks at digital communication*. Cambridge: Cambridge University Press.

Paltiel, M., Cheong, M., Coghlan, S., & Lederman, R. (2022). Teaching digital ethics in information systems. *ACIS 2022 Proceedings, 25*. Retrieved January 29, 2023, from https://aisel.aisnet.org/acis2022/25

Peek, L. E., Peek, G. S., & Horras, M. (1994). Enhancing Arthur Andersen business ethics vignettes: Group discussions using cooperative/collaborative learning techniques. *Journal of Business Ethics, 13*(3), 189–196.

Rawls, J. (2001). *A theory of justice*. Cambridge, MA: Harvard University Press.

Reid, A., Brown, J. M., Smith, J. M., Cope, A. C., & Jamieson, S. (2018). Ethical dilemmas and reflexivity in qualitative research. *Perspectives on Medical Education, 7*(8), 69–75.

Romele, A. (2021). Technological capital: Bourdieu, postphenomenology, and the philosophy of technology beyond the empirical turn. *Philosophy & Technology, 34*, 483–505.

Roschelle, J., & Teasley, S. D. (1996). The construction of shared knowledge in collaborative problem solving. In C. E. O'Malley (Ed.), *Computer supported collaborative learning* (pp. 69–97). Berlin: Springer-Verlag.

Sadowski, J. (2019). When data is capital: Datafication, accumulation, and extraction. *Big Data & Society, 6*(1), 1–12. doi: 10.1177/2053951718820549

Sadowski, J. (2020). *Too smart: How digital capitalism is extracting data, controlling our lives, and taking over the world*. Cambridge: MIT Press.

Sawyer, J., & Obeid, R. (2017). Cooperative and collaborative learning: Getting the best of both methods. In A. S. R. Obeid, C. Shane-Simpson, & P. J. Brooks (Eds.), *How we teach now: The GSTA guide to student-centered teaching* (pp. 163–177). Washington, DC: Society of the Teaching of Psychology.

Stephansen, H. C. (2016). Understanding citizen media as practice: Agents, processes, publics. In M. Baker & B. B. Blaagaard (Eds.), *Critical perspectives on citizen media: Diverse expressions of citizenship and dissent* (pp. 25–41). London and New York: Routledge.

Sullivan, E., & Alfano, M. (2021). A normative framework for sharing information online. In C. Véliz (Ed.), *The Oxford Handbook of digital ethics* (online edition). Oxford: Oxford University Press. doi: 10.1093/oxfordhb/ 9780198857815.013.5

Tammeleht, A., Rodríguez-Triana, M. J., Koort, K., & Löfström, E. (2019). Collaborative case-based learning process in research ethics. *International Journal for Educational Integrity, 15*, 1–22. doi: 10.1007/s40979-019-0043-3

Tammeleht, A., Rodríguez-Triana, M. J., Koort, K., & Löfström, E. (2021). Scaffolding collaborative case-based learning during research ethics training. *Journal of Academic Ethics, 19*, 229–252.

Tromble, R. (2018). Thanks for (actually) responding! How citizen demand shapes politicians' interactive practices on Twitter. *New Media & Society, 20*(2), 676–697.

Verbeek, P. P. (2015). Beyond interaction: A short introduction to mediation theory. *Interactions 2*(3), 26–31.

Véliz, C. (Ed.). (2021). *The Oxford Handbook of digital ethics*. Oxford: Oxford University Press.

von Unger, H. (2021). Ethical reflexivity as research practice. *Historical Social Research*, 46(2), 186–204.

Waight, N., Kayumova, S., Tripp, J., & Achilova, F. (2022). Towards equitable, social justice criticality: Re-Constructing the "blackise box and making it transparent for the future of science and technology in science education. *Science & Education*, 31, 1493–1515.

Williamson, B. (2019). Datafication of education: a critical approach to emerging analytics technologies and practices. In H. Beetham & R. Sharpe (Eds.), *Rethinking pedagogy for a digital age* (pp. 212–226). New York: Routledge.

Yüksekdağ, Y. (2019). *Doctors behind borders: The ethics of skilled worker emigration*. Linköping: Linköping University Electronic Press.

15 Transmedia charity initiatives in Turkey

The case of *Adım Adım*

Dilek Gürsoy

Civil society organisations (CSOs) are essential to societal development. They are also an important part of democratic life in Turkey and can only indeed survive through individual giving. However, it has been reported that civil society and the charity ecosystem in Turkey do not have the desired strength for a variety of reasons, including individuals' disinterest in being a part of social change, deteriorating trust in the donation system, fear of volunteering and donation due to political polarisation and poor visibility of CSOs (Aytaç & Çarkoğlu, 2020; CAP et al., 2017; Uncu, 2019). An overview of recent reports on giving suggests that Turkish civil society is perceived as an insignificant, remote and uninteresting concept.[1] A considerable part of society does not participate in charity activities due to a lack of interest in civil society and faith in its effectiveness. There are also significant concerns over the transparency of CSOs' activities since publishing a public report about an organisation's resources is not a common occurrence. The political division within the country also cannot be overlooked. This polarisation can be observed more clearly when people are less trusting of charities linked to political events in recent Turkish history, such as the Gezi Park protests. Additionally, the supporters of the ruling party, the Justice and Development Party (the AKP), are reported to have a high level of faith in the government and its institutions, such as the Grand National Assembly of Turkey, whereas the supporters of the opposition parties have a low level of trust in the government and its institutions (Aytaç & Çarkoğlu, 2020). Furthermore, the European Commission's 2021 report expresses worry[2] about potential constraints on civil society and human rights defenders' actions under the legislation on the non-proliferation of weapons of mass destruction (Directorate-General for Neighbourhood and Enlargement Negotiations, 2021). Another factor influencing the donation ecosystem is the visibility of CSOs. Due to a lack of media exposure, CSOs' credibility and funding levels are poor. People in Turkey do not use social media to be aware of and publicise the activities of CSOs (Çarkoğlu & Aytaç, 2016).

In the face of all these drawbacks and constraints, the way forward is based on the empowerment of engaged individuals and the organisation of civil society. It is equally critical that active citizens collaborate with CSOs

DOI: 10.4324/9781003389972-18

to mobilise civil society and raise awareness of its potential. It is, therefore, necessary to develop communication systems that will facilitate being and doing together. This research herewith delves into Turkey's donation culture with a focus on transmediality. It examines the *Adım Adım* charity platform, a civil society development[3] in Turkey, within the framework of Freeman's transmedia charity model. It explores possible expansions to the concepts of community media, participation media and documentary media in the context of Turkey.

Transmedia charity as a social enterprise

The communication strategies of CSOs among themselves, with their volunteers and potential donors, have become a phenomenon that needs to be reconsidered with the development of media technologies and audience behaviour. This evolution is apparent in the manuals published in the past decade, which intend to educate members of CSOs in Turkey on how to make the best use of the communication channels that are available to them (Antalya Sivil Platform Derneği, 2020; Güder, 2006; Tunović-Bećirović et al., 2013). Effective communication, however, relates not only to the mass circulation of content that appeals to the target audience but also to conveying the message at a deep and immersing level. At this point, the concept of transmedia charity can be mentioned. However, to understand this term, it is necessary to examine its building blocks, one of which is transmedia storytelling.

Transmedia storytelling was popularised by Henry Jenkins (2007) in the mid-2000s. Initially, the term was associated with the fictional storyworlds of the entertainment industry. It involves distributing unique narrative fragments across distribution channels to create a coordinated entertainment experience. Each medium contributes something unique to the story. Getting the right content to the right people at the right time, connecting fans and rewarding them are the key strategies to constructing a transmedia storyworld. *Star Wars*, *Harry Potter*, *The Matrix* and *Pokémon* are popular examples of this approach.

In time, scholarly works on transmediality found their way into stories of non-fiction, such as documentaries (Karlsen, 2018) and journalism (Gürsoy, 2020; Moloney, 2019). This is where the principles of fictional transmedia storytelling are adapted to non-fictional content. Matthew Freeman's (2018) research re-conceptualises what transmediality means beyond basic notions of storytelling. Within the context of charity, he scrutinises the term from a socio-political stance and labels it as a social enterprise. Transmediality, in other words, is positioned as an interactive approach with implications for 'people, leisure, activism, politics and society itself' (Freeman, 2018, p. 426). After examining a charity event in the United Kingdom, Freeman develops his notion of a conceptual model for understanding transmedia charity initiatives. The model is constructed by non-fictional forms of *participation, documentary* and *community media*.

Developing media technologies and converging media spaces have sought to empower audiences by granting them the means to participate in the vast world of content production, distribution and consumption (Jenkins, 2006). Transmediality positions this opportunity as one of its defining features. In fact, one of its main purposes is to offer a heightened sense of engagement for lasting audience participation. Participation media plays a leading role in the concept of transmedia charity as well. This notion of participation manifests itself in various ways, from a potential donor who watches an online video posted by a CSO to the 'prosumer' volunteer who expands the charity campaign by creating new content (Scolari et al., 2014). A transmedia charity campaign offers many channels of participation through diverse forms, such as a TV infomercial, a social media post, or a performance event. This distribution lengthens the lifespan of the campaign narrative and allows the audience to choose the parts of the campaign story they want to engage in. The goal in this scenario is not only to persuade the audience to donate but also to encourage them to help grow the campaign to other audiences and identify new contributors and resources. Tactics often used in commercial transmedia storytelling, such as merchandising, can also be observed in this process to broaden a campaign's storyline across media.

Charity campaigns include a series of messages that concern members of the public, such as children, LGBT individuals or women. According to Freeman (2018), these messages are linked by an overarching transmedia estate led by a brand identity. The estate disseminates the campaign's meanings and messages over multiple platforms, tied together by specific themes such as education, health or social services. Within the pool of content, documentary media provides the balance of a storyteller throughout content delivery. The estate organises which messages to transmit, in what form and channel, how to connect them, in what order and where to inform, educate or entertain the audience, much as one does when creating a documentary film. The campaign structure is constructed in such a way that the aftermath of each charity event is documented to showcase the effect of the donations.

Transmedia charities promote community interaction, collaboration and solidarity. Community media are local outlets that promote free expression and participatory democracy (Freeman, 2018). Using these channels, donors, volunteers and organisation members build a community around a cause. This macro-perspective allows donors to move between charity campaigns by drawing an abstract link between their messages. Freeman calls this abstract link *transmedia ethos*. According to his definition, shared underlying meanings, beliefs and values are what circulate messages through familiar actors and close encounters. He even claims that community media extends the impact of a charity event beyond its borders to other campaigns with a similar ethos. The unifying power of shared ideas, according to Freeman, is a fundamental component of transmedia charity. According to him, more than the story itself, it is the ethos that pushes potential contributors from one message to the next. The idea of collective intentionality is similarly comparable to Freeman's description of transmedia ethos. It contributes to transmedia ethos by forming a shared identity and understanding within communities, shaping how members interact with and understand the transmedia storyworld.

Eventually, transmedia communication strategies that can be implemented in charity campaigns promise positive results in terms of delivering the campaign message, exposing the campaign's impact and fostering collaboration and participation among those involved in the process. The model provides a fresh look at the role of media technologies and relationships in the charity ecosystem. This study investigates whether participation, documentary and community media can help build a sustainable charity system that inspires individuals and civil society to accomplish their goals by standing together. It explores Freeman's transmedia charity model by applying it to a civil society initiative, *Adım Adım*, within Turkey's context.

Adım Adım platform

In 2008, *Adım Adım* was launched as a collective charity-run initiative in Turkey. It is a collaboration network that brings together CSOs and volunteers who want to run for charity. It provides financial resources and promotional support to important social responsibility projects through not only running but also swimming, cycling and mountaineering. Since its initiation, *Adım Adım* (2019) has reached many volunteers and donors. The collected donations situated *Adım Adım* as an intermediary force that provided help for many individuals.

This initiative constitutes a suitable case for this research because it resembles a transmedia charity enterprise. In the context of transmedia ethos, it defines its foundation on values such as trust, solidarity, belonging, goodness, diversity, entertainment and success (Adım Adım, 2019). According to its official website, *Adım Adım* is built on the mission of guiding the development of donation resources by raising awareness and recognition of CSOs. *Adım Adım* also claims to have the vision of inspiring social solidarity by encouraging individuals and institutions to take collective action through sports. Furthermore, immersive storytelling plays a role in its charity events. During these events, CSOs and volunteers work together to reach individuals in society through stories and engagements via carefully planned communication strategies. While *Adım Adım* has its own online spaces, such as *İyilik Peşinde Koş*[4] (Run for Aid) platform, to guide the volunteers through their campaigns, it is also open to collaboration with other online social platforms, such as *İhtiyaç Haritası*[5] (Needs Map) or *Açık Açık* (Openly).[6] As one of the founders of *Adım Adım*, Itır Erhart indicates that all this endeavour is directed towards a single macro goal: the strengthening and emancipation of Turkey's civil society (I. Erhart, personal communication, March 9, 2021).

Erhart claims that, at the micro level, *Adım Adım* aims to encourage everyone to take action on social issues, regardless of political, ideological or religious beliefs.

Methodology

This study investigates the donation statistics and CSO details published on *Adım Adım*'s online web platforms (*adimadim.org* and *IPK*) as well as the posts related to the CSO marathon campaigns published between March 2019 and March 2021 on its social media accounts (*YouTube*, *Twitter*, *Instagram* and *Facebook*). The data are used to understand the overall operational structure of *Adım Adım* and the roles of its counterparts within its ecosystem.

In addition to content gathered from online sources, the study greatly benefits from in-depth interviews conducted with six donors, five volunteer runners, a founding member and a CSO member joining together under the ethos of *Adım Adım*. The CSO member, *Adım Adım* founding member and volunteer runners were asked about the communication tools they use for charity campaign distribution. They were asked to describe the channels or environments through which they received support and motivation during the campaigns. Donors were also asked what communication tools they used to access and participate in these campaigns. CSO members and volunteer runners were asked what methods they used to persuade donors to act. *NVivo* software was used on the interview transcriptions for qualitative data analysis. The transcripts of the interviews were filtered to show the most frequently used words and the concepts in which these words were used.

The content gathered from the sources mentioned above is categorised under the three components of the transmedia charity theory: *participation*, *documentary* and *community media*. This categorisation method aims to reveal the sub-layers that connect under these three main headings. Thus, it seeks to determine the potential of transmedia charity practices in Turkey's donation ecosystem and to identify areas for improvement.

Exploring Adım Adım through Freeman's transmedia charity model

Before implementing Freeman's transmedia charity model, it is necessary to understand how *Adım Adım* operates its charity campaigns. A thorough investigation into *Adım Adım*'s official website (Adım Adım, 2019), *IPK* platform (Adım Adım, 2015) and social media posts reveals the overall operational structure of the enterprise (Figure 15.1). While *Adım Adım* receives financial aid[7] from sponsors, it also receives operational support from associations such as *Açık Açık*. With the help of the assistance it receives, the initiative develops its own brand. It offers an environment for CSOs and volunteers in need to become stronger in the domains of strategy, communication and analysis. The *IPK* platform informs volunteer runners about CSO campaigns while providing donors with detailed info about the runners they

Transmedia charity initiatives in Turkey 207

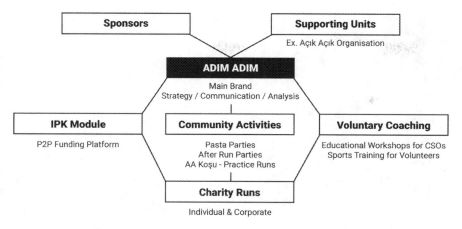

Figure 15.1 The operational structure of *Adım Adım* charity enterprise.[8] Diagram by the author.

support in charity races. The platform also keeps track of how much funds CSOs and volunteers raise during each campaign. Pasta parties, after-run parties and *AA Koşu* practices are all places where CSOs and volunteers can interact and share ideas and experiences. Voluntary coaching provides CSOs with a collaborative setting where they can learn from one another. It also offers volunteers a training environment to enhance their performance in accomplishing additional donation milestones. All these preparations result in the *Adım Adım* brand, the CSOs it supports and volunteer runners taking centre stage in individual and corporate charity runs. All parts of this operational structure lay the groundwork for the *Adım Adım* ecosystem to strengthen and expand while adding new members to its chain of goodness.

Within this operational structure, one can see various channels through which a donation campaign can be fragmented and dispersed by various characters. The content displayed on the *IPK* platform and *Adım Adım*'s social media accounts is useful for determining the flow of the overall campaign narrative.[9] Furthermore, a study of the CSOs' and volunteers' media activity reveals a donation process cycle with a beginning, a middle and an end to each campaign (Figure 15.2).

First, (1) the *IPK* platform is activated during donation campaign preparation. (2) CSOs update their campaign themes and invite volunteers to help them reach their donation goal on this platform. (3) After reviewing CSO financial and administrative histories on the *Açık Açık* website, volunteers choose a campaign theme to collect donations. (4) At the Pasta party, CSOs and volunteers discuss the campaign and their goals. (5) *Adım Adım* organises educational workshops to help CSOs enhance their operations. (6) Volunteers receive physical training through *Adım Adım*'s voluntary coaching in addition to workshops. (7) CSOs and volunteers meet to discuss campaign

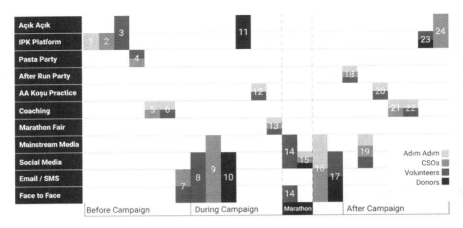

Figure 15.2 A course of the narrative in donation campaigns.[10] Diagram by the author.

strategy and donation letters before the campaign begins. (8) Volunteers send donation letters to their contacts after campaigns are started. (9) CSOs share campaign stories through various channels. (10) Donors share edited campaign messages with acquaintances from preferred media channels to share stories. (11) Donors research the credibility of the CSO on the *Açık Açık* website before submitting donations through the *IPK* platform in the name of the volunteer they wish to support. (12) On the first Saturday of each month, volunteers run *AA Koşu* practice runs for the marathon. (13) A fair is held days before the marathon, where *Adım Adım* distributes t-shirts and displays activities (ex., collecting donations on the treadmill). (14) Volunteers perform with *Adım Adım* t-shirts and banners during the marathon. (15) CSOs, *Adım Adım* and donors share marathon stories on social media to spread the narrative. (16) *Adım Adım* and CSOs continue to request donations for 15 days after the marathon. (17) Volunteers use their marathon performances to ask for donations from their friends and family until the campaign ends. Donors also share campaign narratives with their friends and family, either directly or through the content they generate. (18) After the campaign, volunteers and CSO members celebrate and discuss results at an after-party. (19) Volunteers, CSOs and *Adım Adım* announce donation reports and outcomes. (20) Volunteers return to the regular *AA Koşu* practice until the next charity race. (21) *Adım Adım* educational workshops provide CSOs with ongoing opportunities to enhance their knowledge. (22) Additionally, *Adım Adım* volunteers train with their coaches to prepare for the next charity run. (23) Donors can register as 'volunteers' on the *IPK* platform to participate in *Adım Adım*. (24) CSOs can join *Adım Adım*'s ecosystem by adhering to the *Açık Açık Association*'s transparency standards on the *IPK* platform.

While the course of the narrative displays the transmedial nature of *Adım Adım*'s operational structure, the research has embodied concepts that

Transmedia charity initiatives in Turkey 209

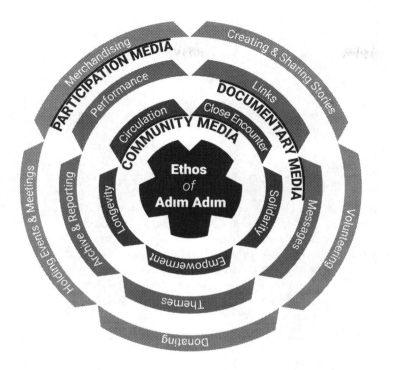

Figure 15.3 Distribution of sub-layers under Freeman's transmedia charity model.[11] Diagram by the author.

Freeman had defined abstractly under the transmedia charity model. Common keywords surfaced in the interview transcripts, revealing more specific sub-layers for Freeman's transmedia charity model (Figure 15.3).

Participation media

The interviewees discussed donation campaign participation by mentioning *donating, volunteering, story creation and sharing, events and meetings* and *merchandise*. Under the category of *donating*, it is discussed how to solicit donations from people as well as the crucial role volunteers play in this process. Sezen Öktem, a volunteer runner, stated that a lively, inviting environment encourages donations (S. Öktem, personal communication, March 24, 2021). She suggests that individual competitions and gamified goals can motivate donors and make it easier for volunteers to ask for donations. Campaign theme and volunteer runner identity are other contributor motivators. Itır Erhart, a founding member of *Adım Adım* and volunteer runner, suggests that a familiar campaign theme may inspire first-time donors (I. Erhart, personal communication, March 9, 2021). Furthermore, Aslı Tunç, another donor, states that donating in person to known volunteers enables her to delegate campaign selection and feel involved (A. Tunç, personal communication, March 21, 2021). However, there are also situations where participation is limited. Öktem cites the elderly as a concern due to their difficulty adapting to modern technology.

In *volunteering*, volunteers participate through distribution and trust-building. As a volunteer runner, Sinan Aşçı sees himself as a liaison between CSOs and donors, as many lack the resources to reach remote areas (S. Aşçı, personal communication, March 17, 2021). He shifted from donating to volunteering to achieve this goal. According to another volunteer runner Ali Eğilmez, volunteers serve as a link between CSOs and donors, building trust through their stories and personalities (A. Eğilmez, personal communication, March 16, 2021). However, the connection between volunteers and their goals is thin. Volunteers list several ways this connection can break. According to Aşçı, focusing solely on a CSO rather than a goal can lead to a loss of motivation. Additionally, Öktem believes that pressuring individuals to donate is unethical. Sinan Abra shares that he has lost his active spirit due to a lack of intellectual satisfaction when communicating with other volunteers (S. Abra, personal communication, March 28, 2021). He struggles to dedicate time and effort to fundraising throughout the campaign.

During the process of *creating and sharing stories*, participation occurs through genuine interaction among small groups. The campaign stories reach the most remote places this way. Erhart claims that volunteers divide a CSO's campaign narrative into many personal stories and share them with their friends. Eğilmez and Öktem prefer direct communication methods such as SMS, WhatsApp groups, or emails for distribution rather than targeting large audiences. As a donor, volunteer runner and CSO founding member, Buse Kaçar receives donation notifications through various channels during campaigns (B. Kaçar, personal communication, March 23, 2021). She and Tunç say they will share these messages with their friends if they believe in their mission. Tunç says hearing CSO stories from strangers is more convincing than hearing from friends. However, she is reluctant to donate to or promote CSOs with a politicised identity in the general assembly or campaign theme. In other words, politics can cause doubts in narrative distribution.

Pre- and post-campaign *meetings and events* encourage CSO and volunteer participation. Common buzzwords for these contexts are community, motivation, transparency, awareness and familiarity. Gathering at events makes Abra, Aşçı, Eğilmez and Kaçar feel like a family or community. According to Aşçı and Eğilmez, meeting new people and discovering shared interests motivates them. As a CSO founder, Kaçar stresses the importance of plenary meeting openness and inclusivity. She believes these gathering places are crucial to educating people about CSOs and civil society.

The *merchandising* of Adım Adım is often mentioned in relation to participation. Erhart, Tunç and Aşçı explore how the Adım Adım name, logo and t-shirt evoke family, belonging, solidarity, trust and power. According to Aşçı and Abra, wearing a bright red t-shirt while exercising on the street can boost confidence and attract positive attention. Erhart and Aşçı state that displaying donor names on t-shirts and the marathon's overall performance offer volunteers psychological support and a sense of solidarity with strangers. Erhart, a volunteer runner, and Tunç, a donor, indicate that the t-shirts' names are a symbolic and practical way to thank donors.

Documentary media

When asked how CSO members and volunteer runners try to persuade donors to donate, their answers revealed joint statements relating to documentary media regarding *themes*, *messages*, *links*, *performances* and *reports*. Volunteers and donors choose campaign *themes* for many reasons. Eğilmez believes the CSO should be independent of the government and well-managed. Aşçı suggests that donation campaigns should be relevant, personal and relevant to disadvantaged individuals. Öktem, on the other hand, donates to the first campaign she encounters, leaving the decision to chance.

The overall campaign story's *messages* develop gradually before reaching donors. According to Erhart, the first stage involves *Adım Adım* distributing visual and structural story templates to all CSOs. CSOs use these templates to collaborate on campaign narratives. Volunteers share their stories with donors via familiar channels. They ensure the donor understands why they are collecting donations, whom they are doing it for and how they will perform. To build trust with donors, Eğilmez, Abra and Aşçı share personalised stories with heartfelt facts. As the final layer, donors receive these donation messages from multiple close sources. Tunç says each campaign expands the variety of messages and sources. She also thinks that too many messages are exhausting.

The concept of *links* emerges as a means of connecting the narrative and the characters. According to Erhart and Eğilmez, *Adım Adım* is a network that promotes healthy communication between CSOs and donors. All interviewees share a common opinion: volunteers in this network serve as mediators, decision-makers or awakeners for dialogue between CSOs and donors. Tunç argues that an organisation's suspicious history or political stance could quickly break this narrative link.

The *performance* concept frequently referenced in the interviews is based on the volunteer's devotion and symbolic position. According to Tunç, charity-run volunteers' physical and mental challenges deserve respect. Erhart believes respect is inevitable because the performance's difficulty shows donors' dedication. Apart from respect, Tunç and Kaçar watch and encourage volunteer performances to share excitement and motivation. Eğilmez, Abra and Aşçı feel solidarity, responsibility and belonging during these performances. Successfully completing a performance gives Aşçı courage for future campaigns. Finally, Kaçar recalls how they, as CSOs, use various methods in charity runs to attract attention, such as wearing unusual costumes during the marathon.

All actors in this process must record and archive campaign and donation results transparently through *reports*. Erhart says transparency must include financial and board member information. She contends that CSOs should be held accountable not only to their donors but also to the general public. Tunç and Abra agree that donors are hesitant because confidentiality causes uncertainty and they want their money to go where it should. The archives offered by *Adım Adım* and *Açık Açık* are also beneficial for volunteers. Aşçı uses the stories and numbers of those he has impacted in his future campaigns as leverage.

Community media

When volunteer runners, CSO members and donors were asked in which channels or environments they experienced support and motivation during campaigns, their answers were about *circulation, close encounters, solidarity, empowerment* and *longevity* within the framework of community media. Eğilmez suggests that focusing on doing good everywhere is more effective than being tied to a specific CSO. This pure focus ensures that volunteers support different CSOs and themes during campaigns. Erhart points out *Adım Adım*'s operational structure, highlighting the contagious effect of goodness as donors become volunteers and *circulation* increases. She notes that this impact is caused by stories being shared only within a close circle.

In *close encounters*, interviewees note that collaboration has pros and cons. Tunç is pleased to see that people can still approach strangers with positive thoughts despite Turkey's negative image. Aşçı and Abra assert that working towards a common goal can foster close friendships between strangers. The volunteers also discuss the drawbacks of intimacy. According to Abra, people who can't talk about anything other than sports can lose their sense of community. He says prolonged, frequent interactions with the same people can cause boredom. Furthermore, Aşçı asserts that inappropriate *WhatsApp* messages can lead to emotional alienation.

Eğilmez and Tunç view *Adım Adım* as a way to channel their energies. According to Eğilmez, individuals with similar experiences and baggage tend to gather under this structure. This gathering is a *solidarity* spirit and collective kindness, according to Erhart and Tunç. Eğilmez defines this endeavour as individuals demonstrating social responsibility and adding value to others. Öktem recounts donating a significant amount to her volunteer friend's campaign, which helped her achieve her goal. Eğilmez and Aşçı emphasise that they find common ground through compassion and democracy when interacting with people of diverse religions and political views. Erhart says the idea that 'we are stronger when we stand together' permeates nearly all layers of this enterprise. Unfortunately, Erhart says, past tensions and rivalries may prevent CSOs from coming together under this roof.

Based on Eğilmez, civil society in Turkey is linked to leftist culture and the street. He claims that street performances create the notion of protest and that people are afraid to participate. Kaçar, Aşçı, Tunç and Eğilmez view the *Adım Adım* initiative as a noble fight against negative factors. Tunç finds it empowering to see the positive changes and progress after so much struggle and exhaustion. Kaçar agrees that it does not concern CSOs to exist in the same place for different purposes if non-discrimination remains a core value in this *empowering* process. Öktem emphasises that the 'run for me, too' message greatly motivates donors and volunteers.

The *longevity* of this endeavour is also among the concepts that came up for community media. Erhart believes that the *Adım Adım* initiative, which promotes cultural and systemic change, can enhance society's view of giving. She cites the annual growth in participation and the COVID-19 epidemic-flattening participation statistics. She adds that the enterprise's pluralistic culture prioritises social and environmental values above all else. According to Eğilmez, *Adım Adım*'s ongoing activities indicate a recurring cycle of hope. He also considers it risky for certain names to identify with *Adım Adım*. He stresses that this ecosystem must be self-regenerating to survive.

Influence of transmedia charity on Turkey's donation culture

The practice of transmedia charity in the chosen case study shows positive potential to promote donation culture and support the development of civil society in Turkey. Participation, community and documentary media work together to encourage charity campaigns and cultural change. This study also highlighted the sub-layers of Freeman's (2018) participation, documentary and community media structure. These layers have raised awareness of civil society's potential and its positive impact on society. These media tools contribute to sustainability and positive change by encouraging engagement and community. This section discusses how these many media formats and sub-layers can promote social involvement and support.

Focusing on fundraising goals rather than emotional engagement with the cause may explain the donation culture's decline. Thus, many organisations are still seeking ways to improve their fundraising and donor relations. Charity organisations can improve audience engagement by using digital and multimedia storytelling. Participation and documentary media may help people engage with the giving culture. Interactive storytelling may assist them in connecting with the audience emotionally. By combining performances, social media and gathering events, the cause can be told more intimately. Customised story fragments can be shared with acquaintances to penetrate society. This strategy can improve public understanding of the cause and increase engagement. Since it aligns with their values and beliefs, emotional involvement can improve the chance of individuals taking action. Building confidence in CSOs is also crucial to this initiative's success. Lack of faith in these organisations and religious and cultural beliefs may limit public funding. People sometimes misunderstand the impact of donations, and many CSOs are hesitant to share their personal and financial information.

Giving can also be hindered by doubts about where and how funds are spent. These traits may make it hard to get support and donations. To build trust and show the impact of charitable donations, transparency and good communication are needed. The study shows that familiar themes and faces can build trust. Using famous people, influencers and friends to promote the cause may help build trust and support. Actively connecting with the community and sharing true stories about donations' impact may build trust with future donors and boost confidence in the organisation. Another important factor is contribution transparency. Documenting funding distribution and use helps CSOs build trust. These strategies can be combined to increase public support and help organisations meet fundraising goals.

Turkey's disinterest in civil society may be due to a lack of awareness of its benefits and community impact. Lack of information, resources and apathy or cynicism towards political and social issues may present problems. Women and marginalised groups may also be discouraged from civil society participation by social and cultural norms. Education and communication will be needed to raise awareness and foster community involvement to overcome this indifference. Community and documentary media may empower citizens to participate in Turkey's cultural change. They use various communication channels to position volunteers as mediators and facilitators of CSO-donor dialogue. These volunteers' dedication, shown in various media formats, inspires others to participate. Documentary and community media promote 'doing and being together' and social responsibility in the community. This promotes civic participation and civil society activities, empowering citizens to shape their communities and effect positive change. Furthermore, documentary and community media may help fight prejudice by offering volunteers and donors a variety of ways to support their causes. Individuals are empowered to take responsibility for their communities and make a difference, transforming society culturally.

The lack of an active and engaged citizenry in Turkey, which fails to recognise civil society's role in social and political change, hinders civil society's growth. Individuals' lack of comprehension of their role and responsibilities in moulding their communities and fighting for change is reflected in this. The lack of alliances and partnerships between civil society, government and the private sector to address society's diverse issues also hinders progress. Lack of networks and alliances among CSOs can also hinder idea sharing and the formation of a unified voice. These networks enable civil society to influence policy and decision-making through collective action and advocacy. Participation, documentary and community media are essential for a diverse and efficient civil society. They can operate as a forum for conversation and communication among various actors. These media types can help CSOs, government agencies and the private sector form networks and collaborations through outreach and community development. Addressing individuals directly is another goal to raise awareness of civil society's relevance and potential. Small groups meet, experience and participate in activities that foster community development, network expansion and bonding through shared interests. These media formats also remind people of their past successes and inspire them to build on them, boosting CSO exposure and empowering volunteers as message bearers. Additionally, branding and merchandising efforts through these media promote 'doing and being together'. These media forms bring people together, encourage pluralism, prioritise social and environmental values and are independent of politics by fostering solidarity and a common goal. The ultimate goal is to build a strong, extensive civil society one person at a time through engagement, support and social responsibility.

CSOs, volunteers and donors must work together to sustain and activate civil society. However, transmedia charity initiatives face several obstacles to sustainability. Digital technology infrastructure can be difficult for the elderly to adapt to, affecting inclusivity and democratic participation. Volunteers' vital role in CSO–donor relations also presents a challenge. Volunteers can become emotionally alienated if they lose sight of the common goal, losing motivation, spirit and community. Volunteers are needed to keep CSOs and donors connected, which is another issue. A transmedia campaign relies on volunteers for custom content, systematic message distribution and training. However, overreliance on volunteers can lead to burnout, threatening the initiative's sustainability. Political identity and themes of CSOs are still major decision components for donors, and these can induce doubts in the process of disseminating the campaign message, breaking the links of the overall campaign story. The initiative's brand should be independent of its founders and executors, who may represent a political party. Donors can be overwhelmed by campaign messages, and CSOs may refuse to collaborate due to past conflicts. To sustain a transmedia charity initiative, inclusion, democratic engagement, volunteer motivation and independence from political identification must be addressed.

Adım Adım's transmedia strategy effectively raises awareness and engages donors, but a critical perspective is also required. Critics may argue that Adım Adım's transmedia strategy prioritises emotional appeals and narrative over providing concrete information about its programs and services. This can make it hard for potential contributors to understand their impact and lose faith in the effort. Critics may argue that Adım Adım's transmedia approach primarily targets the middle and upper classes, failing to reach marginalised and disadvantaged communities. This has the potential to prolong socioeconomic disparities and leave people in need behind. Adım Adım, like other charity platforms, operates in a complex environment, and its transmedia strategy may not fully address its social and political context.

Conclusion

CSOs in Turkey help society develop. However, they face challenges such as a lack of interest, mistrust in the donation system, apprehension about volunteering due to political polarisation and a lack of visibility. This research advocates for facilitating being and doing together to overcome these challenges by empowering engaged individuals, organising civil society and developing communication systems. The framework draws from Freeman's (2018) transmedia charity model and the *Adım Adım* charity platform in Turkey, examining community, participation and documentary media. It examines whether they can help create a sustainable charity system that inspires individuals and civil society to collaborate.

In the chosen case study, the practice of transmedia charity demonstrates the positive potential to promote donation culture and support the development of civil society in Turkey. Community, documentary and participation media encourage citizens to participate in charity campaigns and lead cultural change. Additional sub-layers to Freeman's (2018) participation, documentary and community media structure were also highlighted in this study. The combined efforts of these layers have raised awareness of civil society's potential and its positive impact on society. These media tools promote participation and community to promote sustainability and positive change.

Transmedia charity initiatives also face issues like digitisation for the elderly, volunteer burnout, political identity influencing donor decisions and conflicting interests. For inclusivity, volunteer motivation and political independence, these issues must be addressed. This study focuses on a single case, which investigates the concept of transmedia charity in Turkey for the first time. More research into transmedia charity cases worldwide is needed to understand this new phenomenon. Addressing these issues may be a starting point for strengthening transmedia charity studies and understanding civil society mobilisation within the field of media research.

Acknowledgements

The author thanks the interviewees Sinan Abra, Sinan Aşçı, Ali Eğilmez, Itır Erhart, Buse Pınar Kaçar, Sezen Öktem and Aslı Tunç for their contribution to this research.

Notes

1 There have been a few reports, books and articles published about the donation culture in Turkey; however, this research includes the most recent and relevant academic sources.
2 It has been argued that the law in question, which came into effect in 2020, may impose new restrictions on the freedom of association and have a negative impact on fundraising. The law on the collection of aid imposes harsh conditions on permits to deter CSOs from fundraising activities. Prior notification and long-lasting permission processes for each fundraising activity are among these conditions (Directorate-General for Neighbourhood and Enlargement Negotiations, 2021).
3 On 6 March 2022, *Adım Adım* announced that it would continue its operations not as a development but as an association.
4 *İyilik Peşinde Koş* (IPK) platform is a charity-run web platform that is used by volunteers who want to run for the charity campaigns of CSOs supported by *Adım Adım* (2015).

5 *İhtiyaç Haritası* (2015) is a social cooperative that was founded in 2015 to connect people in need with individuals, institutions and organisations that want to help. Through map technology and community-based verification tools, it promotes cooperation and solidarity in domains such as education, health, culture and the arts.
6 *Açık Açık* (2016) is an association established with the aim of increasing the number of transparent and accountable CSOs in Turkey. The association also owns an online platform, which was established to spread the culture of donation. *Adım Adım* gets support from *Açık Açık*, as it has decided to work only with CSOs that sign donor rights.
7 *Adım Adım* Executive Committee members, *Adım Adım* CSO members and other volunteers receive no financial compensation for their voluntary work. *Adım Adım* accepts financial support and requires that the cash payment for the product or service from which the aid is obtained be provided directly by the sponsor.
8 This diagram shows the interrelationship of the parts that make up the general structure of *Adım Adım*.
9 This chapter focuses not on the narrative content used during the campaign but on when, how and by whom this narrative was distributed among the media within the *Adım Adım* structure.
10 This graphic depicts the steps involved in the creation, distribution and consumption of a campaign. It separates the campaign into three major stages (before, during and after), with a particular emphasis on the charity race (Marathon). The colour coding reveals which actors are involved in whatever stage of the campaign and via which communication channel. The processes depicted in the figure are not identical in every campaign process.
11 This diagram illustrates the sub-layers that emerged from the interview data within the context of Freeman's transmedia charity model.

References

Açık Açık. (2016). *Açık Açık STK*. Açık Açık. https://acikacik.org/stk/
Adım Adım. (2015). *Homepage*. İyilik Peşinde Koş (İPK). https://ipk.adimadim.org/
Adım Adım. (2019). *Home Page*. Adım Adım. https://adimadim.org/
Antalya Sivil Platform Derneği. (2020). *SivilAnT Eğitim Kitleri* (STK'lar için İletişim Becerileri ve Sosyal Medya). https://portal.sivilant.org/uploads/cms/main.ant/48102.pdf
Aytaç, E. S., & Çarkoğlu, A. (2020). *Individual Giving and Philanthropy in Turkey 2019*. Istanbul: TÜSEV.
CAP, IPC, & IAI. (2017, July 10). *Trends in Turkish Civil Society*. Center for American Progress. https://www.americanprogress.org/issues/security/reports/2017/07/10/435475/trends-turkish-civil-society/
Çarkoğlu, A., & Aytaç, E. S. (2016). *Individual Giving and Philanthropy in Turkey 2015*. Istanbul: TÜSEV.
Directorate-General for Neighbourhood and Enlargement Negotiations. (2021). *Turkey Report 2021*. European Commission. https://ec.europa.eu/neighbourhood-enlargement/turkey-report-2021_en
Freeman, M. (2018). Transmedia Charity: Constructing the Ethos of the BBC's Red Nose Day across Media. In M. Freeman & R. R. Gambarato (Eds.), *The Routledge Companion to Transmedia Studies* (pp. 306–313). New York: Routledge.
Güder, N. (2006). *STÖ'ler İçin İletişim, İşbirliği ve Kampanya Yürütme Kılavuzu*. STGM | Sivil Toplum Geliştirme Merkezi. https://www.stgm.org.tr/yayinlar/stoler-icin-iletisim-isbirligi-kampanya-yurutme-kilavuzu

Gürsoy, D. (2020). *Transmediality in Independent Journalism: The Turkish Case.* New York: Routledge.

İhtiyaç Haritası. (2015). *Homepage.* İhtiyaç Haritası. https://www.ihtiyacharitasi.org/

Jenkins, H. (2006). *Convergence Culture: Where Old and New Media Collide.* New York: NYU Press.

Jenkins, H. (2007, March 21). Transmedia Storytelling 101. *Confessions of an Aca-Fan.* http://henryjenkins.org/blog/2007/03/transmedia_storytelling_101.html

Karlsen, J. (2018). Transmedia Documentary. In M. Freeman & R. R. Gambarato (Eds.), *The Routledge Companion to Transmedia Studies* (pp. 25–34). New York: Routledge.

Moloney, K. (2019). Designing Transmedia Journalism Projects. In M. Khosrow-Pour, S. Clarke, M. E. Jennex, A. Becker & A. Anttiroiko (Eds.), *Journalism and Ethics: Breakthroughs in Research and Practice* (pp. 872–892). Hershey, PA: IGI Global.

Scolari, C. A., Bertetti, P., & Freeman, M. (2014). *Transmedia Archaeology: Storytelling in the Borderlines of Science Fiction, Comics and Pulp Magazines.* Basingstoke: Palgrave Macmillan.

Tunović-Bećirović, S., Aygül, M., Bulut-Bican, A., & Fazlić, A. (2013, January 1). *STK'lar için Medya İlişkileri Rehberi.* STGM | Sivil Toplum Geliştirme Merkezi. https://www.stgm.org.tr/yayinlar/stklar-icin-medya-iliskileri-rehberi

Uncu, B. A. (2019). *Polarization in Turkey.* KONDA. https://konda.com.tr/uploads/eng1901-barometer94-polarizationinturkey-df6ed1e-cea62e0b778e84441ed99ccb4d12b781e722fceed6bd03a58c6f33e97.pdf

Index

Abra, S. 210–212, 216
academic support 44
accountability 56, 92, 96, 212, 217
acculturation 157, 166
acting: acting together 2, 8, 10, 120, 157, 161–165, 169, 173, 175; actor 24, 28–34, 36–39, 41–42, 81, 95, 128, 130, 136, 143, 212, 217; on others 165, with others 163–165
adaptation 4, 51, 156, 158, 165
Adım Adım 202–217; AA Koşu 207–208; IPK Platform 206–208, 216–217; operational structure 206–208, 212
affect studies 109, 160
Ahmed, S. 144, 159, 161, 164
alienation 48, 54, 83, 164, 212, 215
Anderson, C. 61
Anglophone Caribbean 171
Anylabtalks 7, 64, 67, 70
app store 130
appearing 82–83
application program interfaces (API) 130, 132, 135, 137
arbitrary 45, 77, 79, 89
architectural space 61
archive 19, 22, 23, 212
art: aesthetic art 144–146; applied arts 27–28, 30; artists' book 27–43; artwork 7, 27–33, 37–38, 40–41, 145, 152; mechanical art 27–28
Aşçı, S. 210, 216
audience 6, 24, 64–69, 81, 83, 92, 95–96, 108, 124, 130–131, 135, 144–145, 149–152, 203–204, 210, 213
audio 64–65, 67–68, 70, 92, 98, 107–108, 111, 112–113
authenticity 82, 183
awareness 8, 49, 55, 78, 89–91, 95–96, 109, 162, 180, 203, 205, 210, 213–216

Bauman, Z. 74, 76–77
belonging 75–76, 102, 105, 113, 205, 210–211
Benkler, Y. 129, 138
black box 48, 53, 56
blog 65, 68, 70, 132–133, 135, 146
Brecht, B.: Brechtian theatre 81
broadcast 6, 17–25, 64–65, 69, 131–132
buggery law 171

campaign 204–217
Caribbean 169–172, 176, 178, 180–182
Cariglobal 180
charity: campaign 204, 206, 213; ecosystem 202; platform 203, 215–216; run 10, 207–208, 211; transmedia charity initiatives 202–218
child 23, 78–79, 82, 94, 119, 204
circulation 68, 203, 212
citizen 76, 92, 110, 129, 143–144, 173, 202, 214, 216
city 76, 110, 112–113, 115, 172, 177, 187, 192
civil society 10, 90, 202–203, 205, 210, 212–216
coexistence 162
coding 131–133, 135, 217
collaboration 1–2, 4–7, 10, 17–18, 21, 27, 29–34, 38–39, 41, 44–46, 48, 52–57, 59, 61, 65, 67–68, 70, 74–75, 83–84, 107, 109, 112, 122–124, 128–129, 143–144, 147–149, 151, 170–171, 183, 186–187, 195–197, 204–205, 212; collaborative community 4–5, 109, 122, 134; collaborative ethnography 7, 45–46; peer-to-peer 45, 47, 52–56
collective: action 3, 9, 77, 106, 129, 174, 180, 183, 214; collective

Index

intentionality 2, 6, 9, 134, 205; creativity 38, 133, 145–158; effort 44, 129, 136–137; knowledge production 5, 18; reflection 21, 24, 106, 171, 183
colonial 9, 164, 171–172, 174, 183
commodification 128, 135, 138, 187, 193–194, 196
commons-based peer production 129
communal joy 178
communication 1–10; dynamic 165; intercultural 156–161, 163, 165; macro-level 156, 161, 165; media technologies 10, 59, 108–109, 116–117, 126, 186–198, micro-level 156, 158, 161, 165; strategies 203, 205
community 3–11, 21, 49, 53, 59, 61, 62, 66, 70, 74–78, 89, 91, 102–107, 110–113, 119–122, 124–125, 131, 135–138, 143–144, 146–147, 152, 170–177, 180, 203–217; communitas 178, 185; community-led company 8, 61, 128; company-led community 128–129, 131, 133, 135–137, 139; engagement 52, 61, 119, 137, 144, 173; online brand community 129, 136; support 102, 132, 205–208, 211–216
complementor company 8, 128, 131, 135–137
conflict 49, 82, 89, 91, 93, 98, 106, 164, 192, 213, 216
congruence 75, 79
connection: connectivity 116–118, 125, 190; disconnect 120
constructivist paradigm 62
consumption 68, 120, 130, 204
content 22, 23, 28–30, 32–34, 36, 38–41, 61, 64, 66–69, 121, 128–130, 136, 179, 189–191, 195, 197, 203–208, 215, 217; curation 31, 48, 67
convergence culture 129
conversation 17–23, 44–45, 48, 61–64, 66, 69, 120, 148, 183, 214
cooperation 120, 127–128, 217
Couldry, N. 7–8, 186, 188–191, 193, 195
creativity 32–33, 61, 80, 129, 133
credibility 202, 208
critical theory 160–161, 165, 193
critical turn 156
crowdsourcing innovation 135

culture: cross-cultural 158, 166; cultural difference 156, 165; cultural relativism 172; dominant culture 162–164; sociocultural 157–158, 160–162, 172; strangers 157, 159

dancehall 174, 178, 183
data: datafication 186–187, 190–194, 196–197; relations 187, 89, 193–194, 196–197
Death Stranding 8, 116–127
Deleuze, G. 53, 75, 83
Derrida, J. 76, 80
Dervin, F. 157, 160, 163
design: design product 28–32; designer 7, 27–41, 66, 70, 189, 193, 196–198; elements 28–30, 32, 34, 38, 40; process 28–34, 38, 41–42
deterritorialization 83–85
dialogue: building dialogue 41, 143; dialogic 5, 7, 17, 19, 44–46, 48, 55, 58, 143–145, 147, 151–152, 154, 164, 170
dichotomy 75–76, 82, 158, 172, 194
digital: digital communication technologies 9, 108–109, 166–167, 186–198; digital ethics 186–188, 191–195 (*see also* ethics); digital platform 128–129, 134, 137, 186–190, 194; digitalization 187, 189, 190
discourse 7–8, 55, 60, 70, 74–75, 79, 89, 97–99, 145, 157–158, 161–163, 165, 171–172, 182; discursive construction 132, 159; integration 158, 162, 165
discrimination 21, 90, 94, 169, 173, 194, 213
dismissal 18–19
displacement 8, 95, 103–105, 111–113
disposal 77
dissonance 81, 164
diversity 62, 75, 147–148, 156, 164
documentary 17, 18, 23, 24, 204, 211–212, 214
donation 131, 204, 205, 210, 212, 214–215; campaign 207–209, 211; culture 203, 213, 216; ecosystem 202, 206
Dougherty, D. 61
duo autoethnography 44, 46–47, 55–56

early intervention 104
Eco, U. 83

Index

education 2, 5, 9, 23, 30, 41, 44–52, 66, 71, 94, 96, 98, 144, 195, 204, 207–208, 214, 217
Eğilmez, A. 210–213, 216
el secreto abierto 180
Emancipation Park 174–176
emotion 9, 17, 19–21, 24–25, 27–28, 44, 46, 56, 90, 92, 94, 98, 102, 105–106, 108–109, 114, 124, 148–149, 151–153, 161–163, 165, 174, 179, 187–188, 191, 212–213, 215; ethics of 82, 94; feelings 50, 55–56, 63, 90, 94–96, 102–105, 109–113, 134, 148, 173, 175
empathy 8, 74, 89, 90, 92, 95–96, 98
empowerment 95, 98, 106, 112, 145, 173, 202, 212
enactment 81, 107
encounter 1, 9–10, 76–77, 145, 204, 212; intercultural 156–157, 159–165
engagement 1, 6, 44, 52, 55, 61, 67–68, 96, 119, 128, 132–137, 143–144, 173, 180, 186, 195, 204–205, 213, 215; engaged individuals 202, 214, 216
entertainment 59, 136, 203, 205
entrepreneurship 61, 70
episode 22–23, 59, 64–70
Erhart, I. 205–206, 209–213, 216
essentialist 156, 163
ethics: dataficaction 187, 192–194; digital communication technologies 9, 108–109, 166–167, 186–198; *see also* digital ethics
ethnography 170; duo autoethnography 44, 46–47, 55–56
ethos 68, 186, 193–194, 196; transmedia ethos 204–206
everyday 2–3, 9, 18, 33, 44–45, 56, 59, 63–64, 92, 95, 102, 105, 120, 129, 150, 158, 191, 193, 199
exclusion 74–75, 90, 97, 115, 159, 164, 187, 194
extension 129, 131–133, 135–137

Facebook 129, 137, 189, 194, 206
faith 202, 215, 215
fear 23, 55, 74, 94, 98–100, 102, 104, 174–175, 177, 179, 202
Ferri, G. 156–157, 159–160, 163–164
Flash Mob 9, 169–170, 173–179, 181–183

Flickr 129
foreign 78, 164
Foucault 180, 183
Freeman, M. 3, 203–206, 209, 213, 216–217

Gauntlett, D. 60, 70
gay liberation 172, 180
gay pride 9, 172–173, 177, 179–180, 182–183; EuroPride 173
Geçtan, E. 78–79
gender: agency of women 18, 20, 24, 177; equity 61, 70, 170; feminist politics 17, 20–21; gendered body 20; identity 34, 49, 51, 172–173; inequality 21; women's activisim 17, 24
ghost 76, 80
gift economy 129; gift-giving community 129, 136
Google 66, 111, 130, 181
government 89, 91, 92, 95, 147, 202, 211, 214
Guattari, F. 75, 83
guest 63, 65–66, 68–70, 170

Habermas, J. 77–78
hackerspaces 61, 70
Hamlet 6
hate 77, 89, 133, 197
hauntology 76, 80
heterosexuality 171–172
hierarchy 28, 30, 32–33, 41, 81
homo homini lupus 75, 83
homogenised 78
homophobia 9, 169, 172
homosexuality 171
host 22, 59, 64, 66, 68–70, 133, 143, 158, 165, 172
human rights 8, 89, 91–98; violation 90

identity: brand 204, 210, 215–216; identity, collective 102, 105–106, 112–113, 152, 157, 205; individual 34, 45–46, 48–52, 75–77, 79–80, 82–83, 172–173, 187–188, 194, 209
immigration 156
in-betweenness 80
individual: identity (*see* identity); individualisation 74, 116, 120, 126; individualism 28, 44–45, 117, 119, 121–122, 129, 158
inequalities 92, 96–97

inertia 80
information: design 32–33, 39; privacy 194–196
inside 82–83
integration 156–158, 162, 165, 189
interaction 7, 9–10, 18, 29, 39, 62–63, 67–68, 97, 105, 110, 116, 121, 134, 143, 156, 160–161, 163–165, 180, 188, 195, 204, 210, 212
interactivity 108, 129, 133–134
intercultural: competence 157, 163, 165; dialogue 157, 163–164; interculturality 156, 160–161, 165
interdisciplinary 1, 3–4, 7, 9, 31, 33, 41–42, 62, 64, 70, 97, 150, 198
interface 27, 32, 39, 42, 130, 189
interrelation 97, 160, 217
intervention 19, 21, 23, 40, 60, 95, 102–104, 106–107, 109, 112, 120
interviewe 17, 19–22, 24, 63, 66, 69, 111, 209, 212, 216
IPCC 3–5, 42
isolation 8, 44, 46, 48, 116, 118–119, 125, 157
it statement 7, 75, 78, 80, 83–84

Jamaica 5, 169–183
Jenkins, H. 60–68, 129–130, 203–204
JFLAG 170, 173–178, 181–182
Jones, D. 169, 173
journalism 90–93, 96–97, 203; ethics 91–92; narrative see narrative

Kaçar, B. 210–211
Kojima, H. 119–121, 124; Kojima Productions 8, 116–117

labelling 77, 84
labour 4, 21, 24, 30, 130, 135, 151, 187, 195; immaterial 129
Lacan, J. 77, 79
language 51, 77–79, 83, 97, 153, 158, 160, 162, 164, 181; visual 28, 32, 34, 37–42
LGBTQ: community 170, 172, 175; Jamaican LGBTQ people 169–183; rights movement 171–172, 182
liminality 80
listener 18, 20, 22–24, 64–65, 112
loneliness 8, 46, 48, 55–57, 116–121, 124
long tail 68
longevity 212–213

majority society 157, 162
makerspace 2, 59–64, 66, 70
Markman, K. M. 68
Maroons 173
me: me statement 7, 75, 78, 80–81, 83–84; my thing 79; my world 79
meaning 7, 29–32, 75, 78, 82–83
media: consumption 68, 204; doing media together 7–8, 10, 65, 69, 186, 194, 197, 212, 216; doing radio 68; mediatisation 116, 122, 125–126; mediator 83, 214; texts 75
memory 6, 18, 21–22, 102–103, 194; collective 105–107; embodied 174; project 107; remembering 6, 17–19, 169, 183; transactive 19
merchandising 204, 210, 215
methodology 3, 6, 7, 18, 27, 28, 31, 33, 41, 46, 59–60, 62–64, 67–69, 96, 143–144, 152, 157, 170–171
Miller, V. 160–162
mirror 78–79, 83
monetization 129, 135–136
Mühlhoff, R. 160–161
multi-case study 62
mutual understanding 9, 156, 161, 164

name 77, 82, 84
narrative: journalistic 8, 90, 96–98; space 19–20
nation 119–120, 158
negotiation 50, 80, 90, 157, 179, 182, 202
neighbour 76, 144, 146–147, 149–150, 202
Nein, L. 81, 84
network 8, 18, 55, 66, 98, 116–118, 123, 125, 129, 131, 136, 187, 205, 211, 214–215; broadcasting 131
newcomer 76–77, 131
news 90–91, 93, 96, 178, 181, 182, 190

O'Neill, O. 188, 190
Öktem, S. 209–213, 216
opponent 76
opposite 75, 81, 84
oral history 6, 17–19, 22, 24–25
other 74–84, Big Other 80; The Others 76
outside/outsider 2, 53–54, 74–77, 79–80, 82–83
ownership 78

paromasis 82
participation 1–2, 55; participant engagement 10, 59–60, 63, 69, 203; participatory culture 1, 68, 204–205, 209–210, 213–216; participatory methodologies 2, 6, 9, 143, 147–149, 151–152; *see also* methodology
pedagogy 144, 195, 197
peer to peer support 34, 41, 48, 52–56
Pekerman, S. 83
perception 45, 48, 55–56, 77, 106, 109, 160, 192–194, 196
performance 20, 24, 50, 67, 74, 81–83; performer 75, 80; studies 7, 75–76, 80
phenomenology: experienced difference 159–160; post-phenomenology 193; sociocultural difference 157, 160–161
physical space 5, 61
pinkwashing 172
place 103, 105–108, 110–113
platform 8, 23, 31, 64–66, 68–70, 92, 124, 128, 131–133, 135–137; affordances 5, 103, 113, 122, 134; power 128, 130, 133, 137–138; work 129
pluralised societies 9, 156–158
podcast 7, 59–70; episode 64–70; independent podcasters 68
political: polarisation 202, 215; stance 203, 211
possession 78–79
postcolonial 164, 171, 183
postpositivist paradigm 158; neo-essentialist 158
power 8, 18–21, 24, 54, 56, 60, 66, 68, 90–91, 95–97, 102–104, 106, 109–110, 112, 129, 132–133, 145, 149, 151, 157–160, 162, 164–165, 171, 173, 180, 190–191, 202, 204, 210, 212–216
presence 18–19, 75–76, 84, 109, 117, 131, 159, 162, 196
production 7, 17–18, 23, 27–28, 32–33, 37, 39, 41, 59, 61–68, 110, 129–130, 137, 193–194, 204; knowledge 1, 5–6, 18–19, 144, 147–148, 170; producer 18–21, 28, 64, 67–68, 90, 197; produsage 60, 67–68, 130
protest marches 179
psychoanalysis 77

public: publicness 177–178, 181–182; sphere 7, 20, 59–62, 77, 92, 130, 177, 179, 181–182, 190

qualitative: analysis software 132; data collection 47–48, 60, 62, 64, 69, 133, 136; research 6, 195; *see also* data
Quijano, A. 75

racism 90, 97
radio: broadcasting 17–18, 20–22, 64–65; women broadcasters 17–19, 21–24
Rainbow House 174–175
Rancière, J. 77
reassuring 76
reciprocality 81–82
recognition 39, 76, 78, 81, 89, 93, 95, 131–132, 146, 152, 161–162, 187–188, 191, 205
Reggae 169, 174
rejection 77, 179
relational modes 160, 163, 165
reporting 91–94, 97
research methodology 59, 64, 67–70, 147, 149; *see also* methodology
resistance 83, 106, 144
resonance 9, 156–157, 160–163, 165; affective 162; descriptive 156, 161, 165; discourse 157–158, 161–163, 165; intercultural 9, 156–157, 160–162, 164; macro-level 156, 161–162, 165; micro-level 156, 158, 161, 165; normative 156–157, 161, 163–165; recognition 161–162; relational mode 163; resonance-alienation-continuum 164; transformation 164
respectability politics 171–172
Rorty, R. 90, 94
Rosa, H. 161–162, 165

Sadowski, J. 186, 189–190
Sarıkartal, Ç. 81
Saussure, F. d. 79
Schechner, R. 80, 146
Searle, J. 2, 134
self: self-authorship 50; self-discovery 78; self-recognition 78, 81; self-representation 68
semiology 75, 78–79, 84
sentiment 94
sexuality 23, 171–172, 177, 179–180
Shakespeare, W. 80

shared memory 170; *see also* memory
sign: signified 75–76, 79, 83–84; signifier 75–76, 79–80, 83–84, 172
Slade, G. 118, 120, 126
Slater, P. 119–122
Soca 174, 178
social: capital 137; change 91, 104, 202; innovation 70; media 33, 65, 69, 122, 124, 131, 133, 136, 176, 190, 202, 204, 206, 208, 213; networking 129; responsibility 205, 212, 214–215; sociality 1, 116–117, 119–126, 145; social-phenomenological 161 (*see also* phenomenology); sociocultural 157–158, 160–162, 172
society 1–2, 10, 50, 66, 70, 75, 77–78, 90, 93, 96, 109, 119, 123, 126, 143–155, 156–168, 174, 202–218
software development kits (SDK) 130, 132
solidarity 8, 10, 89–90, 94, 98, 120–121, 124, 149–151, 173, 175, 183, 204–205, 211–212, 215, 217
stereotypes 84, 97
storytelling 8, 18, 33, 47, 96–97, 203–205, 213
stranger 78, 157, 159, 210, 212
streaming services 67, 128, 137
suffering 89–91, 94–97, 103, 106
surplus value 128, 136–137
sustainability 56, 61, 70, 173, 205, 213, 215–216

Tepenin Ardı 76–77
territorialization 76, 82–84
tether 116–117; tethered self 116–118
thematic analysis 137
third-party: apps 131; developer 8, 128, 130–135, 137–138
together: living together 9, 156, 159, 162; reflecting 17–26, 169–185; *see also* collective reflection
togetherness 1–2, 5, 10, 27, 44, 48, 54, 56, 102, 104–105, 112, 116–117, 122, 124, 126, 152
track 67, 174
transcultural 158
transdisciplinary 6
transformation 4, 50–52, 67, 126, 130, 145, 164

transmedia 10, 23–24, 202–218; Freeman's transmedia charity model 203, 205–206, 209, 213, 216–217; participation media 203–204, 209, 216; storytelling 203–204; storyworld 205
transnationality 83
transparency 39, 46–47, 209–210, 212, 214
trauma: collective 8, 102–104, 106; compressed cultural 104; cultural 102–115
TRT 17–26
trust 20, 42, 46–47, 63, 74, 111, 149, 152, 202, 205, 210–211, 214, 216
Tunç, A. 210–213
Turkle, S. 8, 116–118, 124–126
Twitch 8, 128, 131–138; Twitch Developers 8, 128–129, 131–133, 135–138

uncertainty 53, 76, 110, 158
unconscious 79
unsettling 76
user 27–43, 68, 71, 107–109, 130, 135–137, 188–189, 193–196, 198; experience 30–32

value-capture 130
victims 8, 84, 89–90, 92, 94–98, 107
viewer 21, 24, 27–33, 39, 41, 131, 135–136
Virtual Reality (VR) 102, 108–109, 113
visibility 173, 177–178, 202, 216
visual: content 29; language 29, 34; literacy 29; art 27, 31, 42; communication 27, 31, 33; communication design 27, 31, 42; visualisation 65
voice 20–24, 38, 46–47, 63, 92, 102, 107, 112, 214
volunteering 202, 209–210

war 89–101; correspondent 91, 98
Wittgenstein, L. 79

Yalan 82–83
YouTube 61, 129, 137, 206
Yücel, T. 82